BY ELLEN GOODMAN

Value Judgments

Turning Points

Close to Home

At Large

Keeping in Touch

Making Sense

BY PATRICIA O'BRIEN

Good Intentions

The Ladies Lunch

The Candidate's Wife

Staying Together: Marriages That Work

The Woman Alone

I KNOW JUST WHAT YOU MEAN

The Power of Friendship in Women's Lives

ELLEN GOODMAN ✦ PATRICIA O'BRIEN

SIMON & SCHUSTER

New York ✦ London ✦ Toronto ✦ Sydney ✦ Singapore

SIMON & SCHUSTER
Rockefeller Center
1230 Avenue of the Americas
New York, NY 10020

Designed by Carla Bolte

Manufactured in the United States of America

1   3   5   7   9   10   8   6   4   2

Library of Congress Cataloging-in-Publication Data

Goodman, Ellen.
I know just what you mean : the power of friendship in women's lives /
Ellen Goodman, Patricia O'Brien.
p.   cm.
1. Female friendship. 2. Woman—Psychology. I. Patricia O'Brien. II. Title.
BF575.F66 G66 2000
158.2'5'082—dc21   00-024859
ISBN 0-684-84287-4

Contents

What I Know About My Friend Pat 8
What I Know About My Friend Ellen 9

Introduction 11

1 ✦ Beginnings 15

2 ✦ We Talk, Therefore We Are . . . Friends 31

3 ✦ Why Are Men's Friendships So Different? 50

4 ✦ Taking Chances 67

5 ✦ Playtime 88

6 ✦ What's a Little Competition Between Friends? 104

7 ✦ Are We Traveling in Different Directions? 132

8 ✦ The Bad Stuff 161

9 ✦ We're in It Together 182

10 ✦ Testing the Limits 209

11 ✦ The Wider Circle: Friends and Family 239

12 ✦ The Long Run 257

Epilogue 289

Acknowledgments 295

Bibliography 297

I Know Just What You Mean

What I Know About My Friend Pat

+ That she has four essential food groups: orange juice, potato Air Crisps, wine, and broccoli.
+ That in parochial school the nuns taught her how to change her clothes without exposing one immoral inch of flesh.
+ Her real hair color.
+ That she loves fireworks and once went scuba diving after only a half-hour lesson and that she wants to take a balloon trip across the Serengeti Plain.
+ That she has four only children with four different careers: lawyer, doctor, documentary producer, banker—but names that all begin with M.
+ That she was a girl scout. I mean a Girl Scout.
+ Her weight. Within a margin of error. Give or take the watch and earrings.
+ That once, when she was press secretary for Mike Dukakis's presidential campaign, she met Ted Danson at a fund-raiser and had no idea who he was.
+ She once entered the Pillsbury Bake-Off.
+ She hates olives and pickles.
+ She is the only person in recorded history who went on Robin Leach's cooking show to prepare a signature dish of Kraft macaroni and cheese.
+ That when she went from journalism to writing novels, the biggest hurdle was giving herself permission to make things up.
+ She wears shoulder pads even in t-shirts, even when she isn't wearing makeup.
+ That she has six grandchildren—and counting—and actually spends Christmas with her husband, her ex-husband, his wife, their four daughters, four sons-in-law, and the grandchildren.
+ That she reads the horror stories in the newspapers and can't get them out of her head. Especially since she's had six grandchildren (and counting.)
+ That she wears a 10 AAAA shoe. And dorky shoes.
+ That she gets more catalogs than anyone I know.
+ That since I've known her, her phone number has changed eleven times.

What I Know About My Friend Ellen

- That she is wide awake obscenely early in the morning.
- That she eats carrots like normal people eat chocolate and is happiest chopping fruits and vegetables into tiny pieces.
- That she's the only person in America who lost her Pulitzer Prize citation instead of framing it.
- She scorns my Air Crisps and then eats half the bowl.
- That she hates television hockey, basketball, football. Really hates. But not women's soccer.
- That she is absentminded to the point of crossing the street when the light turns red.
- That on her way to deliver the commencement speech at the University of Pennsylvania, she accidentally got on a plane to Albany—and in a total panic refused to sit down until the pilot relented and taxied back to the gate.
- That she swore me to secrecy on the above for three years.
- She wants a small dog. I mean, she stops and talks to every small dog we pass on our walks.
- Her witching hour is 10 P.M. After that, she tends to drop off in the middle of a conversation.
- She searches relentlessly for a jacket with sleeves long enough to fit her.
- That she's a compulsive berry picker on her island in Maine.
- That the only beauty routine to which she is faithful is getting her nails done.
- That her closet is filled with green and mustard-colored clothes.
- She interrupts anything to point out a blue heron or a nuthatch.
- And buys only bird-friendly shade grown coffee.
- Her secret desire is to sing doo-wop in one of her daughter Katie's productions.
- And to produce the perfect bowl at pottery class. Many efforts are accumulating.
- Her real hair color and her real weight.
- That she has had the same telephone number for twenty-six years.

Introduction

This book began as an act of friendship.

Long after we met, after we launched and relaunched our children, after we reached the harbor of second marriages, after we had achieved a certain measure of success in our journalistic careers, we looked at each other and said, "What about writing something together?"

We had done everything else together. Lived through our thirties, forties, fifties. Struggled through single motherhood. Been confessors and advisers through our daughters' adolescence and each other's love affairs. We had traveled together, drunk wine together, edited each other's newspaper copy. We had shopped for mother-of-the-bride dresses together, debated hormones and hem lengths, and argued over the fine points of politics, sexual and otherwise.

Neither of us can remember who had the idea first. Somehow it just came up, on a long walk or after a long dinner, those times that seemed to be the backdrop against which we learned things about each other—things like our shoe sizes and the places where we were tough and where we were vulnerable. Somewhere in the first lighthearted conversations about "writing something," the notion of writing our own story began to emerge. Maybe it was the logical outcome for two writing friends—especially when they've spent the last several years realizing slowly what they created without a road map, a Triptik, or architectural drawings. We are, after all, at midlife, and midlife is a moment of reevaluating, taking stock. In some curious way, surrounded by family and work, we've taken our friendship for granted—not taken each other for granted, but the friendship itself.

It amazes us now to look back and see what we've been building: the story of our friendship is the story of our divorces, our children, careers, loves, losses, remarriages, knee injuries, and even our differing opinions on such earth-shattering matters as pickles and olives. At a dozen times, we might have taken a different course without each other's advice—wrecked a love affair, accepted the wrong job, or made the wrong decision for a child.

We knew precisely how important this ongoing conversation, this running commentary was to the person each of us had become. But it was a bit of a jolt to recognize that we had become the joint owners of a respectably long and grounded friendship. We had moved from youth through middle age with each other, becoming stronger than we would have been alone. We had talked and talked and talked, and finally talked our way through a quarter of a century—and in that time, we had become fluent in the language of female friendship.

It is that language we want to share. We already share it with our other friends, and have for years, because this is by no means an exclusive friendship. Moreover, in writing this book, we discovered how eager other women were to talk about their friendships, how delighted they were to have their authenticity recognized, how strong a desire they had to give voice to something that goes far deeper than the sentimental or cynical.

Friendship *matters* to women; it matters a lot; women today—with lives often in transition—depend on friends more than ever. Many who once believed family was *the* center of life, with every myth and movie and fairy tale having the same married-happily-ever-after ending, now know that friends may be the difference between a lonely life and a lively one. As they turn over the Big Birthdays, women are taking deep breaths and looking around at the other women who are their fellow travelers and saying— sometimes for the first time—this person is important to my life; indeed this may be my most sustaining relationship of all.

That isn't to say friendship doesn't come with contradictions; they are as complex and as embedded in this relationship as in any other. Nor does friendship always play a consistently strong role in women's lives. There are times when women can barely find time to make friends, let alone nurture them. Many have known the frustration of not having room in the datebook for the people they care about. Our fondest hope is that women will see themselves and their friends in these pages, and perhaps be better able to voice to each other what those friendships mean.

Yet even as we began, we became uneasy with people's reactions. Some would say, "Oh, that's a wonderful subject," and promptly ease into a story, a name, a memory of their own friendships. Others would react either warily or with a quick, startled laugh. "Well, I hope you're still friends at the end of it." Or: "So much for the friendship!"

Were they telling us friendship was warm and wonderful as long is it came without any obligations? That you could ask for only so much from a friend?

Were they right? What would happen if we added partnership to friendship? Our relationship had taken us through so much dicey terrain. Would it be risky to cross over into new territory? We had rarely even lived in the same city, and now look what we were getting into.

We decided right off the bat—although we didn't tell our editor—that at any time, *any time,* the book and the friendship collided, we would dump the book and save the friendship.

What we wanted to do was show the way friends travel with us through life—all of it or parts of it—not only with our story, but with the stories of other women: a remarkable group, ranging from a United States senator and her best friend to two former welfare mothers who have seen each other through many lean years. We wanted to get at the fragility and the strength of relationships that are not assigned at birth, not officially blessed at ceremonies, not granted any legal status, nor invested with social demand for permanence, but which "merely" carry us through life.

In our conversations, one phrase kept echoing: "I know just what you mean." We said it; they said it; so did all the women we knew. It was a universal bridge of connection—and we finally realized the title of our book had emerged. It was there all along.

Two artists who are both collaborators and best friends shared an intriguing phrase with us one afternoon around Pat's dining room table as they described how they worked together. Every day began with a discussion of their latest concerns or thoughts or what was going on with a husband, a mother, another friend, whatever. They thought of these early-morning emotional bulletins as a daily sharing of finely ground grains of emotional detail—their own daily news report, which they dubbed the Women's Fine Feeling News.

We found it a challenge at times in writing this book to hold on to our own fine feeling news. Not only did the crises and everyday cycles of our separate lives have to compete with the job of writing together, we had to make sure we didn't siphon the pleasure out of friendship even as we wrote about it. We came to believe that fine feeling news—so clearly on the wire that ran back and forth between our brains—was at the center of the closest female friendships, the place where women do the work of their lives, the growing, the understanding, the reflection. It's how we know each other and ourselves. And we came to realize that we weren't just writing this book, we were living it. So it really became a journey of friendship: there was no safe catbird seat from which we could pronounce and expound, and there were some jolts and surprises along the way.

But that is only the latest part of our story, and, as with most stories, it's probably a good idea to start with the beginning. For us, that was a crisp fall day in Cambridge in 1973.

1

Beginnings

Ellen

The sun was setting when I pulled my battered red Chevy Vega station wagon out of the driveway of the brown shingle house that I had just bought with every last nickel to my name, and headed off for Cambridge. The hands on the steering wheel were still speckled with the red paint that I had been rolling onto the living room walls that day, paint financed by the sale of an engagement ring from a former marriage and life.

I was thirty-two years old, a single mother, with a five-year-old daughter and a brand new puppy, living less than a mile from the house in which I had grown up, and I was going back to Harvard ten years after graduation. An adult now, a journalist, a reporter for *The Boston Globe,* I had hustled and won a prize—a mid-career Nieman Fellowship in journalism—and I was off to meet the other members of my "class" for the first time.

In those days, I was breathless. Coping with work and family and love— what Zorba the Greek would call the whole catastrophe. I was not at all sure how the pieces of my life fit together. At work, I had learned to say what I thought and to write about ideas. I was by no means as confident when it came to the messy business of feelings.

But this September of 1973, I knew, in some inchoate way, that I was on the edge of something more than a year "off." Perhaps a year "on."

Pat

While Ellen was driving from Brookline, I was on the bus coming from my rented house in Belmont, marveling at the fact that I had landed in this place, at this time, in this way. Harvard was only a few miles south of the working-class town of Somerville (known locally, I learned later, as "Slumerville"), where I had been born—geographically close, but in the days when my Irish immigrant mother and father lived there, Harvard might as well have been on the moon.

That was the past, this was now. I was thirty-seven, a newly divorced mother of four children working as a reporter for the *Chicago Sun-Times* with a year ahead of me as a Nieman Fellow. For a woman who had not graduated from college until she was thirty, this new venture felt like a huge leap across a class divide. Getting here had taken a certain amount of audacity, and even though I had an officially punched ticket of admission, I half expected someone to snatch it away at the last moment.

I also had two teenage daughters living for the year with their father back home in Evanston, Illinois, and two younger girls nervously tiptoeing through a strange house, wondering what the year ahead would hold for them. This was by no means a carefree venture. But as I walked down those narrow streets toward the home of Jim Thomson, the head of the Nieman program—the brick sidewalks scraping the backs of my high-heeled shoes—I also knew there was nowhere else I wanted to be. I was literally walking into a major life-changing experience, not knowing what would come next. I knew that from here on, everything would be different. I just didn't know *how* different.

Ellen

I remember when I first spotted Pat. She was wearing some kind of full skirt, heels, and bright lipstick; her long, wavy brown hair was parted in the middle. This was Harvard Square in the black-turtleneck, ripped-jeans, straight-hair, early-'70s era. She was ironed and starched.

I added it all together and, in the way women will sum up the totality of

Nieman class, 1974. (Pat is 5th from right; Ellen is 7th from left.)

someone's personality through their shoes and suit jacket, I came up with this: perky California cheerleader. Suburban mom. Smiling, pretty, very Little League, station wagon driving. Verrrrry straight.

Yet I knew she had to be a good reporter in the competitive atmosphere of Chicago to have made it through this process. And from the bios we'd been sent, I also knew that Pat was the only other woman in the class with children. We were both divorced. Cheerleader or not, we had these things in common.

I wasn't looking for or expecting a friend, just a classmate, but I was curious. Maybe there was something below that conventional surface. She had four children to my one and, as if *my* life were not overloaded enough, had just published her first book. There was a long year ahead of us, so who knew what I'd find out.

Pat

I first saw Ellen as I stood in the front hallway of the house, exchanging stiff little pleasantries with a few people whose names I hadn't absorbed. She was tall, with long straight hair and blue aviator glasses, dressed in some kind of loose pants, clearly not wearing a girdle. (I was only weeks away from shedding mine.) I knew there were three other women in my class, but she certainly didn't look as nervous or uptight as I felt. Craftsy orange earrings; no makeup. An in-charge, what's-it-to-you type. I fingered the piece of paper in my pocket that listed all the class members, and glanced around for a bathroom so I could duck in and check them out. But the minute Ellen opened her mouth, there was no question—she stood out from the crowd.

"Well," she said in an easy, cheery voice, "I wonder what bullshit everybody threw to get here?"

How blunt were you allowed to be at Harvard? Not that I wasn't wondering myself how the others had parlayed their credentials into this prize. But here was somebody who actually said it out loud. The thought crossed my mind: How can she be so irreverent in this rarefied environment? But still she had an engaging air that relaxed me, that made me listen for what she would say next. When I learned she was the Nieman who had gone to Radcliffe, I thought, well, no wonder she's so casual. This is her turf. It must all be easy for her.

This is how we met, but it's not how or certainly why we became friends. Pat saw a confident, breezy insider, but she couldn't see the missteps or wrenching changes. Ellen saw Pat's conventional surface, but not the rebellious soul, and certainly not the pulls of tradition and independence that had defined so much of her adult life and that would be a running dialogue of our twenty-six-year conversation.

Would we ever have sought each other out after a chance meeting at some ordinary cocktail party? We doubt it. But we had the gift of time to discover and to get to know—that oddly flat statement—each other. We had a chance to become friends.

Friends? What's a friend? If the Eskimos have twenty-six different words for snow, Americans have only one word commonly used to describe everyone from acquaintances to intimates. It is a word we have to qualify with adjectives: school friends, work friends, old friends, casual friends, good friends.

But this catch-all word doesn't catch everything, especially how we describe a truly intimate friend. A chosen relative? Bonded, but not by blood? When we asked women how they define what a close friend is, they leaped past such qualifiers to describe the impact: being known and accepted, understood to the core; feeling you can count on trust and loyalty, having someone on your side; having someone to share worries and secrets as well as the good stuff of life, someone who needs you in return.

This special person is not always easy to find. "Every so often you run into someone from your tribe, a magic person," said actress Carrie Fisher. "People who give without keeping lists and receive with gratitude." These "magic people," these close friends, she said, become like family.

The longing for close friendship begins early and goes deep. In the much-loved children's classic *Anne of Green Gables,* the young heroine is newly transplanted to Avonlea and pining for a "bosom friend." With a yearning that has resonated through several generations of young readers, Anne confides her hope of finding "a kindred spirit to whom I can confide my inmost soul. I've dreamed of meeting her all my life."

The most famous young diarist of the twentieth century, Anne Frank, herself yearned for a close girlfriend with whom to share her feelings when she and her family went into hiding to escape the Nazis. Deprived of that intimacy, she turned to her diary, making up imaginary friends and writing them letters chronicling life in the claustrophobic, secret annex. "With them, she could laugh, cry, forget her isolation," writes biographer Melissa Muller.

The desire for love, trust, and intimacy is at the center of all close relationships, and friendship is no exception. But because friendship has no biological purpose, no economic status, no evolutionary meaning to examine or explore, sometimes we see a curious vanishing act.

A friend who might have been privy to every nuance in a courting relationship is not in the receiving line at the wedding; the friend who delivers a heartfelt eulogy may have been banned from the hospital room because she wasn't "family." We have many ways of celebrating family milestones, but not the milestones of friendship. "It's your silver anniversary? Let's make the toasts and get out the presents!" Nobody does that for friends.

We wanted to. We found ourselves walking away from interview after interview, feeling we'd just had some of the best conversations of our lives with women telling us the stories of how they met, joking and laughing with each other, thoroughly enjoying the pleasure of sharing their histories together.

✦ Boston publicist Sally Jackson first laid eyes on Melanie L'Ecuyer when, as a scared five-year-old, she came into her mother's hospital room and saw two-year-old Melanie, dressed in a camel-hair coat and leggings, throwing a tantrum under her mother's bed. The howling child, she was told, was the daughter of her mother's nurse.

✦ Nadia Shamsuddin and Maddie Hammond met as two women glaring at each other on an elevator, wondering who would be able to write a check faster to snare the choice apartment they were about to see.

✦ Mary Landrieu was boarding a bus with a group of strangers heading for a high school leadership conference when, drawn by a friendly face, she sat down next to Norma Jane Sabiston, the girl who would become her lifelong friend and, eventually—when Mary became a U.S. senator from Louisiana—her chief of staff.

✦ Author Mary Gordon took one look at Maureen Strafford when she met her in grammar school and made a firm, instant decision to ignore her totally. Why? Because Mary was wearing a mohair sweater and Maureen was wearing plaid.

✦ Eileen Fennelly and Jenn MacDonough, now college students, were five-year-olds wearing party hats when Jenn mistakenly called Eileen "Elaine." Eileen decided right there that she hated her. By the time they graduated from high school, the longest period of time that went by without their talking to each other was exactly, by their actual count, seventy-two hours.

Some of these women felt an initial spark of connection, and for some it was just a spark, but it's with great relish that they remember these stories of meeting each other. They were not so different in their exuberance from a young child recounting the thrilling fact of what she has in common with a friend—"Do you know we were born on the same day?" "I can't believe she uses ketchup on her hot dog, too!"

Certainly the two of us were very different; in an earlier era we might never have met. We grew up a continent away, Ellen on the older, colder side, Pat in the sunny California world of shallow roots that had drawn her parents west when she was a child. If we had followed the prepared scripts, we each would have stayed in our place. We might have remained in our circumscribed ethnic groups, our neighborhoods and family circles, holding little in common. Pat was, after all, expected to stay in Catholic schools, and when Ellen went to college, she was assigned a roommate with whom she had only one thing in common: they were both Jewish.

Looking back at the trajectory we were on, it was Pat who made the moves. She was the one who moved in great upheavals from one place to the next. Ellen stayed put, spending all but four years of her life in her hometown. Pat's life was charted by its uprootings, willful and imposed. Ellen had traveled intellectually, but her feet remained on the same, familiar ground.

It wasn't just ethnicity or geography that made for some of the degrees of separation between us. In our early twenties, we had nothing in common. When Ellen was starting college at Radcliffe in September of 1959, Pat was changing diapers for two small babies. Pat cannot imagine what she would have had to say to the young college freshman from Brookline as she stood at a changing table in Eugene, Oregon, with a wiggling baby in front of her and diaper pins in her mouth.

At twenty-seven, Pat was a full-time mom with four kids, learning the wonders of Hamburger Helper and Simplicity sewing patterns. Ellen had started working in the early '60s, and had one child at twenty-seven. She stayed home after Katie's birth for a total of six weeks; Pat was at home for nine years. Pat had the Feminine Mystique, while Ellen had a ticket on the first anxious flight of Superwoman before the myth came crashing to earth.

By the time Pat ventured back to school, juggling those four children and final exams, Ellen was married to a medical resident, living in Ann Arbor, and commuting to her job as a reporter for the *Detroit Free Press*—never quite accepted as one of the doctors' wives raising babies at one end of I-94, and never quite accepted as one of the boys covering fires at the other.

By 1968, we would at least have understood each other's language. We were both working mothers, trying to do what we wanted to do: work and keep our families intact in an atmosphere still hostile to the effort. Pat had broken from the Catholic Church with a prescription for birth control pills—and deep ambivalence. For Ellen, Judaism had become more a celebration of family and food than formal ritual.

By 1971, the women's movement was changing both of our lives, and—even before we met—we already had more in common than liking ketchup. Each of us in our own city was covering the first "happenings." Pat wrote an article on being ejected from a Chicago church because she was wearing a "Women's Strike Day" button, and Ellen also visited a church, to write a piece for the *Globe* about radical feminists teaching sexual politics and karate.

You could say we had the classic first day of school meeting. We were starting something entirely new, with hors d'oeuvres rather than shiny lunchboxes in our hands. It's the familiar story of friendships that emerge as natural by-products of a new venture, antidotes to the fear of being alone in an uncertain if not totally unfamiliar environment. We've seen this happen with small children, even our own. Recently Pat's granddaughter Charlotte, at the end of her first day of school, tugged her mother, Marianna, by the hand and pulled her into the classroom. "Come meet my new best friend," she implored. "What's her name?" Marianna asked. "I don't know, let's go ask her," Charlotte replied. The connection was made; details to come later.

As grown-ups we were not afraid of starting school alone, but we did realize we were in a privileged, special moment of our lives. We had come to Harvard well aware that the changes in our own lives reflected larger changes taking place in the society; certainly as women we already had more choices and more freedom than any other women in history. As proof, we only had to look at the photographs of earlier Nieman classes on the wall of the Nieman House: up until our year, in the entire history of the Nieman Fellowship program, there had been only ten women—and ours was the only class since 1947 to have more than one. In all those years, there wouldn't have been another woman with whom to share the experience. In our class, there were four.

We met in a landmark year. Richard Nixon had been elected to a second term, and the first of the Watergate conspirators—the tip of the iceberg ahead—were found guilty. The U.S. Supreme Court ruled for the first time that women had a legal right to an abortion. The divorce rate had soared 8 percent from the year before. The most popular television shows in a changing America included *The Waltons* and *All in the Family,* while on the big screen, Ingmar Bergman's stark *Scenes from a Marriage* was making people uneasy with hard truths of this rapidly evolving age.

Against this backdrop of change, women were going through a major cultural transition. It wasn't just laws and political sensibilities that were changing. So were ideas about human development. The view that women had grown up with—based on a male model—had taught them that humans mature to sturdy, independent adulthood by growing away—from family, from friends, from connections.

But most women didn't experience life that starkly. They didn't one day arrive at a static state of adulthood and say to themselves, "Well, that's that," and they certainly didn't want to be "grown-ups" alone. In the 1970s, women like psychiatrist Jean Baker Miller first challenged the idea that women grow up by separating. Carol Gilligan, charting the moral development of girls, began to hear "a different voice."

It's been easier since then to see the female reality, that women develop *in* relationship, *through* connection. Women don't "find" themselves or "understand" themselves all alone but by interacting with others. They forge and reforge their own identity in concert with others, engaged in a long dance of mutuality.

Sociologist Lillian Rubin argues in her book *Just Friends* that friends are central actors in the continuing development drama of adulthood. Women are born daughters, they recite vows that make them wives, become mothers through giving birth—but they choose friends. They aren't just picked out of a line-up or sought through the personals column—wanted: a friend. Women *become* friends.

Is there a moment between that first meeting and the time when you *become* a friend? Is there a dot on the time line that says, right here and now, from this point on, we *are* friends?

Psychologist Judith Jordan has what she describes her "crazy fantasy" about the moment of becoming friends. "I think we're going to be able someday to do CAT scans of people when they're connecting . . . you know, where you can actually get imaging of different things that go on in the brain and they can say this person's in a good alpha place!"

Ellen

A good alpha place? The stage setting for our very first alpha lunch was the much too tweedy and wood-paneled Harvard Faculty Club. It was no more than two weeks after we had met.

We had planned this lunch as no big deal, a quick salad before a two o'clock class. It lasted until four—the first of a dozen times when I remember being delighted that this time in college, I wouldn't be penalized for cutting class.

In my journal I report with little detail the "highlights" Pat told me about that day, but I remember them vividly. She talked about motherhood, how as a young Catholic mother she finally got contraceptives from the doctor "for regulating her period," and for the first time realized with a lifesaving, emancipating joy that she wouldn't be the mother of nine after all.

We shared the war stories of our divorces, in which neither of us was entirely innocent. She confided that she still loved her just-ex-husband and showed me the locket around her neck that carried his photo. I told her about the end of my marriage and the lingering, troubled relationship that followed, one that I was neither in nor out of.

I would date the real beginning of our friendship from that lunch. No, she was not the cheerleader I had expected, not so verrry straight. We became friends the way adult women do, telling the stories of our lives. Pat had no idea how unusual it was for me to share those experiences or how vulnerable I felt that autumn afternoon revealing things I had never said out loud to any but family or my closest friends. And certainly not to a stranger from Chicago.

I didn't make friends quickly or confide easily—chalk it up to Boston conservatism. Or to family. My sister, Jane, and I were so close as kids, I didn't feel the need of another friend. They used to say that Boston women didn't buy hats, they *had* hats. So it was with friends. I made friends slowly and carefully. But virtually from the outset, I felt absolutely certain I could trust Pat.

In many ways, that first lunch set the tone of our friendship: vulnerability and trust. The mutual baring—slowly—of darkest secrets seemed lightened by the knowledge that they had been accepted. Pat had a way of taking a thought and running with it that I found delightful. She was a natural storyteller, dramatic, even melodramatic. I didn't do melodrama. I did wry. But Pat saw through wry.

I had the first intimations Pat would give me something I could not give myself when I cautiously shared with her the grand finale to a marriage that was already dying from lack of attention. I shared it in the spare and tamped-down emotional detail I often used, but she got to the dark heart of it instantly. She gave me the acknowledgment of the pain from the ending of my marriage that I had put aside in a need to get on with life, to put one foot in front of another, holding a small child by the hand.

In that first lunch, Pat offered up an expression that dotted so many of our early years. It's one of those ordinary phrases that takes on a new truth when repeated much as one would a motto. "Life," she says to this day, when describing something that can be amusing, bizarre, or even deeply troubling, "is so interesting."

We were each bold and timid in different ways. But her adventurousness, her lust for experience, her energy, and a love life that was a soap opera without the tragedy all appealed to my cautious soul. She offered both courage and consolation, as each was needed.

Somehow my journal that year was filled with other relationships, especially with men who swiftly became incidental. But scattered throughout are the words, "Pat said," or "Pat thought." We began to explore the world through each other's eyes and minds. We were becoming part of each other's DNA.

Pat

It was late one afternoon in that same first couple of weeks when I walked up the stairs to the second floor of the Nieman House and saw Ellen curled up in a chair, seemingly absorbed in a book. I recognized the book jacket immediately—I would have known it from a mile away. What if she hated it? Writing *The Woman Alone* had been my first tentative effort to understand the changes taking place in women's lives—including my own—and for all I knew, the breezy blonde from Radcliffe was groaning at its naïveté, even as my sudden, unexpected appearance demanded some response on her part. I also knew I cared what she thought—a lot.

"This is good," she said simply, and then asked a question that got right to the heart of the issues I had tried to raise. I knew instinctively she would not stick to polite comments. I had my first glimpse that afternoon into a wonderful, ruminating mind that took other perspectives seriously; a woman who was on a learning curve, as I was. The confident Radcliffe insider who had loomed in my first impression was not an intellectual know-it-all. She was willing to explore a topic on terms other than her own.

I think this open-mindedness is one of Ellen's great gifts, and it comes from more than intellectual curiosity. It comes from a deep charitable core. I felt almost right away there was a level at which I could trust her, which meant there was a level at which I could be myself without softenings or embellishment. As a child, I was too awkward, too bookish, too different to attract many friends. Home, not school, was my refuge. It was with my younger sister, Mary, that I played, rode tricycles, baked chocolate chip cookies. She was my first friend. As I grew, I expanded the circle, but it was never large. Feeling accepted didn't come easily.

With Ellen, I could talk about family and politics and change and loss and get back much more than supportive echoes. More than that, she needed me, which is no small thing. When she broke up with her boyfriend a few months after we met, I was home for the holidays in Chicago. She called and we talked for hours.

In all our conversations, she would offer a thought or point of view, often unexpected. I would ruminate, take the idea further down the road, hand it back to her like a baton in a relay race, and then she would juggle it for a moment before taking it further herself. This was fun, but fun of a different kind. We were exploring our minds as well as our hearts.

We began actively to seek each other out. Many mornings, after the children were in school, we would meet at the Pewter Pot restaurant next to the out-of-town-newsstand off Harvard Square, order one muffin each, and sit there until noon, drinking cup after cup of coffee. The waitress would glare at us and slam down a check, but we couldn't pull ourselves away. We offered each other advice, came close to tears, laughed like crazy at some funny or forbidden memories now shared. I found myself angry at whatever had hurt her, and soon we were viscerally on each other's side. We discussed Watergate, Vietnam, newspapers, editors—all the evils of the world. We scribbled notes on everything we talked about on the back of napkins—how to help my Maureen, who was being teased in school; whether we would have published the Pentagon Papers; the myth of the vaginal orgasm—and tucked them into the pockets of our jeans, and we would walk out of there feeling invigorated, and more than a little buzzed on caffeine. I consider those mornings at the Pewter Pot the best seminars I've ever attended.

I see now how we got each other right—and wrong. She saw me as the risk taker in life, while I saw her as braver than I in her career. She liked my penchant for nostalgia, while I felt she was more fearless of letting go of the past. The truth, of course, was more contradictory for us both. We would later understand both ourselves and each other much better, even at times swapping strengths and weaknesses.

One thing never changed: I always felt closer to cataclysm. Once during that first year, for all my brave-new-world feminism, I realized I couldn't balance my checkbook. I had to march into the bank and get some officious guy to help me straighten out my finances. I was amazed by Ellen's blithe advice, and envied her ability to follow it: "Just open up a new account, wait until everything clears, and then if there's any money left in the old account, you just transfer it to the new one." What an interesting idea . . . maybe, I thought, I might try it sometime.

We had clicked, not just once, but time and again as we continued to meet over coffee, attend classes together, and share seminars. At some point in that year, we started talking about "my friend Pat" and "my friend Ellen." So, too, the women in this book told of their tremendous delight when they knew they had made a true connection, at the point where they realized they had gone from liking each other to bonding.

Jane Mansbridge, a political scientist at Harvard's John F. Kennedy School of Government, remembers dropping by to see Sharland Trotter, an acquaintance stricken with cancer, expecting to chat for a few moments and be on her way—and instead connected instantly and deeply with a woman who had no time to waste on trivial relationships.

Barbara Corday, a young mother in Los Angeles in the '70s, showed up at the offices of an antiwar organization run by a dynamo named Barbara Avedon, and was so swept up in the passion of Avedon's commitment that within weeks she was flying to Washington for a protest demonstration with her baby in a backpack. The two Barbaras went on to become partners as well as best friends, writing a hit television show about partners and best friends: *Cagney and Lacey.*

At a statehouse demonstration in the '70s, two back-to-school welfare mothers, Dottie Stevens and Diane Dujon, were side by side under a desk, practicing for a protest skit. At the peak of the protest, their arms—one white, one black—were linked. It was a life-changing contact.

And there was the time of the huge snowstorm in Baltimore, when Oprah Winfrey, then a local television anchor, invited a stranded production assistant named Gayle King to spend the night.

"Yeah, but I don't have any underwear," Gayle said.

"I have underwear, it's clean, you can wear it," replied Oprah. "But I draw the line at the toothbrush." They stopped at a drugstore and bought a toothbrush, then went home and stayed up talking until four in the morning.

We could go on, but you will meet these people and many others at length in the chapters ahead. They are women who have made the kind of contact that keeps them coming back, knowing they have connected at a deeper level than usual, that something new and special has come into their lives.

Maybe this is Judith Jordan's "CAT scan"—the moment when two women feel truly understood. When someone doesn't just say "I know what you mean" . . . but actually does. When she "gets" it, and, more to the point, "gets" you.

A new friend can reintroduce a woman to herself, allowing her to look at herself with a new pair of eyes and a different mindset. The younger sister cast as "daffy" by the family is seen as "funny"—and fun—by a friend. The melodramatic wife is welcomed as a rich storyteller. More often than not, through close friendships, women see themselves through another lens, experience a new kind of self-consciousness. Flaws can be recast as strengths, self-doubts lifted by acceptance. Friends help define and motivate each other.

In recent years, a small group of researchers at Wellesley College's Stone Center has been breaking conceptual ground on women's research, putting together a new dictionary of words to describe the "good stuff" that comes out of connection: a sense of mutual empowerment, movement, change, clarity, and zest. It is the last of these that applies here. Zest? It wraps up in four letters much of what friends mean as they describe the excitement and energy flow that occurs in connection, when we take pleasure in each other's company.

We very quickly felt the pleasure of both understanding and being understood, of helping and being helped. Looking back, we realize now that in some ways, during our early time together, Ellen was looking to Pat for emotional reinforcement, while Pat was seeking an intellectual partner. In talking about men or writing, feelings or ideas, we would add our own freight to the other's train of thought until occasionally it brought about a change of direction. We came quickly to respect each other. If Pat had an idea, it was not to be dismissed; if Ellen had another viewpoint, it was worth mulling over. We changed each other's minds—and came to value the fact that we could. We were each other's teacher.

After one Nieman seminar, Pat learned from Ellen how to draw the distinction between being honest and being nice. ("You don't have to smile when you're asking a speaker a tough question.") It was a shock for Pat to realize that she had for too long masked her mind by presenting to the world as ingratiating a demeanor as possible—trying, in a sense, to sneak in under the wire.

We also had laid-back, time-off playtimes together. There was the time Ellen introduced Pat to the bizarre ritual of cooking lobsters. "Here, just put the bag between your feet," she said one memorable afternoon, handing Pat a wiggling bag of her first lobsters after coming out of the fish market. Pat couldn't take her eyes off that sack all the way home, convinced it took some kind of savage bravery to cook the damn things. But Ellen showed her true colors when the cooking began. The lobsters went tumbling into the pot, Ellen banged the lid on, and grabbed Pat's hand. "Here's the way you do it," she said. "You stick them in the pot and you run out of the room until they're done."

We spent weekends taking our kids to museums and sharing sleepovers, and we did the duet of guilt before hitting Bailey's for sundaes with fudge sauce that ran like brown lava over the rim of the stainless steel bowl (should we, oh god, I'm so fat, will you get one if I do?).

In that incredible year off—and on—we gorged on the smorgasbord of seminars and classes and weekly meetings that brought the world to our privileged and temporary Cambridge door. We had plates full of politics and philosophy and family law. We enjoyed our classmates and their wives—who were rightly included as Niemans themselves. In our small and large adventures, we created stories that form the rich background for our lives.

At the end of May neither of us was ready to leave this "camp." Before the class scattered, before we all returned to our prior lives, we were invited to Europe for an astonishing "freebie," a chance to study the Common Market and then wing off to the country of our choice. Unreal? Absolutely. We knew this would be an adventure of the first order.

We were both excited. Pat began packing for the trip the way she had packed when she went away to college in the '50s—throwing everything in the suitcase that she might possibly need under any circumstance. With the cabdriver waiting to take us to the airport honking his horn outside, Ellen, whose possessions were crammed in little more than a backpack, was throwing things out of Pat's bulging suitcase. "But I need that!" Pat kept protesting. When Ellen ran downstairs to placate the cabdriver, Pat shoved as much stuff back in as she could. Her vindication? Ellen was borrowing from her for most of the trip.

The day we flew off to Brussels was Pat's birthday, and one member of our troop decided we absolutely must have a cake to celebrate. Well, not exactly a cake. She baked a batch of brownies and laced them with marijuana (perhaps as a complement to airplane food?). Some of us, feeling very adventurous, began nibbling away at the brownies in the waiting lounge. Hopefully the statute of limitations has expired (does this qualify as a "youthful indiscretion"?) because by the time the Nieman Class of 1974 staggered on board the plane, half of us were capable only of giggling through the flight attendant's instructions. Pat was scared we would all be thrown off the plane. Her conservative side reasserting itself, she made it back to the bathroom and flushed away what was left of her brownie. She then collapsed into her seat and remembers absolutely nothing about that flight to Europe.

Our trip lived up to its billing, and all our adventures obscured the jolt of the partings that were to come. With time winding down, our class had one rollicking farewell dinner in Brussels, and then the two of us boarded a train by ourselves for Amsterdam.

On that dark train ride through the European countryside, we shared an ominous flashback: only thirty years earlier, Ellen, as a Jew, could not have made this trip without peril. We could not have been friends. We looked at each other, the truth jolting us out of our easy tourist mode. That sense of time and place followed us up five flights to our Amsterdam room where we stared out over the rooftops, startled by the accidental and fragile nature of connection. How casually this frienship had bloomed. How much we had come to mean to each other. Our friendship had been nurtured in a cocoon of privileged time off; we knew there was no structure, no institution, to anchor it.

We had premonitions that we were going to have to go back to who we were—when we knew, deep in our bones, that, thanks to each other, we were different. And we made a pact. We would not let each other return to the "old" self. *These* friends would *stay* friends.

Although we didn't quite see the Big Picture yet, on that train ride we were "reupping." We were going into our first voluntary reenlistment.

2

We Talk, Therefore We Are . . . Friends

Pat

I returned home to Chicago that summer of 1974 with a thud—actually, a series of thuds. I walked in the door of my home in northwest Evanston to almost barren rooms (the prior owners had reclaimed the furniture they had left temporarily in the house), and even though I knew the place would look empty, I hadn't realized *how* empty. The naked rooms only underscored the fact that a new life had to be put together for myself and my children in the aftermath of my divorce. I remember sitting down on the dingy gray carpet in the living room, looking around, and thinking, the bubble has burst. It's time to get busy equipping the kids with school supplies and restocking the larder, heavy on SpaghettiOs.

So okay, poor me, the glamour was gone. The handsome Italian I had dated in Rome was an ocean away, Harvard was but a misty memory, and the roof needed replacing. I also had four great kids and a good job and the roof wasn't collapsing. Time to get on with it.

My new job at the *Sun-Times* was writing editorials, a job I approached with some wariness. I felt removed from the bustling, energizing newsroom, and a bit like a phony as I wrote editorials exhorting Congress to pass some bill or other in a newspaper that was barely noticed in Washington. It was like putting on a virtual-reality pin-striped suit. I was expected to adopt the mien of the rest of the guys, and approach the job like they did. Yet I also now had my own once-a-week column, which gave me a chance to talk about the social and family issues that were my true interest, even though this wasn't considered as "important" as editorial writing.

It was a confusing time. The clarity and excitement of a year of being taken seriously on my own terms was fading rapidly. The editor of the editorial page thought former Niemans needed to be taken down a peg or two, especially women, and it frustrated him that I wasn't obsessed with politics and economics. Plus my math was terrible (I once wrote an editorial deploring a Pentagon budget in the millions. Oops—it was billions. I left off a few zeros on my copy.) Back on the job, in low moments, I wondered if my brief flight to the sun had been a fluke.

But now I had a reality check at hand, a new reference point for myself. I had someone in my life who actually knew who I was. I couldn't get on the Belmont bus and meet Ellen down at the Pewter Pot anymore, but I could call her—and I did, as often as I could. In what was to become a habit for the next quarter century, I would pick up the phone and wait for her voice.

"Hi, you busy?"

"Not that busy, what's up?"

And for the next thirty minutes or so, I would tell her what was going on. How I was learning that even though I was a member of the "editorial board," I couldn't sit in with the all-male inner circle that met separately to set policy because—oh, this is rich, listen to this, Ellen—there weren't enough chairs in the room.

"They didn't have enough chairs??? Are you kidding me?"

We could laugh together, get mad together, plot subversive strategy together—and then we could talk about what was in the latest issue of *Ms.* magazine and what was going on with the kids, boyfriends, and ex-husbands before hanging up and getting back to the job of living our separate lives in our separate cities. Thank God for the telephone. It was our lifeline.

Ellen

I think of it now as postpartum depression. Or postparty depression. The party was over, the other kids had all gone home, and I was back at work. It was the summer of Watergate and the whole newsroom was on resignation watch. There were long nights when my daughter called from home, asking sleepily, "Mom, has he resigned yet?" This six-year-old's only political interest in Nixon's fate was in getting me home in time to read her another chapter of *The Trumpet of the Swan.*

I was back with my *Globe* friends, but there was a new city editor to impress or else—and there I was, assigned to churn out features on families fighting inflation. Hadn't I done this series before? Just to make this reentry truly depressing, I was experiencing the wonderful opportunity of sharing the newsroom with my old boyfriend . . . and his new wife.

In one of our last days as ladies of leisure, Pat and I had put together a list of all the things that we wanted to remember from our "seminars." The things we wanted to do and to be. The ways that we had begun thinking about life and our lives. Spooked by how easily we both could fall back into old habits of thinking—even about ourselves—we'd written a list of where we would go from here. It was a list of things we would do and things we wouldn't do.

Impressed by Pat's book—if she could do it, I could do it—I had a book contract, but no idea of how I would begin, let alone finish. I looked at my list from time to time and realized that I was checking off the wrong side: I was accomplishing too many of the things "Not to Do."

Unlike Pat, I was not at all sure that our friendship would retain its flavor after she had gone back to Chicago. Friendships had to fit, didn't they? Chicago? I'd been there only once in my life. My other friendships had room on the schedule. I had wonderful lifesaving lunches in the office cafeteria—taco salad again?—with my lanky and lively friend Otile McManus, where we did daily bulletins on everything from clothes to story leads. My friend Helen Strieder and I had begun a ritual of Wednesday night pizza with the kids—they played, we talked. And my sister and I shared everything from shopping to child care. Blame it on skepticism—or experience—or an overdeveloped fear of loss—but I didn't have much faith in long-distance friendships.

But sometime that first year, I realized that when I needed a reality check, damn the phone bill, dial ahead.

"Pat, tell me if I'm completely out of my mind," I said, and repeated the conversation I'd just had with an editor who said it was fine for me to work but that *his* children were so smart they needed a mother at home.

"*Whaaat?*"

When I needed a booster shot of bravery, I would pick up the phone: "Okay, what do you think? Can I write about shaving my legs in a family newspaper?"

"Go for it."

When a man I broke up with insisted we had to get together—again—for another long analysis of why it was over, I was already punching in the 312 area code.

"Do I have to?"

"Enough is enough."

In some ways Pat and I had already become old friends, two women who knew each other when and knew each other well. But we were also co-conspirators in change, who knew what was on those lists. We got over the first of the highest hurdles of separation because of the fun we found in our friendship, the pleasure principle of sharing thoughts, but we endured also because we needed to keep up the fuel, the energy for our lives. We were on each other's side.

So we simply decided to keep it going. We let our fingers do the walk-ing—telling ourselves always "it's cheaper than therapy." And so it was. Barely.

There was no one other than ourselves, of course, who would have cared if we had become "reunion friends." There was no institution that would have demanded an accounting. No one would have appeared at the door with a summons or forced us to sign a separation agreement. No one else would have suffered if we had lost touch. We could have simply stopped talking.

That didn't happen. We were friends; we had to talk. It was the single most important—and most obvious—connection. Talk is at the very heart of women's friendships, the core of the way women connect. It's the given, the absolute assumption of friendship. "I never have to *ask* my best friends to talk, nor they me; the talk just happens without preamble, without formal beginning or end, flowing richly and immediately back and forth between our separate lives and shared experiences along a *living* current of conversation," writes therapist Lois Braverman.

We like that idea of the "living current." We've seen it and felt it in our own lives, and we know other women have, too. In the flow of conversation, back and forth, women hear each other out, take each other seriously, care and feel cared for. When a friend calls with a serious problem while you're cooking dinner, the pot goes on the back burner. When something happens at work or home that you can't quite, exactly, figure out, you take all that raw undigested feeling to a safe place—a friend—and come away clearer. Talk is what we all take for granted and yet it is precisely what makes women value and feel valued in friendships. In these ongoing dialogues, women reveal themselves. Gradually, trust is tested and won; an intimate comfort zone is created.

Women know this intuitively—and they've had the language to express it for a long time.

"Oh, the comfort—the inexpressible comfort of feeling safe with a person," wrote George Eliot, "having neither to weigh thoughts nor measure words, but pouring them all right out, just as they are, chaff and grain together, certain that a faithful hand will take and sift them, keep what is worth keeping and then with a breath of kindness blow the rest away."

We poured those thoughts out, chaff and grain, knowing the faithful hand was at the end of a long-distance telephone line. For the sake of our bank accounts, we tried letters, that technological precursor to e-mail. But inevitably we reached for the phone. Whenever possible, we picked up the phone at the office—justifying the expense with shop talk—to cut down on our long-distance bills. But we did it.

In truth, talk between women is easily trivialized by our culture. There is a drumbeat of disapproval—sometimes mixed with bewilderment or even envy—that surrounds women who spend long minutes, hours, on the phone. It trails after women who sit down together with pizza or coffee, women who stand in the ladies' room at work mulling over the details of their daily life. They are chattering, indulging in a gabfest, gossiping, prattling. Their telephone bills are waaay too high.

So it is hardly surprising that Kurt Vonnegut, that fine-tuned satirist, offered up his own answer to Freud's classic question: "What do women want?" with this rejoinder: "I know what women want. They want lots of people to talk to." We add one elaboration: women want to talk to friends.

There are impediments, all sorts of interruptions, times when the "living current" can turn into a busy line or a disconnection. A friend moves away, gets too busy with children or work, or many of the other things that fill the often frenetic lives of women.

The fact that a friendship is a chosen relationship also makes it more fragile. Remember the homemade marriage ceremonies of the 1970s pledging union for "as long as we both shall love"? It was never quite true for marriage, but it was always true for friends.

From childhood on, friendship is relegated to the backseat. Children are expected to have "friends," but they are by no means required or expected to *keep* them. Parents who arrange for play groups and worry about the "social skills" of their children rarely make those friends a priority when schools are chosen, or when they buy new houses or take new jobs. No statistics are kept at any age on lost or broken friendships—which often last only as long as a summer vacation or a yoga class. It's assumed that old friends will be replaced with new ones. No harm done.

In one sense, this casualness toward friends is of a piece with our highly individualistic and mobile society. Political scientist Jane Mansbridge says we see friendship as a lifetime elective: "I voluntarily enter, I voluntarily leave. It's perfect for the American fantasy of the individual who can enter into friendships as long as they're good for you and then leave them. Not like family."

Lillian Rubin described this cultural attitude with a particularly crisp phrase: family is sacred; friendship is secular. Family does come first. Indeed, adult women are expected to transfer the energy invested in young friendship to the search for a husband and the job of building a family. When we were growing up, this was a given. During the decades and in the neighborhoods where women's lives revolved primarily around family, it was faintly disloyal to spend time talking with friends that could be spent on cleaning and errands and child care.

Not every woman knew what she was missing. In those first years of childraising, long before we met, Pat remembers struggling to explain to her husband why she felt lonely surrounded by four children and a dawn-to-dark day; she told him she needed to hear the sound of an adult voice. And in a gesture as well-meaning and loving as it was desperately off-point, he bought her a radio.

Women have wider lives now. And busier lives. Friendship still has to be squeezed into a schedule that puts family and work first, and in the time crunch of modern life, friendship can be the first thing women lose. In the movie *One Fine Day,* Michelle Pfeiffer plays the very model of a stressed-out single mom with a schedule so tightly wrapped that when George Clooney asks her about friends, she snaps: "I don't have *time* for friends."

Time for friends? Women can't help but see friendship as the "treat" they can allow themselves only after the business of the day is done—if it's done.

And yet . . . when we ask women the best part of the workday, many say it is lunchtime, which gives them the excuse to "grab a bite" with a friend at work, to sit down and talk. Young mothers set up play dates for their infants and toddlers that are, in fact, mom dates. Women pencil each other in around work and kids and men and doctor appointments and trips to the supermarket.

In spite of all the time pressure, women go to great lengths to make new friends and keep old ones. The need for connection with other women, to live lives in relationships, is so great and the pleasure of these connections is so real, that women make remarkable efforts to counter the centrifugal forces of our society.

Every woman whom we ask, "What do you do with your friends?" answers first, "We talk." A woman friend calls another and says, "I have to talk." And what they both know is, if she doesn't, the big problem or the small dilemma will stick in her throat like a fishbone.

We talk, therefore we are . . . friends. Talk can be serious or funny, painful or exuberant, intense or joyous. But at the heart of the connections made is one sentence that women repeat over and over: "I know just what you mean."

Deborah Tannen, the linguistics expert who so perceptively chronicled the difference in the language of communication between men and women, struck a real chord with the title of her book: *You Just Don't Understand.* Women recognized that phrase of disconnection at a gut level. It wrapped up the dead end of misunderstanding and frustration women have often felt with boyfriends, husbands, fathers, co-workers.

"I know just what you mean" says the opposite. It is almost a mantra—said laughingly to a pal on an elevator giving a fast reprise of last night's date, said sympathetically to a friend with job troubles, said with deep, heartfelt emotion to a friend struggling in her marriage. "I know just what you mean" resonates for women because it conveys what friends offer each other at the core: understanding, empathy, care. "I know just what you mean," one woman says to another—and a burden is lifted. Both feel lighter in spirit. They are not alone.

Girls realize early in childhood that their friendships are rooted in talk. Friendship is defined at a very early age as the ability to comfort each other, to share feelings, to understand the world of school or family. As Tannen writes, "For grown women, the essence of frienship is talk, telling each other what they're thinking and feeling and what happened that day: who was at the bus stop, who called, what they said, how that made them feel."

One Halloween morning we listened to a class of fourth grade girls on a day when their thoughts were mainly on costumes and trick-or-treat bags. But as they sat cross-legged in the hallway of their suburban school, each jockeying to be next to her closest friend, the subject switched easily.

When Emily, a chubby-cheeked girl with long, polished blond hair, was asked what a friend is, she never missed a beat. "A friend is someone you can play with and trust to talk about things. Like if you got into trouble or something, like if you forgot your book, you could tell a friend before a teacher. And also, if they don't listen, then they aren't your friend."

Hilary, brown bangs flopping over her eyebrows, chimed in, "Well, if you feel kind of sad or something and you just need someone to talk to and your parents are at work or something, you can call your friends."

One after another, the girls (we have changed their names) added small stories about playmates who were also friends in need. "This year for Halloween we made a great mummy and put it out on the porch and it got stolen and my whole family was kind of upset. So I called Hilary. . . ." And Olivia remembered when her mother was in the hospital and "I was crying that night and I called Emily. . . ."

They are trying to understand their lives out loud, to forge their own identities in tandem with friends, and to make sense of the world—together. By the time they are teenagers, as Mary Pipher wrote in *Reviving Ophelia*, "Girls discuss the smallest details of conversations and events—who wore what, who said what, did he smile at her, did she look mad when I did that. The surface is endlessly combed for information about the depth."

It may often seem like prattle, the kind of chatter that makes parents and teachers roll their eyes, wondering when the kids will grow out of using the telephone as a lifeline. But it is in reality the first act of what we know will become a sustaining force in their lives as women.

Eileen Fennelly and Jenn MacDonough.

Many women remember early childhood friendships with longing, wistfully wondering whatever happened to the girls they once felt fused to forever. Do childhood friendships have to disappear? Can they be sustained?

We talked with two young women who have made it past some of childhood's basic turning points—two energetic, almost siblingest college students who are passionately determined to remain lifelong friends. Eileen Fennelly and Jenn MacDonough have been bonded since they were both five years old. Connection is so much part of their everyday lives, they use each other's phone number as their ATM password. They describe themselves as "having the same brain. We think the same things at the same time."

On a summer night at the end of their freshman year—at two universities in two states, six hours apart, they sit at the Fennelly dining room table, demonstrating what has held them together since they were almost literally first expressing their thoughts in full sentences.

"We talk all of the time about everything," says Jenn.

"All of the time," echoes Eileen.

"One morning we talked on the phone for three hours straight, we never have any silence or anything. We just talked, talked and talked. And we'd seen each other the night before," Jenn adds.

"And we were going to see each other in like an hour," says Eileen.

These young women, who grew up only five houses apart in the Boston suburb of Arlington, were thrown together in first grade when Jenn came to Eileen's house for after-school care. There were times Eileen resented this mandatory playmate—with whom she had to share both her mother and her Barbies.

To this day, they can cheerfully list their differences: Jenn has a straightforward personality and Eileen is the self-described "moody" one. Jenn "does" English and plays the piano. Eileen is good at math and field hockey. Jenn is the planner; Eileen is the one who starts a paper at 2 A.M., the morning it's due.

When they were kids, they had a volatile relationship with breakups and makeups. But they also created their own secret language. Their friendship survived the ups and downs of grammar school, even the time Jenn read Eileen's diary. By their senior year in high school, they had "watched" innumerable segments of *Beverly Hills 90210* with open phone lines and talked through every boyfriend.

"I got the first boyfriend, and you were mad at me that I met him, I don't know what it was," Eileen remembers, looking sideways at her friend.

"You were being a jerk," Jenn promptly responds.

"Yeah, probably," says Eileen. "Maybe when I was going out with him I had a lot more confidence and that made me act like—"

"Yeah," says Jenn. "And maybe I was a little jealous."

They shared the small stuff—what he said and she said—but also the big stuff: one parent's cancer threat, one sister's bulimia. In this "language lab," they acquired absolute knowledge of how the other would react to any given situation—and the absolute security of each other's company, each other's ear.

They faced their first separation when college came around. Jenn chose Ithaca; Eileen was accepted at Villanova. And suddenly they realized they were expected to handle disconnection the way adults do: with some sadness, but with their energies focused outward and away.

So they packed their parents' cars and, in tears, took off separately for New York and Pennsylvania, promptly calling each other from their new dorms the next day. "When I got there I was sobbing," says Eileen, glancing at Jenn. "I don't know why I was so sad. I guess it's just because it was a milestone."

They made new lives, new roommates, new friends—and each racked up a $300 phone bill to the other. In hock to their horrified parents, Jenn and Eileen learned to limit their calls to a twice-weekly half hour. The rest—and it was a lot—went to e-mail.

Each had wondered what it would be like to reunite after their freshman year. Would they have changed too much or replaced each other? "But it wasn't like that, it's like we picked up exactly where we left off," says Eileen.

Jenn and Eileen picked up where they left off because they didn't truly *leave* off—witness the phone bill. But this phrase, often stated with happy surprise—"we picked up just where we left off"—is one we've heard again and again. We have come to realize that friends often carry each other in their minds and hearts through long separations.

These two young women illustrate for us not only the energy—from the earliest ages—that women will put into establishing connection with each other, but how hard they will battle to keep it going with the central tool at hand.

"We talk for comfort. That's how girls figure things out," says Eileen. "It's like talking to yourself, but you are talking to someone else." Jenn says simply, "I can't analyze a situation if it's just myself. I need Eileen's feedback."

They still get mad at each other and make up, but they are learning how to argue and stay together, how to look at the world through two sets of eyes. Together they are figuring out not just what they want of men, life, relationships, but their basic values and beliefs. Will they make it as lifelong friends? We don't know, but we're willing to place a bet on it

———

The need, the capacity, to discover and create an identity by talking over time and distance and telephone cords may start early, but it is lifelong. Small talk? Imagine being a suburban housewife and mother in the 1950s who has just begun to believe tenuously, and against all the world's expectations, that maybe she can also write poetry. Imagine then meeting someone else who believes the same thing. What are the odds of that?

In the 1950s, poets Anne Sexton and Maxine Kumin were two such young mothers, each trying to find a creative voice. After meeting in a writing workshop, these housebound women began literally talking their way through their days and their early fragile hopes for themselves and their poetry.

On an open phone line—a lifeline—they read their work to each other. They wrote, read, rewrote, reread. Years later, in a joint interview, Kumin remembered with pleasure how they finally did a "wicked thing." What was it? "We put in a second line because our husbands complained we were always on the phone." Chortled Sexton, "We used to talk for two hours sometimes."

On that second line, they validated each other's work and life. They were each not "the only one." They not only understood but empowered each other. They spoke the same language and yet supported the search for their own different poetic voices. Years later, after some estrangement, after Sexton's long struggle with depression had led to her tragic suicide, Kumin could still remember those days fondly: "I confess we sometimes connected with a phone call and kept that line linked for hours at a stretch, interrupting a poem talk to stir the spaghetti sauce, switch the laundry, or try out a new image on the typewriter: we whistled into the receiver for each other when we were ready to resume. It worked wonders."

The isolation that Kumin and Sexton felt and fought has many modern echoes. Most women aren't as inventive as the two poets—or perhaps can't whistle that well—but many women recognize themselves in that story. Only the technology has changed.

In Maryland, two first-time mothers, Melinda (Mendy) Thaler and Jane Khoury, made the decision to quit their jobs and stay home with their babies. Mendy, who had been a concierge in a Washington office building, and Jane, a lawyer, actually met through their "matchmaker" husbands. "I was at home with the baby," remembers Mendy, "and Paul was desperately trying to find me friends." As it turned out, Jane was the wife of one of Paul's high school pals, and when the two husbands brought their wives together, they knew immediately they would be friends.

They talked, how they talked. They talked about the decision to quit work ("You feel guilty no matter which way you choose," said Mendy), about what comes next ("I don't need the validation of a job, I get it now from volunteer work," said Jane). They talked in the park, at Gymboree, at the mall, at the aquarium, while pushing strollers, changing diapers. When they couldn't be together, they talked for hours on the telephone. They began calling themselves members of the Society of the Cordless Phone.

They talked while making beds, doing dishes, tucking their cordless phones under their chins while they scrubbed the kids in the bathtub. "Gradually we opened up and talked about more than kids and work and whether we'd get any sleep that night," said Jane. "We would have long, intense conversations, and then my husband would come home and I wouldn't have that much to say." She added with a laugh, "Why can I talk forever to Mendy and not to him?"

They each have two children now, and Mendy has become a teacher. As they look back, these charter members of the Society of the Cordless Phone think about what it must have been like for their mothers. "My mother couldn't talk with her friends that much," mused Mendy. "She was restricted by the cord."

We look back on our earliest conversations with each other now with a new understanding of what has kept us coming back, dialing back, continuing a conversation over nearly three decades. In that first luncheon at the faculty club, a comfort zone opened up. The two of us could pass our stories across the tabletop like a salt shaker. If empathy is the ability to get into another person's emotional state, to walk a mile in her feelings, the best of friends have that ability.

The connections between women are not the passive dialogues that even women seem to downplay when they say we are "just talking." Women are not just venting their feelings, like sheets taken out for an airing. Among the best of friends there is that dance of mutuality we described before and can almost chart. One woman tells a story to the other, but even in the storytelling she pays attention to how it's received. The second woman listens and adds to it another thought, a question, an open-ended idea. As each understands the other, eyes lock, attention is paid, elbows go up on the table.

In that first year back when Ellen was calling Pat, sharing uncertain feelings over the long-distance line, she wasn't looking for an instant solution or a facile answer. The quick exchanges that we describe at the beginning of this chapter—Ellen's question about whether to get together for yet another postbreakup meeting ("Do I have to?") and Pat's answer ("Enough is enough.")—were by no means that abrupt. We would stay with each other, thinking and feeling out loud. When we were stuck, we were each other's engine. When we couldn't figure out what was going on by ourselves, together it became clearer. We could both give and receive help, and feel energized by both roles. And when we said good-bye, it was with a sign-off: "Thanks, I feel much better."

This is the pattern of women's relationships. Even with that cry—"I don't have time for friendship!"—in their ears, women are able to make quick, sometimes intense connections. In a plane, two mothers, strangers in assigned seats, launch into a conversation about the trials of traveling and mothering. At a conference or seminar, the shop talk crosses back and forth into personal talk.

Women have brought this style of connection to the workplace, which is now so frequently the primary "neighborhood" for working women. While researching her book on the workplace, *The Time Bind,* Berkeley sociologist Arlie Hochschild was struck by how many harried working mothers seemed starved for friendship and how frequently they made great efforts to seek each other out. "Friendships at work between women are becoming enormously important," she told us. She described the women at the company she studied as having "tremendously intimate conversations" with each other over quick cups of coffee, "doing rehearsals and postmortems" on everything going on at home—even when their co-workers didn't know their families.

Women often erase the distinctions between workplace and private relationships. And sometimes we see a kind of seamless talking-and-working friendship that truly bridges both the personal and the professional worlds.

We were lucky to see this in action in the most unlikely place: the high-rise office of two legal headhunters in Atlanta, Melba Hughes and Linda Sloan-Young, businesswomen who have merged their careers and their fortunes into one firm.

———

The day we visit them, Linda is a little nervous. Intense, volatile, her wispy blond hair pulled back tightly, earrings swinging, she leads us from a closed conference room—"we only put prisoners in here"—to one with windows. Rooms are on her mind.

For years, she and Melba have worked together in the same room, their desks at 90-degree angles, talking, talking, sharing; their separate conversations and separate meetings with others all blending together. It might drive other people crazy, but it worked fine for them. But now that business is

Linda Sloan and Melba Hughes.

booming and they are holding more separate meetings with separate clients, they need to cut back on the noise level—so partitions are going up.

"I have horrible separation anxiety," Linda moans. Melba points out patiently that they will be separated only by a folding door that can be left open. Linda looks doubtful. Then she brightens. "Okay, I've decided it's going to be very nice not to have to share an office with Melba anymore. She's the one who's going to be suffering because I won't be there."

Melba, the mellow, contained one, rolls her eyes. "We'll probably never close the door," she says.

Life at Hughes & Sloan jumps. It starts the same way every morning. They sit down together for what other business partners would call the "regular morning meeting." They review. They plan. They worry about their client list. They discuss expansion. But that's just the beginning.

"Talk to me," Linda demands. "Tell me something. What's going on?"

She isn't just talking business. She means kids, husband, the little pockets of resentment or worry or delight that thread through their lives. She pulls and prods; and Melba responds, taking her own sweet time. In her black suit, every inch the businesswoman, she offers the first real sharing of the day.

"I come in and I'm pissed off at Jim and she goes, what's wrong with you, I can tell something's wrong with you, tell me what it is," says Melba, settling back in her chair, grinning as she discusses their routine. "And I'm going, leave me alone, and she goes, well, all right, when you're ready to tell me, I'm here. And then at two o'clock in the afternoon, I'll say to her, let's take a break. We'll close the door and then I'll put my feet on the desk and I'll tell her."

Their names may be linked with an ampersand on the door of their office suite, but their lives are linked with talk. They began as boss and employee over ten years ago, sizing each other up in an interview that could win a prize on how not to get the job. Melba, very, very pregnant, was already in the business of matching lawyers with jobs. But her business needed help. Linda was just barely out of a marriage and "desperate"—"I was talking to the greengrocer to get out of the house."

"She was nontraditional, nonconventional," Melba says.

"Tell them what I looked like," urges Linda.

"She came in with a skinny ponytail and a safari hat, and she had on shoes with heels that were THIS high and she was very tanned—"

"You asked me about my shoes. I said these are my fuck-me shoes."

They are laughing now.

"As soon as she said that about her shoes, I said, oh, you're hired," says Melba.

Then, one glitch: Melba, who was about to have a baby, told Linda she was going to name her baby Amanda.

"That's my daughter's name," Linda said.

Melba decided instantly—forget Amanda. She and her husband, Jim, would choose another name.

It was love at first conversation.

Melba is black and Episcopalian; Linda is white and Jewish. Linda's life has been lived on a roller coaster; Melba's is rooted in family and structure. Linda does the hiring; Melba does the firing. Linda hates lunching with clients; Melba enjoys it. Each describes the other as the bossy one. They go

on diets together. "We're obese right now," says Linda (describing five excess pounds as "obese"), "but we lose weight at the same time."

That's the light stuff. But they did not get to their positions as heads of a
respected legal head-hunting firm through fun and games. Nor did they
reach the depth of the friendship they have by joking about shoes. The true
and personal connection was forged in the process of a rough lawsuit that
pitted the two of them against Melba's former partner.

When Linda came to the original firm, she says, "I couldn't figure out
why Melba was doing all the work and giving somebody else all the
money." She was uncomfortable with the setup and told Melba she was
leaving. "I told her the only thing that would make it better is if she would
come with me," Linda remembers. That was a wake-up call for Melba, who
was forced to admit to herself her own discontent. She resigned herself, and
the two women started their own firm

Later the sheriff showed up at their new office and served them both
with subpoenas. Melba's former partner was suing them. Melba and her
husband had just bought a house. Linda had a child to support. How could
they handle an expensive lawsuit without damaging their new business?

They decided to take no money from the business for six months, living
on savings. Then they countersued. They were partners in a crisis now.

"We'd deal with the lawsuit over the weekend," says Linda. "We spent
every weekend together eating pizza with the kids. I mean, her child's first
word was *litigation*. It was amazing."

"We were working day and night, and all this time, our relationship was
getting stronger, stronger and stronger," says Melba. "When I would lose it,
she would just be there to carry on, and in the beginning, I would lose it for
a day every couple of weeks, and then she would lose it for a day."

Finally, they settled the lawsuit. They were free of the strain and worry it
had caused. But for just a little while, Melba admits, she wondered what
would happen next, when they didn't have the litigation to hold them together. "I was really, really worried about what was going to happen to us,"
she admits.

But these two were on the same side and stayed there. They argue routinely, and fight full-blown. And they admire each other and praise each
other unstintingly.

"My parents think she's their kid," says Linda. "We're interchangeable in
a lot of ways. In the way we bring up our kids. The way we were brought
up. My parents couldn't love her more if she were their daughter. They
think of her like that. They talk to her like that."

To which Melba replies, without missing a beat, "They like me better."

Linda promptly laughs, "They do. They say, 'Why can't you stand up straight like Melba? Why do you have to swear? Melba doesn't say that.'"

They take care of each other's children. When Melba first hired Linda, she did what she had to do to give the professional/personal partnership its best shot—and that meant immediately finding someone to take care of Linda's small daughter. Years later, Linda returned the favor—"stealing" a nanny for her friend. "I was driving carpool and one of the families in the car pool had a really great nanny from Trinidad," she told us mischievously. "I hated the two kids in the car pool because they messed up my car real bad. So I stole the nanny and gave her to Melba."

How many times have they been each other's child-rearing adviser and expert? When Linda found herself embroiled in a fight with her preadolescent daughter over whether she could wear a bra, it was Melba who counseled, "For God's sake, buy the child a bra, what do you care?" and, years later, ran interference for the girl when Linda complained that the bra strap was showing under her daughter's tank top. And when Melba is too strict with her daughter, it's Linda who takes Ashley's side.

No, it isn't just that they take care of each other's children, they point out—they feel each one's child is their own. There was the time Linda blurted out to Ashley, "Oh, you really *are* my child," and only then the little girl looked at her, puzzled. "But how can I be?" she asked. "You're white, and I'm black."

So what happens if one of them leaves the firm, tries another career, moves to a different city? Linda laughs. "Oh God," she says. "We'd call each other six times a day." As we leave, Linda casts another mock-apprehensive look at the new office; we can tell she is already pushing open that folding door.

This was a friendship that took off immediately but really solidified in the crisis of the lawsuit. If they had been different people, that could have ripped their partnership apart. Their exuberance, their ability to be light-hearted and yet absolutely committed to their work, to create a workplace that seems both successful and "friendly," comes from the trust that experience forged between them. They have been through troubles together, knowing each can count on the other to deliver.

Trouble. Whether at the office or simply in their personal lives, that is the time when women most need to reach out to friends.

There is an expression that Ellen likes to use: "Thanks for talking me back off the window ledge." We have done that for each other when we needed a confidential ear or a reality check. When Pat was dealing with the turbulent teenage years of her youngest daughter, sometimes she crawled into bed, reached for the telephone, dialed Ellen's number, and asked, "What do I do now?" The conversation would range all the way from strategy—how do you get a sixteen-year-old to agree to a sane curfew hour without triggering defiance—to the emotional: what do you do and say when she's had a fight with her teacher and you think the teacher was right?

A friend calls a friend at the raw stage of experience: "I have to tell someone." Talking it out is feeling out loud. "I don't know what I'm feeling until I hear what I'm saying." She wants what Toni Morrison's character in *Beloved* once called a friend of the mind: "She gather me, man. The pieces I am, she gather them and give them back to me in all the right order."

For the big stuff, for the am-I-crazy stuff, the problems that are so difficult to unwind alone, we go to people we trust. Not simply trust to keep our confidence. But trust to stay with us and understand and put it into "the right order." Not tell us what to do, but figure it out together.

And sometimes what we need from a friend isn't talk at all. It's listening.

Pat

Ellen and I were sitting together on the beach in Michigan City, Indiana, watching my children playing in the surf. It was 1975. I hadn't been this close to South Bend in years, and even as I stared out at the lake my mind was elsewhere. It was back in the years of my marriage when my former husband had been on the faculty at Notre Dame and we had lived together, the six of us, in a grand old Dutch Colonial with sagging shutters. Way back. Ellen prodded me gently, and I said I had a hankering to see the place again.

She pulled her toes out of the hot sand and said, "Well, you've got to do it sometime. Let's go now."

I asked a neighbor to watch the kids, and we climbed into the car and drove to South Bend. We walked around the campus of the university first, revisiting places that held importance. I pointed out the spot where in the 1960s we attended outdoor Sunday mass with the kids sitting in the trees. I told Ellen how radical we all had felt. And I told her how, in the later days, I would wear dark glasses at mass because everything I had believed in felt as though it were slipping away.

I took her by the old Dutch Colonial. The house looked tired and sad, and I wasn't doing much better. I could almost see my children crunched companionably together on the porch, an umbrella over their heads, looking up delightedly at the sky. I told Ellen about the day I saw them there when I was coming home from Chicago just as a rain shower was ending, and how I knew at that moment I had been lucky enough—and all working mothers wonder about the moments they miss—to arrive in time to take an unforgettable mental snapshot.

We walked slowly around the house. I pointed out where the old swing used to hang. I told her about how the kids used to run after fireflies on hot summer nights and we would bring them home in jars, and they would go to sleep watching them glow.

I was only now becoming aware that I was carrying on a monologue, my friend silent by my side. "I'm talking too much," I said. "Oh, please," she said in her best tender/scathing way. She fell silent again, letting me find my own way through the memories.

We went back to the university and walked the leafy path up to the stadium, and I started laughing about the vanity that used to send me forth in a new too-warm fall dress at the beginning of each football season, only to languish, perspiring, in the stands. I told her about the time my ex-husband and I were roped into playing "chaperones" at a football game for a Notre Dame sophomore who had won a date with the Playboy Playmate of the Month. She later said to me, "You know, you ought to talk to Hef. You could be in the magazine." Ellen gagged.

I showed her the golf course where women were barred from playing (I started a polite furor by writing an article about it), complete with Notre Dame's excuse: they didn't have any bathrooms for women on the course.

The stories tumbled out now: not all sad; not all bittersweet. Some were wonderful; to be treasured; even funny.

When we finally got back into the car and sped off for the vacation cottage in Michigan City, it occured to me that only Ellen could have shared that day. She had come back with me into my past and helped me—simply by sticking by my side and respecting the experiences I was reliving. She didn't try to comfort or readjust those memories; she was too wise a friend for that. She didn't try to solve what wasn't solvable. She simply listened, as I talked.

3

Why Are Men's Friendships So Different?

Ellen

"Guess what I have in my hot little hand?" I call Pat as soon as the freelance check clears the envelope—$250, big bucks in 1975. Enough for a nonstop flight to Chicago while Katie is visiting her father in Florida. "It's burning a hole in my pocket," I say, and we both laugh. I had plenty of use for that money; there was a bathroom in disrepair, and the indoor-outdoor rug in the basement had seen a bit too much of the outdoors. "The hell with it. I'll be there on the first."

I line up two interviews for the book that was still—still—in its preliminary phase and explain to a man I'm dating that I am taking that rare weekend for a friendship hit in the Midwest. The day before I take off, I run into a newly divorced friend at the market. Brian and I stand at the counter; I tell him I'm headed for Chicago. Work? He asks. No, I answer, friendship. There is a quizzical look. It's not a wedding, a birthday, an illness? Just a visit?

Well, sure, I say, wouldn't you go visit your best friend? At that, he tells me about Mark. He and Mark go way, way back, back to their hometown of St. Louis, where Mark still lives. They've been through everything together. They skipped classes together in high school, they forged an ID that passed muster at the local liquor store. They spent college summers together mowing lawns and tarring roofs. Mark introduced Brian to his exwife, and was the best man at their wedding.

The line we are standing in moves slowly toward the checkout counter. How does Mark feel about the divorce? I ask. There is a small pause. "I haven't actually told him yet." I must look startled; it's been five months. Brian adds quickly, "I'm going to call him, soon."

When I arrive in Chicago and Pat and I are finally, blizzardbound, sitting across the table from each other, glad to be together, I began, "I have to tell you this story." And told her.

"Five *months*?" she says, astonished. "How is that possible? A woman wouldn't go five minutes!"

Pat

What a day that was. By the time we slogged through the snow to a restaurant and settled ourselves damply in our seats, we couldn't wait to start down our lists of things to talk about. Work, the kids, what wine to choose—it all came tumbling out in no particular order as we forgot the weather and relaxed into sharing the pleasure of each other's company. Naturally (it always happened sooner or later), we talked about men.

Ellen proceeded to tell me the story about the missing best man. "What do you make of it?" she asked. We began puzzling over a big question: *Did* men share the important stuff of life with their friends? How did they do it?

I told her about Richard, a neighbor in Evanston, whose parents had both been killed in a horrible auto accident. One morning shortly after that, as I walked to the train, I noticed that Richard and another neighbor had started scraping the old paint off his house. For the next two weeks I watched them out there early every morning, scraping, and then painting one coat and another, up on ladders, near each other. I never saw them talk, and once I wondered fleetingly if there was some tension between them. Then I ran into Richard's wife on the train one day, and commented on how nice her newly painted home looked.

"Yes," she said quietly, "Jerry spent two weeks of his vacation helping Richard get the job done."

I asked her whether the two men, old friends, talked much about the loss.

"Hardly at all," she said. "But I don't think Richard could have made it through without him."

I told this story and looked across the table, knowing Ellen's quizzical look must match my own. "How can they do it that way?" I said.

Why do men and women, on the topic of friendship, puzzle each other so much? Let us start with the obvious: women do friendship differently than men. Among women, friendship is conducted face-to-face. But as Carolyn Heilbrun once wrote, "Male friends do not always face each other: they stand side by side, facing the world." While women tend to *be* together, men tend to *do* together.

We have thought about this friendship divide ever since that dinner back in 1975, a time when sex differences were just beginning to go under an intense cultural microscope. We know that men's feelings of closeness and connection are real; that painting a house or watching a ball game together can be an act of friendship. But we also know we would feel lonely if we couldn't talk to each other about everything, through good and bad times.

The two of us have wondered over the years just what is going on between men. And the truth is, we have disagreed with each other about whether men are missing something so central to friendship that it amounts to almost a fatal flaw, or whether they are handling friendship just fine—in their own, mysterious way. Do men, as Letty Pogrebin wrote in *Among Friends,* deserve "Incompletes" in the subject of friendship? Are women in the business of grading?

"What on earth do you have to say to each other?" men ask. Women have their own counterquestion for male friends: "You spent all day together on the golf course and never told him you were worried about your job?"

When we first began telling people that we were writing about women and friendship, the second or third question would invariably be, "What about men? Are you writing about them, too?" Sometimes it was asked with a smile or a teasing challenge; sometimes defensively. We could hear a distinct subtext: if you're writing only about women, are you saying your friendships are better than ours?

We answered that we were writing about women because, if you write about what you know, what we know are women's friendships. We would leave it to men to write about their own friendships. The contradictory, complex differences between the two sexes in a time of such change is a topic for a different kind of book. Yet here we are, looking across the gender divide with curiosity and sometimes bewilderment.

Let's give comedian Rob Becker the first take on this subject. Becker plays Darwin to the sexes in the theatrical hit, *Defending the Caveman.* He announces to his audiences at one point that—at last—he has the gender-friendship gap all figured out.

So, here's how it works, he says. Men were the hunters, see? They were required to stand side by side without talking for fear they'd scare off the prey. Women? They were gatherers, out there foraging in the jungle for food. So they HAD to talk while they worked, for safety.

You get the picture? "If a woman goes for very long without hearing the voice of another woman, she knows she's been eaten by an animal," Becker announces. So women are genetically allotted some five thousand words a day, while men are allotted only two thousand. No wonder women talk more, he triumphantly concludes.

Well, hunters and gatherers aside, if there is one prototypical image of women sharing friendship, it's that of two friends sitting across a table from each other, clutching their coffee cups, talking feelings. If there is a similar image of men, it is of buddies sitting together watching television, talking football.

We know these images are simplistic and women and men are both guilty of stretching them to make assumptions about each other's friendships that range from the stereotypic to the bizarre. Men never talk about anything but sports, women say in frustration. Women talk only about clothes, men retort. Both sexes get trapped in vast generalizations. But the differences between the same-sex friendships of men and women are real. Decades of research can't be ignored.

A long list of studies tell men and women what they already know: men and women talk about different things in different ways. Men are less likely to talk about personal subjects with other men than women are with other women. As Pogrebin summed it up, "The average man's idea of an intimate exchange is the average woman's idea of a casual conversation."

What else do the researchers show? Men's friendships are based on shared activities, women's on shared feelings. Men who do things together, paint that house, change that tire, feel close; women who share secrets, troubles, relationships, feel close.

If you had a camera you could videotape the gender gap. Women literally touch each other more; they sit closer together, focus on one-to-one sharing. But when men talk about what they do with their friends, you get a different portrait: men doing things together in groups.

The research list goes on. Men do not criticize their friends as much as women, but neither do they communicate the kind of acceptance women count on from their friends. Men put shared interests highest among the reasons they bond with a friend, while women first want friends who share their values. And even men tend to view their friendships with women as closer and more intimate than those with other men.

And yet—here's the counterweight—at least among grade school boys, a study shows that a relative lack of intimacy and affection doesn't affect the importance or the satisfaction boys get from their friends.

Every friendship is as different as the people involved, and not all men are caveman hunters and not all women are cavewoman gatherers. But differences between male and female friendships have remained constant and consistent. What has shifted are the values placed on those differences. What's striking now is that the culture has gone from seeing men's friendships as superior to seeing women's friendships as superior. Is that just a swing of the pendulum?

It's not surprising that philosophers in the past routinely dismissed women as incapable of true friendship. They were certain that, because women led more "trivial" lives, they had limited capacity for elevated feelings. The classical idea of friendship was heroic, and the greatest thing a man could give a friend was his courage and loyalty. Montaigne once wrote in a spirit of superior regret, "To speak truly, the usual capacity of women is not equal to the demands of the communion and intercourse which is the sustenance of that sacred bond; nor do their minds seem firm enough to sustain the pressure of so hard and so lasting a knot."

Women, on the other hand, often idealized their relationships with each other. Historian Nancy Cott describes how educated women in the nineteenth century passionately poured out their feelings, often expressing their firm belief in the superiority of female relationships. "I do not feel that men can ever feel so pure an enthusiasm for women as we can feel for one another," wrote one woman to another. "Ours is nearest to the love of angels."

The idea that friendship is defined by intimacy has become, in our time, less fervently defined—but more solidly understood. As a result, the gender gap has been focused on the intimacy gap. And men's friendships are indeed often given an "incomplete" grade.

Carol Shields captured this swing of the pendulum in her novel *Happenstance,* a tale told from the two points of view of Brenda and Jack, a husband and wife in their thirties trying to understand themselves and each other. At one point, Brenda presses her husband Jack on his relationship with his best friend, Bernie, calling it "incredible" that they so rarely talk intimately. Jack is troubled by the challenge and broods over it:

> Perhaps it was really true that men seldom make close male friends after the age of twenty. . . . Was it in one of Brenda's magazines? Or a *Time* essay? . . . Men were failures at friendship. . . . The drive to compete and conquer or something like that was what did it. It froze the spontaneous bonds of affection that eased the friendships between women. (He had observed Brenda closeted with her friends; even on the telephone she leaned, sympathetic and nodding, into what seemed a sealed, privileged bathysphere.) . . . Brenda seemed to have the idea that close friendships had something to do with the baring of souls; somehow she'd never grasped the fact that something else was involved in his friendship with Bernie. And having this single and unique friendship, he realized that he was more fortunate than many of the people he knew.

"Failures at friendship?" The traditional western model of maleness has been one of independence. From Erik Erikson to Daniel Levinson, the old school assumed that children grew from being dependent to being independent—to "becoming your own man," as Levinson put it.

How did this shape the friendships of adult males? At the most extreme, there is the lonely image of Richard Nixon, a truly friendless man who was unable or unwilling to trust. "I never wanted to be buddy-buddy," he once said, "even with close friends, I don't believe in letting your hair down, confiding this and that and the other thing—saying, 'Gee, I couldn't sleep because I was worrying and this or that and so forth and so on.' I believe you should keep your troubles to yourself."

The new wave of psychologists that emerged with feminism looked at human development differently. They wondered what it would look like if a woman's perspective were included. Women, they understood, grew *in* relationship, not *out* of it. And while "women have learned empathy," as Jean Baker Miller says, "In the overall, men have been encouraged to turn away from learning about relationships, to develop in other directions, lest they be seen as 'womanly.'"

"Womanly?" Maybe, as some studies suggest, men sit further apart, keep friendship light, hold back affection out of their fear of homosexuality. Gay men's friendships, after all, are more like women's in the desire for intimacy and self-disclosure. Does that add weight to the possibility that much of the fear of intimacy in heterosexual men is rooted in homophobia?

Janet Surrey and Stephen Bergman, who, as husband and wife collaborators, have lectured and written extensively on gender differences, tell of a man in one of their therapy groups who attempted to start a male-bonding group based on the trips to the woods, the drum beating and other rituals encouraged by author Robert Bly. "We drummed and chanted and talked a little, but nothing, you know, grew," he said. "One of the things I suggested once was for each of us to call up the other guys on the phone. . . . Well, it was as if I had suggested we wear dresses or something."

Boys are steered away from "babyish" emotional responses early on in childhood. In the long years between preschool and adolescence, boys are busily building tree houses, playing computer games, competing on the field, all the while learning the boyhood hierarchy: who's up, who's down. They are expected to struggle for a place in that hierarchy.

But girls are not expected to break their early emotional connections. As they move into school and onto the playing fields, they still hold on to a different sense of relationship. In casual play, girls are much more likely to change the rules or even end a game to preserve their friendships. In class, they are small anthropologists, tracking all the relationships, able to share a remarkable peripheral vision, keeping an eye on the blackboard and each other at the same time.

We have two favorite stories about the early differences between boys and girls. One that the cartoonist Dan Wasserman told us is about the day his young son "made friends" with another boy. The two boys ran up to each other in the midst of a gathering, eyeballed each other, and, by way of introduction, bumped heads and then fell on the floor laughing with glee. Compare that with Pat's granddaughter Charlotte's introduction to coed soccer at the age of five. All the boys ran onto the field to play. The three girls on the "team" were feeling shy and uncertain, so they huddled first, whispering. Then they held hands and walked onto the field to join the boys. These are the contrasts that young parents note with bemusement and some chagrin.

Some of those differences are changing . . . and many are not. Step again with us into that classroom of fourth-grade girls. This really is the year, says their young teacher, Carrie Danforth, when the differences seem quite set. Even though Danforth works against this tide, she says, "The boys are still just little boys who would rather go out and play and be rough. They just get together and their bonding is because of what they do together."

When Danforth asks the boys what they did all weekend, she is likely to get a list of activities. When she asks the girls, they will talk about sleepovers, putting polish on each other's nails, what they talked about.

Asked if they think their friendships are different from the boys', the girls express no doubts. Lucy speaks up with total authority: "They might be friends in the same way, but they do totally different stuff together. It's like being a friend as a boy means to sort of go out and do sports all the time. Girls sit around and talk and stuff."

At nine years old, Olivia offers a young version of generic female bafflement. "Well, whenever I get home, I call Emily and Hillary every night and boys don't do this . . . because they . . . I don't know but they just like sports. That's all they think about, sports, sports, cars."

One other girl in the classroom, under the tutelage of Carrie Danforth's efforts to soften the edges of gender, pipes up, "That's a stereotype." Danforth nods approvingly. Encouraged, the girl adds, "Some boys may like to just stroll around the woods or something." Others nod. But almost immediately they click back into comfortable assertions of what they actually believe and experience.

Boys, in turn, get baffled observing all the intensity and drama around girls' friendships. They express bewilderment at their lack of focus on the task at hand; for example, how can talking be more important than winning the game?

At about the sixth grade, these criticisms are voiced more coherently. Surrey and Bergman collected a remarkably straightforward list of questions the sixth- to eighth-grade boys and girls they studied asked about each other. This is what the girls wanted to know about boys:

✦ Why don't boys cry?
✦ Why do boys beat each other up?
✦ Why don't they talk much?
✦ Why don't boys talk about anything interesting?

The boys, in turn, had their own puzzled queries about girls:

✦ What do girls do all day?
✦ Why is everything such a big deal?
✦ Why do girls gossip all the time?
✦ Why do they whisper and giggle?
✦ What's with all that sighing and crying?

The differences in what boys and girls experience and expect of friend-ship seem to harden in adolescence. Boys become anxious about intimacy and girls even more anxious about separation. We saw this one November morning at a high school class outside of Portland, Maine, where the teenage students sitting in a gender relations workshop seemed to be nearly as far across the gender divide from each other as the teenagers in our own high schools in the 1950s. And so was their male teacher.

One of the girls, responding to a question about what a friend is, said, "A friend is someone you tell your feelings to." Countered the teacher: "I don't bother my friends with sadness."

The girl argued the point. "But if you can't talk to anyone, you will feel that you're all alone. Like when I'm upset I would tell friends so I would have the support of other people. Like, they were there and cared enough about me to make sure I was okay and to help me figure out what my prob-lem was."

"There's a satisfaction in dealing with it alone, in knowing that you in-dependently overcame the hurdle," the teacher replied.

A male student spoke up, agreeing with the teacher. "I think sometimes it does feel better. Friends are friends, but they are not always there, men-tally or physically. So I'm not going to sit in a corner. You just keep it to yourself, you can handle it, you can achieve it. It makes me feel better if I can handle it by myself." It isn't right to burden your friends with your trouble, he continued. "Like a friend says, 'How's it going?' and you say, 'Oh it's bad,' and then they'll feel bad. If you are going to go down, go down by yourself. You don't have to drag anyone else down."

Only one boy broke across the gender divide in this brief discussion. He insisted he *did* talk about his feelings to his friends. But when asked how often, he said, "Well, I do it with my female friends."

This classroom reinforces the research saying women are generally ex-pressive with their friends—all across the emotional range—and men more self-protective. Listening to these teenagers, we couldn't help thinking of a Toyota ad that we had just seen flashed on a television screen: "Women

Leave You. Bosses Fire You. Friends Forget You. Trucks Are Forever." The message to men: Stand on your own two feet. Or drive on your own four tires.

What happens when we get to adulthood? All the patterns that men and women learn in childhood are deeply ingrained—even today. Same-sex friendships become the comfort zones where both sexes look for solace or understanding. Women may look for the kind of intimate relationships with men they have with women, while men still find face-to-face, over-the-table dissection of emotions overwhelming.

In a study of college students, researchers found women were less lonely when they had other women to talk to. But, more interestingly, they found that men too were less lonely when they had more interactions with women. Do men know they are missing something?

Becker, our caveman guide, answers that by making us laugh at the stereotypes. "Women get together with their friends and have those creepy talks. Men do not say, 'Hold me, Chuck, I need to cry.' When they greet each other, they say 'Hi, dickhead.' To a guy, that's like pouring your heart out."

You can certainly hear men "pouring out their hearts" if you tune in to guytalk radio. "Imus in the Morning" is pockmarked with a ritual exchange of male insults. In one, Don Imus provokes his sidekick, Charles McCord, until Charles calls him: "A-hole!" Imus retorts, "You're an a-hole!" They go back and forth till Charles says, "You're a constellation-sized a-hole," and Imus tops him with "You're a Stephen Hawking's size a-hole." They both laugh, not a blow struck or an ego offended at this friendship play.

Nevertheless, a man in one of Bergman and Surrey's meetings objects, "I hate to say it, but we men need to learn to just sit on our butts and talk," he said.

An enormous number of contradictory things are going on simultaneously. There is much more self-consciousness about sex roles, and there are changes within each sex and between each generation.

Eileen McNamara, a *Boston Globe* columnist and friend, tells about the time her son Timmy brought home two sex education questionnaires from school—one for her to fill out, one for her husband. What did each of them like best about being a woman or man and what did they miss most? Without even talking to each other, Eileen said what she liked most were the rich friendships women had throughout their lives. Her husband, Peter May, said what he missed most as a man were the kind of friendships that women seemed to have. Their son was astonished. What his mother liked best about being a woman is what his father missed most about being a man.

Talking about differences almost inevitably leads to talking about "better" and "worse." At times, it seems that men and women have entered into that contest. And even women go around and around this discussion: Can women's friendships be too intense? Are men's too distant? The two of us debated this all the way through this chapter.

One evening at a charity event, Ellen fell into a conversation with U.S. Senator John Kerry about this book. "Is the idea that women's friendships are better?" he asked quickly. "Different," replied Ellen. "Yeah, but are they better?" he pressed.

The irony was that we were discussing one of those differences: the sense that men, especially young men, are taught to think in a competitive hierarchy, to struggle with who is up and who is down. This ranking can make it hard to get close. How easy it was to turn this into a competition: "Are women's friendships better?"

Kerry, a Vietnam War veteran, then talked at length about how close men become in combat, when the fear and intensity breaks down traditional male barriers to intimacy. He said that when men leave the battlefield for home, the old ways reassert themselves—except perhaps when they are reunited with their army buddies.

We know the closeness that male friends feel; we've seen it. Men who, as Ellen's uncle Mike, a veteran of World War II, says, "soldiered together" through both terrifying and bonding experiences, have feelings that few women can share. Pat's husband, Frank, a veteran of the same war, remains strongly connected to Dan, his foxhole mate, and always will be.

The men in our own lives are not inarticulate or paralyzed in intimate conversation. Ellen's husband, Bob, and his best friend, Howard, may go to L.L. Bean fishing school dressed up in full trouting regalia, but they also laugh and share love and loss.

It seems to us that men become more emotionally expressive with friends as they get older. The hierarchical struggle that may make younger men wary of intimacy with each other—"What happens if it leaves me vulnerable?"—becomes less important. And so does the concern that if one man expresses empathy for another, he is suggesting that his friend is "in need," the translation for which is "weak."

Historian Stephen E. Ambrose acknowledges that friendship among men is difficult. "I was well into my fifties before I discovered the pleasure of hugging a male friend," he writes. "Now I do it habitually."

In his book, *Comrades,* written in his sixties, Ambrose paid this tribute to his dearest friend: "I love Nick and he loves me. He would die for me and I for him. We have no secrets. . . . Our trust in each other is complete. . . . I can't imagine life without Nick." Ambrose continues, "This is what friendship could, should, might be. Growing together, supporting one another, keeping the other guy's dreams alive. . . . There is no element of struggle in it, no pushing, only lifting, drawing the other guy on, teaching, working in partnership without ever having to ask for help."

Would any women fault that expression of friendship?

Carol Tavris, a frequent writer on psychological issues, offers some fair warnings against "feminizing" the definitions of intimacy and friendships. "Male friendships are scorned as superficial, based as they are on shared interests in, say, the Mets, and Michelle Pfeiffer," she says. But not enough weight is put on the abiding connections of men who show up, who "are there" for each other. She tells the story of the night she and her husband—scheduled for worrisome medical tests—had dinner with an old friend of his. "I watched, fascinated, as male stoicism combined with English reserve produced a decidedly unfemale-like encounter. They laughed, they told stories, they argued about movies, they reminisced. Neither mentioned the hospital, their worries or their affection for each other. They didn't need to," Tavris wrote. She added: "Women could learn a thing or two from this."

In their own lives, women do learn this. Some of the most memorable gestures of friendship are just that—gestures, acts of friendship that require no words. Ellen still remembers the night before her daughter's fourth birthday, when she sat on the sidewalk outside her house, overwhelmed by the challenge of putting together the bicycle she had bought for Katie. The pieces lay out on the sidewalk; Ellen couldn't tell an axle from a fender. It was one of those moments when a single mother is absolutely sure she has failed in the task of being mom-and-dad. But then Otile arrived like a St. Bernard, with a six-pack of beer and a Phillips screwdriver.

That rescue operation required no words, just action.

We too have felt the comfort of side-by-side silence. One evening on an exhausting political campaign, after writing our stories under frantic deadlines, we went for a walk. We covered block after block in dead silence. Not a word was exchanged. And what we realized later was this: women friends have to reach a comfortable level of intimacy to be able to be silent with each other, and men have to reach a comfortable level of intimacy to be able to talk with each other.

We had a chance to observe men practicing friendship one hot August day in Washington. Want to see how male friendship works in action? Come to the softball field.

This is where Pat's stepson, Ben, meets with a group of childhood friends as many times as possible each summer for the ritual of a shared ball game. By now all these men are in their early thirties. They have known each other literally from babyhood, marking the transitions together from the playpen through high school and college. They are all now living different lives in different cities—one is a television anchor, two are lawyers; another is in politics, another an actor. They have flown in from Chicago, Los Angeles, Boston, Miami. Their camaraderie and sense of comfort with each other is seamless. Their greetings are totally casual, as if they had seen each other yesterday. The game begins, stitched with jokes, high fives, and such expressions as "Hey"; "Great catch"; "Way to go."

But they're not just playing a softball game.

Bits of information start going back and forth. Somebody asks about a sick mother-in-law. Somebody else mentions a book he likes. Someone else claps a friend on the back who has just struck out. "Hey. Next time." Someone mentions casually a commuting problem with a girlfriend. An undeniable vein of pleasure runs through the morning. Although they play hard—Ben is known for some spectacular catches—which side wins or loses doesn't seem to matter all that much. It'll turn around "next time."

Dan Hamilton, a blithe young man with a quick mind and a sense of the ridiculous, is leaning against the sagging cyclone fence that surrounds the field, waiting his turn at bat. Ben walks over, pulling off his glove. We talk about how long this group of guys

Sister and brother Rachel Hamilton and Dan Hamilton.

has known each other, how much they've done together, how they are sticking together even as they marry and move away. How, they are asked, would they describe their friendships?

They look at each other, and Dan starts off—hesitantly at first, then confidently. "They're based on a mixture of intimacy and humor," he says. "One of us might bring up a problem, and the others can be listening and caring, and then someone makes a joke, and we go into a joke riff for four minutes." He grins. "We can veer from Mark McGwire to personal stuff and back and it's not belittling. It's just shifting away and back. There's something liberating and genuine in not having a quote 'discussion' unquote. You can't be above being punctured by fast and funny."

Ben agrees. "Almost nothing is a big deal, and we cherish that. If someone stops for coffee and is late, it's okay, if no one is kept waiting long. For us, humor is the whole nine yards, and sometimes women take jokes the wrong way."

"Do we talk?" says Dan, warming to the subject. "Yes. Is it revelatory? Yes. With subjects and verbs? No. It's not female serious. It's our way of being free and uninhibited."

Ben nods. "There's a comfort level that sometimes women can't supply. It works for us."

We hear the crack of the ball against the bat. The runner streaks for first base, then second. Now it's Dan's turn. He tosses a quick joke over his shoulder to Ben, and strides up to the plate.

———

We know about "comfort levels"; we know the ones that work for us. And we're still wondering about the differences. So one crisp fall night, we invited Dan and his sister, Rachel Hamilton, a wonderfully talkative pair with an equal abundance of same-sex friends, to talk with us.

Dan is a graduate student in the history of law, and Rachel is an exuberant actress from Los Angeles who was in Boston for a prewedding gathering that had reunited her with four of her dearest friends from high school.

There's been a generation of change since we were first struck by the silent camaraderie of the two men painting the house in Pat's neighborhood, and astonished by the distance between Brian and his "best man" that Ellen noted. Dan and Rachel were more than willing to sit down with us and—with a lot of laughter and frankness—help put the puzzle pieces together.

So, we ask, how *are* their friendships different?

———

Rachel: Mine are cooler.

Dan: Oh, hey, *thanks.*

Rachel: Well, we're really good at playing. When we met at the restaurant this week, there was a huge amount of affection, tons of "OH, MY GODs"; oh, it was a big scene. We can't get enough of the "*Oh, my God, you are here, you are here*" kind of energy.

Dan: Yeah, I was there. It was incredible to observe. They go at it all at once. Someone is talking about the waiter, someone is mocking the Backstreet Boys, and someone's talking about shoes. They're all draped over each other, and they can *all take it all in.* I felt like Robert Young in *Father Knows Best:* "I have no clue what the kids are talking about these days."

Rachel: Oh, that was our reuniting lunch. But these are *incredibly* nurturing friendships; we're not bitching or Barbieing with each other. We do get very intense.

Dan: When we reunite, it isn't like that. First, there's a handshake. I can't imagine not seeing my friends after a long while without shaking hands. We hug, but it's perfunctory and awkward. We hug to indicate we're close, not to feel an embrace. Then we begin to insult each other—you know, someone is wearing bad pants or has weird hair. It becomes a contest to see who can be funniest and who can win.

Rachel: Well, we do *some* teasing. There are some areas where it's okay—you can say, "What's that, flashdance?" to someone wearing five-inch heels.

Dan: For us, it's playful.

Rachel: For us, the territory can get painful.

Dan: It's not personal, it's fodder. We're not talking about each other.

Rachel: Is it just stuff—like sports stats?

Dan: We're trying to create a little play, a riff, just mixing it up. It's fun.

Rachel: *We* get to the important stuff fast. It's like, let's connect. You have the floor, I have the floor. What's going on, where are you? We get to the core quickly. And if we don't get to the core quickly, we know there is something wrong. "*Seriously,* how are you?"

Dan: I don't want to get to the core unless they want to get to the core. Every once in a while, someone will say something surprisingly needful, and there's a kind of a hush.

Rachel: You get real.

Dan: Not really, we were real before.

Rachel: If you get rejected by a girl, do you think, I have to call Ben and talk about it? Or if you get fired, or something—what do you do about that?

Dan: Well—I might call a friend. But I wouldn't talk about it except in a self-deprecating way. I'd say, "I've been fired." And Ben would say, "Well, you probably deserved to get fired." And I would say, "Probably." But there is a mode in reserve. Crying. Crying is taken very seriously.

Rachel: So maybe it's the knowledge that, if you really wanted to, you could go to your friend, you could use that escape hatch. It's just nonverbal.

Dan: It's a mistake to think just because men aren't speaking, they aren't intimate. I was upset once and Ben said, "Come to Miami," and I was there in four hours. I don't think we talked about what happened for more than twenty minutes.

Rachel: Sometimes I envy that. Sometimes I just want to play and not necessarily talk about everything. Sometimes when I'm in an intense discussion, my capacity is reached, and I feel like a bad friend because I just want to flirt with the bartender.

Dan: Can't you just say, "Is there a car chase coming in your story?"

Rachel: Yeah, *very funny*. So what about your friendships with women? You meet them and want to talk about life?

Dan: I ask them a question, "How's the job going," and when they answer, "There's some good and there's some bad," it catches me off-guard. I think, "Oh, we're going to talk in paragraphs. Oookay."

Rachel: I don't see how you guys actually tell each other anything.

Dan: It's easy. I get a new job. I say to my friends, "Got a big office." They say, "Got a PHONE?" I say, "Phooooone." "DOOR?" "Doooor." You think that's slapstick? It's nurturing in its own way. Guys find their own level. Is that true for women?

Rachel: I don't know if we have just one level. What we share is an ability to form really close relationships with other women. It's huge. It's what makes my life great.

Dan: It's a mistake to think that just because men aren't speaking, they aren't intimate.

Rachel: I buy that. I think the stereotype of men being less sensitive and not in touch with their feelings is pretty much bullshit. I know it's there. But how it's sublimated, I don't know.

Dan: And I wonder about that subterranean world of yours, that "Let's touch base, where are you, how do you feel," which you do a lot.

Rachel: Every day.

Dan: We get to the core with each other by knowing we don't have to talk about something important. The implicitness is more powerful than anything that can be said.

Rachel: I couldn't do it that way, I couldn't. Talking with my friends is like oxygen. I can't think of any other way to live than having a few select friends who know me well.

So, we go back to the puzzle. Male friendships are not as intimate by any of the standard measures we've discussed. Does that mean that men are missing something? Even if they don't think they are? Does it mean that men friends should be more like women friends? Or do we just acknowledge the differences and let it go at that?

We argue it with each other.

Ellen: I *still* think men would be better off if their friendships were more like women's. I still think most of them are missing intimacy.

Pat: You mean our definition of intimacy. This nonverbal stuff isn't all a joke. Aren't we being just a bit smug to say ours is the *only* way?

Ellen: Don't forget, when men really talk, they usually do it with women. If they could really talk to each other too, wouldn't it make life easier for them, *and* for women?

Pat: If they feel their connections are real, on their own terms, why would they want to?

Ellen: Well, it wouldn't be enough for me.

Pat: It wouldn't be enough for me either.

4

Taking Chances

Pat

It was a lazy Sunday morning in midsummer of 1976, the kind of morning where everything is sleepily predictable. The kids and I were finishing breakfast in the dining room, the sun pouring through the windows, the Sunday comics spread in full color all around the table, when the phone rang. It was Ellen. I could hear the excitement in her voice before what she was saying had fully registered—there was a job opening representing the *Detroit Free Press* in the Washington bureau of Knight-Ridder newspapers. Was I interested? She knew the editor and she had recommended me. It would mean more money, a big jump in my career, and wouldn't it be great if we lived and worked in cities that were at least in the same time zone?

I was startled. A job in Washington? Unlike many reporters, I had never been in love with politics. I wasn't yearning for the nation's capital, but I wanted a better job with more money and a better future. Things had grown stale at the *Sun-Times*. People were being moved laterally; there was a lid on salaries and whispers all around that the paper was losing money and would have to be sold. "Maybe," I said, my heart starting to pump faster. "Let's see what happens." My kids were chattering peacefully in the next room and I was feeling simultaneously excited and frightened by the most accurate premonition of my life: I was going to get that job offer and it was going to be tempting. And if I took it, I would leave a city I loved. But most of all, if I took the job, I would be taking my family through major, jarring change.

Things moved quickly. I was interviewed and—my premonition coming true—was offered the job, throwing everything into turmoil. On one track, as part of the courting process, I was being flown to Washington to meet people in the bureau. On the other track, I was trying to find a way to stay in Chicago. My editor at the *Sun-Times* told me I was crazy not to jump at the chance to go to Washington, but I was talking to an editor at the *Chicago Tribune* about switching newspapers. I talked with friends, with my parents, with my children. I knew I was sitting on a plum job offer, but I couldn't decide. I was afraid.

Just before the bicentennial Fourth of July holiday, I turned the job down. But the knot in my stomach didn't loosen. That Saturday I lay on a hot beach listening to my eldest daughter, Marianna, and her friend Susan discussing their plans for college, for life, for the unknown future. I remember saying to them, "Do all the stuff you're dying to do now while you're single and without responsibilities—don't wait." I heard myself saying these words, knowing I was also saying, "It's too late for me," and I didn't like that. I didn't feel virtuous or responsible or at peace. I felt sad. I felt old. I had turned forty that spring, and part of me was just beginning. I wasn't ready to wrap life up into a safe package.

When I arrived at the *Sun-Times* early Monday morning, the newsroom was almost deserted, with just a few of the older reporters, round-shouldered, hunched over their typewriters, sitting at littered desks. I glanced down at the floor. Someone had spilled a cup of coffee on the linoleum the Friday before and it had dried into a splotchy stain. The whole place seemed static; a still life. I stepped over the dried coffee and headed for my desk. Had I just passed up my one chance to move on? To grow in my work and my life? Was that what I had done?

Later at lunchtime I walked into the Loop and started wandering through Marshall Field's department store. I could undo this, I thought. Maybe. But, did I want to? Could I really reverse course and give up everything in Chicago to try something new? I figured that the job had been probably offered to someone else by now. My feet were taking me to a public telephone just outside the china and crystal department. I called the editor who made me the offer, knowing he was already at the Democratic National Convention. My hands were shaking and I had to dial twice, and I sensed a woman waiting impatiently behind me for the phone. "Are you changing your mind?" his secretary asked me. "Yes," I said. "Wonderful!" she said. "He'll call you tonight. Congratulations!"

I dialed one more number: Ellen's. And I told her. This time, it was for real. Her voice coming from that phone reminded me of my strengths. She had never tried to persuade me to take the job; instead she remained what she had been for me through the entire painful time: a steady anchor to myself.

I hung up in a daze and blurted to the woman waiting behind me, "I just made a decision that will totally change everything."

"I hope it was the right one," she said simply.

Not everything in life has a clear answer. The decision was right for me in many ways, but it was a fundamental good-bye. In particular, it was a major uprooting for my daughters. I look back now and think about the sadness this brought to my ex-husband, who was losing daily access to his kids. He hung in there for them, and that helped make it possible for the two of us, years later, to reach our own peace with our past.

I think back to this time not only as a major transition in my life, but as a major transition in my friendship with Ellen. The decision to move to Washington involved a sequence of events set into play by my friend, and perhaps a shakier friendship might have left me with the temptation at some point or another to say, "*What* have you gotten me into?" But she was with me every step of the way. It was in a sense the most significant deepening of our friendship to that point. And she understood the pulls in both directions.

Ellen

I didn't hesitate for a minute. Kurt Luedtke, the *Free Press* editor, had a job to fill. I had a candidate: Pat. It was a no-brainer, a perfect fit. Not just for the *Free Press,* but for Pat. It was a way out of the *Sun-Times* leaky boat, the office that was too small for Pat's ambition, the paycheck that was too small for her family. How many hours had we spent complaining, feeling stuck? This was a big-time job.

I had a wide-angle view of Pat's life that included her family and saw glimpses of the disruption. But I have to say that at the moment I called, my only real emotion was excitement.

That summer of '76, I had just begun to be syndicated. The Xerox tele-copier, that precursor to the fax machine, sent my column from *The Boston Globe* office to *The Washington Post* Writers Group at the top floor of 1150 Fifteenth Street. From there they sent it out to the clients—exactly six—who had signed up that March. It was a stress test of the first order and nearly every one of those early 750-word columns was run by my friends Otile and Bob or tested out over the phone to Chicago.

I realized even then how lucky I was to be able—bless you, Xerox—to step up and onto a larger soapbox without ever leaving home. I am the homebody of the two of us, rooted in my extended family. I was living less than a mile from the apartment I grew up in, in the same town as my mother, sharing backup child care and all the daily concerns with my sister, Jane. I was acutely conscious of my own desire to reach out while staying put.

But Pat? On that day when I cavalierly, cheerfully called her up—ab-solutely knowing that she would get this job—I thought mostly about how this could be *the* move, the one that we had talked about, planned, the one that fit the pact we'd drawn up two years before. After all the complaints, it was a chance to act.

I believed then that Pat was far more adventurous than I. In fact she was. In fact she is. In the way that two people will enjoy each other's differences, I had always seen her as more dramatic, the one who loved fireworks and roller coasters. I was the one who preferred to have her feet on the ground. Still, I had no idea how big a roller-coaster ride this would be.

In the weeks when Pat was interviewed, in the days when she changed her mind, agonizing over the phone line, yes, no, maybe, I listened, did the pros when she did the cons, switched to the cons when she did the pros. But there is no doubt that I hoped she would go for it.

I put my friend first, above her family, or maybe just out of the context of her family. Friends can do that. We talk to each other about our personal dreams, we take them seriously, and the best of friends want those dreams realized. But I remember that call from the pay phone in Marshall Field's when I could "hear" the color in her voice—white as a sheet.

In retrospect, I think she packed up one life for another because of something pretty deep: Pat would rather regret the chances she took than the chances she passed up.

But I do wonder now how much of my own excitement was personal. I was breaking out and I wanted my pal to come along. I was, as well, heading onto the Bos-Wash corridor and it would be, well, fun to be back in the same world, to be within commuting distance.

At no time, during the next winter—when the kids were trying to fit into new schools, when Pat was trying to keep a drafty house warm and a new job afloat—did Pat ever point a finger my way. The Chinese have a belief that you are responsible for the life you save. What about the life you change? Friends do this for each other all the time. We introduce our friends to Mr. Right or Mr. Wrong. We go together to pick out a house. We say, yeah, sure, you can handle another baby, or, listen, you can make it on your own without him.

And sometimes we pick up the phone and say, "Pat, guess what? I just put your name in for a great job."

We have described the classic image of women friends comforting each other; listening, affirming, supporting. Carolyn Heilbrun calls such friendships "societies of consolation."

But there are times when a friend provides more than the warm soup of empathy. She becomes a catalyst for change. Over a long life, full of disruptions, stops, and start-ups, friends can be the collaborators, the instigators who make change possible. They are often the ones who urge us to take a leap, who jump with us or help us scramble back up the other side.

This is especially true for women today who are improvising their lives. Mary Catherine Bateson, author of *Composing a Life,* described her own life as "a sort of desperate improvisation in which I was constantly trying to make something coherent from conflicting elements to fit rapidly changing settings." Women often make repeated course corrections in life without a clear map or guidebook. So they turn to each other.

It was even more true at the time Pat picked up and went to Washington—for a job! For her own ambition! There was little cultural support for a mother to uproot a family and move away for her career. We could both say intellectually, turning the pages of *Ms.* magazine, that a woman had as much right to do it as a man, but it often sounded hollow. The background chorus of disapproval for this kind of move was powerful—and internalized. At such times, friends were the only ones there to provide a small dose of encouragement.

Throughout our friendship, we have encouraged each other to take the next step, to figure out what it should be, how to get there, and how to make it work. And if it was a disaster, how to regroup. We became agents of change for each other, if that is not too academic a phrase, developing a mutual support system that saw us through a lot of rough times. But cheers aren't enough, and this deepened role has risks.

This time, in the decision to move to Washington, Ellen was both instigator *and* collaborator, but it was Pat who took the risk. The stakes are high when one person, at the urging of the other, steps out to the edge of the cliff. The result is a deepened responsibility that can put pressure on the weak spots in a friendship. Certainly this period of upheaval underscored the differences between us.

In part, friends are more likely than family to encourage change because families, after all, have an investment in stability and continuity. They can be essentially conservative, wary of the individual risk and change that can destabilize the whole. Mothers, fathers, sisters, brothers may have old or inflexible ideas of our identity. Even the most loving family may want each member to go on playing a designated role.

Friends are granted private access to the center of women's hearts; they see the pieces that don't quite fit or are hidden from view. Those parts of the self make us push out against narrow confines of family roles toward a wider world. And friends may represent that world. Anaïs Nin once wrote, "Each friend represents a world in us. A world possibly not born until they arrive, and it is only by this meeting a new world is born."

Pat's daughter Margaret can almost precisely pinpoint such a moment in her own life: it happened as she talked with a new friend, Christine, while walking one morning on the cliffs of Catalina Island. Both women, busy wives and mothers in their mid-thirties, were trying to muster up the courage to take big leaps in their careers—Christine, a psychiatrist, yearned to compose music. Margaret, a documentary producer, dreamed of selling an ambitious project on ancient Rome.

"In that one great morning, we realized we were in the same place at the same time," Margaret said. "Our husbands were totally supportive, but it was so exciting to find a kindred spirit—the understanding, the joy of reinventing ourselves—we gave each other the encouragement to break out and *do what we wanted to do.*"

Christine urged Margaret to write a proposal for her project; Margaret encouraged Christine to get the composing software she needed and start writing music. Christine's compositions are now performed professionally, and Margaret got her funding. Now, when she has to spend three weeks overseas on a shoot, it is Christine who urges her on. "Don't worry," she tells Margaret. "I'll be there to take care of the kids' play dates."

"We are driving each other forward," Margaret says. "And when we flag, we call each other for encouragement. I don't understand music, and she doesn't know art and history, but we are learning from each other. And nobody understands the trade-offs like she does."

This excitement, this heady sense of having a partner who makes you stronger, can start early in women's lives. When children—especially girls on their way to becoming women—are ready for change, they often look to friends to see who they really are, or who they are becoming. During adolescence, girls most urgently and famously need someone to see them not as they are,

Maureen Strafford and Mary Gordon.

but as they want to be. They search for encouragement, as they take their first major steps away from their identity within a family, a school, a church. Sometimes they'll find a friend with whom they test limits and take dangerous risks. But they also look for a partner who can share a joyful, liberating moment. There may be a turning point when two are truly stronger than one, and, as in a game of Red Rover, they break for their lives.

To this day, Mary Gordon and Maureen Strafford, a novelist and a doctor, both wives and mothers, remember the precise moment when they held hands and ran. It was a moment they plotted as carefully as inmates planning a jailbreak.

It was 1966. Mary and Maureen were Catholic teenagers in a Queens parochial high school, so smart they left their classmates in the dust. Everyone—the nuns, their families—assumed they were heading for a good Catholic college, maybe Manhattanville, but that wasn't what they wanted. In high school, they felt the walls closing in. They could imagine themselves caught in lives stultified by rote and the confining expectations of their families. They knew any daring actions they might consider were electrically wired for sin. Especially the idea—the shocking idea—of attending a non-Catholic college.

They look back on that time now and describe themselves as turtles, each providing the other with a shell.

"We had the other, that was all the home you needed," says Mary, an angular woman with large, fearless eyes and dark hair. We talk one November day around Ellen's dining room table. "Why would you want another home where somebody else was going to yell at you or tell you to do something? We wanted to get out. We had to get out of our families. We were desperate to get out into the world."

Maureen, soft and pretty, as round as Mary is angular, remembers herself floating a little more placidly with the current. "Mary was much more courageous about stepping out into the world than I was, much more brazen about it. We felt it was so easy to deal with our world as it was, it was easy to be the smartest kids in the class. We ran the school. It was so simple, it was pathetic."

It's easy in retrospect to see why Mary and Maureen formed a company of two in their adolescence. Mary came from a dark home. She is intense, piercingly honest, analytical. She looks at the world without flinching. Maureen is open, generous-spirited, wildly overcommitted. But together they have a lightness of being and a seriousness of purpose that seems whole—a whole grown in concert with each other. Most important, they shared the same irreverent sense of humor.

"We were always trying to figure how we could get out of the house, how we could be someplace together," says Mary. They gave each other permission to laugh at the deadly serious world of religion, becoming each other's counterculture before they knew what a counterculture was. "We bonded over these things," says Maureen. "It's so important because as a teenager, the world is very serious to you, but at the same time you're just discovering it, and you're just a little afraid of what's out there. Mary was my sort of journey person. I wasn't always sure what to take seriously and what to laugh at, and when I had someone who could say, 'this is totally ridiculous,' it was wonderful."

"Maureen was so good for me," says Mary. "When I said I was a poet, she read everything I wrote, and she would cry and say it was wonderful, and she kept copies of my poems. And I told her I thought we should read Kierkegaard, I think that's an important person to read. I didn't know why the fuck you were supposed to read Kierkegaard, but we did. We could try that world of the intellect and culture together, because we couldn't get any help from our families."

They dreaded what they thought was in store for them. Mary was flailing at the boundaries more than Maureen; but she didn't want to flee without her friend. She painted an alternative picture of the future, letting all the skills of her future life as a novelist come into play. "Listen, Columbia, that's where we should apply," she would urge her friend. "Barnard. Remember Franny and Zooey? Our favorite family, the Glass family. We'll go to Barnard and we'll meet the Glass family and we'll be fine." J. D. Salinger, not the saints, captured their imagination.

"We were obsessed with the Glass family," Maureen interjects.

They tried the proper channels. No, said the nuns. We will not send your transcripts to Barnard. It is not a Catholic school.

Maureen might have let it go at that. But she had Mary. "She really said, let's go," Maureen says. "Let's go into the world. So one Saturday—we didn't tell our parents because they would have immediately locked us up and we would have been in big trouble—we just went down to the convent to say that our parents wanted our transcripts sent. We were very good at talking."

Then Mary called Barnard, politely requesting that they put pressure on their school, urging them to release those transcripts, get them out of bondage. The transcripts were sprung, finally, but the battle was just beginning. Scolded one nun: "You want to go to Barnard? You have full scholarships to Catholic colleges, why would you do that? I know a priest who taught at Columbia, and he said a young Catholic girl will lose her faith and her virginity in six months. What can you be thinking of?"

"It was the first time we heard a nun say *virginity* outside of 'Blessed Virgin Mary,'" says Mary. "You know, it was like, *what?* So, that really spurred us on. But, I *mean.*"

"It was just a word you didn't *say*," Maureen adds. "There was a movie then that the church condemned because it used the word *virgin.*"

Talking about breaking out was one thing. Doing it was another. They had to go to Barnard, had to march physically onto the subway and go there and present themselves and believe they had a right to be there.

"It would have been too frightening for me because I was much more of a conformist," says Maureen. She knew Mary wanted her to go, but she also knew that Mary would go on her own if Maureen lost her courage. Should she go with her friend or should she stick with what was safe?

It was time for taking chances. She took the leap, right down into the subway, first getting off with her friend at the wrong stop, in the middle of Harlem, then ending up at the magical, elusive Barnard.

They were sent to sit in on a class. "And here is this professor looking totally fabulous, like Germaine Greer, with boots up to here and a miniskirt, and she looked so smart and she was talking about the city and we were talking about taking a chance—we were thrilled. Just thrilled," remembers Mary.

Later that day, the shadows gathering, they got back on the subway and went home, their decision made. They were going to Barnard, they were moving out, and they were doing it together.

Now at midlife, these two friends—with a repository of old stories, old boyfriends, old escapades—see that event as central to the ways their lives unfolded. They could build a life on their imagination and daring. They gave each other courage.

Mary went on to become a respected and best-selling novelist, breaking through with *Final Payments,* a novel about growing up Catholic, followed by several others, as well as a dead-honest memoir of her father. She is married with two children. Maureen became a pediatric anesthesiologist and the wife of an ebullient lawyer (who especially loves Mary because she describes a former boyfriend of Maureen's as having skin "the color of urine") and is also the mother of two children.

Not all the transitions in their lengthy friendship have been made in tandem. But hitting the subway that afternoon broke through their barriers.

If Mary and Maureen both felt "different" from their high school classmates it's not a surprise. Adolescent girls commonly feel like misfits, searching frenetically for an identity that works. It's one of the reasons why they so often switch friends, trying on one after another, rather like clothes, until they find the one they feel comfortable with. The "different" girls gravitate to each other with a great sense of relief.

At every major transition, a woman's sense of self is up for grabs. There can be a reprise of adolescence when—after divorce, childbirth, widowhood—women are trying to figure out again who they really are. This process of upheaval often means connecting with a new person who can shore up that changing self-image. When Pat met her friend Irene Wurtzel in 1989, she had just made the leap to writing fiction. The two of them launched their friendship—Irene is a playwright—on the joys of exploring such topics as back story, through lines, character development and plot flow, but it quickly became much more. They found they could understand and connect on everything from a love of books to how you choose the right assisted living facility for an elderly parent. Pat had found someone who not only knew what she was about, but who helped her believe she could do it.

But many of the classic stories of women bonding come in young adulthood when the old structures of life—school and family—have begun to fall away. Whether a friend is there to cheer a woman on, go through the experience of transition with her, or be the person on the other side, she is often a crucial link in making the transition work. And is there any more classic story than that of a young woman taking a chance on moving to a strange city—and needing a friend?

———

Nadia Shamsuddin and Madeline Hammond know exactly what that means. They first met standing warily next to each other in an elevator in a TriBeCa apartment building in Manhattan. The open house for the rental apartment they each craved was called for 6 P.M., and they were there—both of them—on the dot. The ad in the paper had sounded too good to be true: "Cathedral ceilings and wooden floors. Female looking for a female roommate, $800 a month." Oh, yes, each of the women thought. Oh, please, let me get it.

Maddie had been in the city for three weeks and had learned one painful lesson: when you're looking for an apartment, and you see a place that isn't too awful, you grab it. This time she had her checkbook in her hand. Nadia knew one thing, too: she was sick of sleeping on a couch in the apartment of her parents' friends. After a month of that, she was ready to pounce on the first decent place she could find.

It was a tense elevator ride. Maddie, tall, with blond curly hair and a pale, unsophisticated, and open face stood next to Nadia, short, brown-skinned, trim, and sleek. Each felt, "Oh great, *she's* going to get the apartment." They were both imagining how they could beat out the other. They stood stiffly at the apartment door as the owner buzzed them in. Then it hit them: no cathedral ceiling. No wooden floors. Just a one-room "dump" and a man with black, slicked-back hair, oozing sweat, sitting in a chair, facing them.

One of them had the presence of mind to ask the obvious. "Where's the spare room?" Mr. Oil Slick pointed to a door that was actually a closet. Maddie and Nadia looked at each other in instant, silent understanding.

Then Maddie turned and bolted for the door with Nadia right behind her.

"Can you believe it?" they said to each other in mutual horror and relief as they took the creaky elevator down to the safety of the street. "What if you hadn't been there? What would I have *done*?"

They stood out on the sidewalk, laughing, going back over the details ("Did you see his *hair*?") for the next forty-five minutes, as they reran their close encounter. Then Nadia said impulsively, "I know of an apartment up in midtown where they need two roommates. Do you want to check it out tonight?" Maddie thought that sounded pretty good. She agreed, harboring the tiniest worry that maybe this stranger might be as "loco" as the guy upstairs in the apartment with the so-called cathedral ceiling.

The rest, as these two like to say, is history. It's the history of two single women in the city. Ever since that close call three years ago, these twenty-somethings have been best friends. As we sit in an East Village coffee shop, jackhammers tearing up the street, they talk about RollerBlading and hanging out and people-watching together, teasing each other. "See that old guy with the lettuce in his teeth, Maddie?" Nadia murmurs. "That's your boyfriend." When things are serious, Nadia says, "I have the kind of comfort with Maddie that I have when I'm alone. I can be completely myself."

There was something more to that initial connection than simple geography and a good apartment horror story. They each arrived at that elevator at a time of great change. Both had been in New York less than a month; both were struggling to find a niche. Neither was sure where she was going.

Nadia was born in London and raised in Seattle, the daughter of a Muslim couple from Bangladesh. She was separating from the childhood friends who were already settling into marriage and motherhood. She came to New York to study social work, but soon found that world and work too grim.

Maddie's own life had been suddenly, painfully disrupted. The fourth of five children, the daughter of religious parents, the granddaughter of missionaries, Maddie had studied in Colorado to be an environmentalist. Maddie's husband was the one who

Nadia Shamsuddin and Maddie Hammond.

wanted to leave Colorado. But in the very last week, in the midst of packing, "my husband ended up cheating on me." The marriage exploded.

Maddie never imagined big-city living; now she was working on Wall Street. She had assumed she'd be married forever; now she was single. All her assumptions about the future were up for grabs. "I was committed to the marriage," remembers Maddie. "When it ended, everything I thought my future was going to be just wasn't anymore. I thought, 'Oh God, what's so wrong with me that this person would cheat on me?' All of that. And I think I was really self-destructive. And I think, now looking back, it was just a really difficult time, I was very angry about what happened to me. And then Nadia came along. I was in this garbage phase of my life and Nadia just helped me sort things out."

"I think we came into each other's life at a time when we both really needed people," says Nadia. "Maddie was there for me when I needed someone to talk to. And seeing how she was going through a hard time made me feel that I wasn't alone."

Together they became New Yorkers and, to this day, Nadia still acts as the fashion police, forcing Maddie to return the shoes that made her feet look like they belonged to a platypus and approving the almond-shaped tortoiseshell glasses before she bought them. They both dress in the uniforms of the big city: Nadia in the all-black skirt and shell, Maddie in more black, with a white shirt and a small pearl necklace. They have known each other for only three years, but it's been a compressed three years. What happens next? Will they marry? Stay single? Live in New York? London? Seattle?

Today Maddie works at an investment firm and Nadia in public relations. This is a fluid time in their lives, and there is no one strong force holding them together—other than the way each sees and reinforces the person the other wants to become.

"I think we're going to look back and say, "Oh my God, ten years ago, remember when we were living in Manhattan?" She glances at her friend. "I hope you have kids and I have kids and they can play together."

"That's my fantasy," Nadia says with a vigorous nod.

———

The recognition in the elevator—what would have happened to me without you?—remains the bedrock of their friendship. Without each other, New York would have felt like a riskier place; a riskier adventure. They grabbed a serendipitous meeting and anchored it. We don't know yet if they will be "friends of the road," as Lillian Rubin puts it, or "friends of the heart." Friends of the road—the people who pass through, whom you are not destined to know forever—"depend on sharing time and place," she says. "When they're with us, they enrich our daily lives, but we can count on them only so long as they are in our lives. With friends of the heart, the connection is more likely to take root around being than doing, around a sharing of self in ways that can be sustained apart from the accident of geography or historical moment."

Every woman we know has had friends of the road. Pat remembers two unlikely fellow travelers she met when she went back to college as a twenty-nine-year-old mother. One was a divorced woman, ten years older than Pat with three children; another, five years younger, was a mother on welfare.

The time was the mid-'60s, several years before the fact of an "older" woman returning to college became commonplace. Pat met them in a registration line at the University of Oregon, and their friendship turned the scary process into an adventure. They studied together, encouraged each other, vied for grades. Each one found herself springing out of her seat to answer questions in class, knowing the other two were silently rooting for her. When graduation day came, they graduated as a Class of Three, honor roll all. For Pat, these friendships were affirmation that she wasn't alone (or crazy) in going back to school. And even though the Class of Three went their separate ways after graduation, they had given each other what they needed.

It can be harder as life goes on to find such a fellow traveler. Lives become more circumscribed and the expectations more rigid. Imagine what it must have been like for Eleanor Roosevelt when her husband was elected president and she was deeply unhappy, uncertain about her own future. Becoming first lady would mean giving up her private life and all of her individual political interests. She would become White House-bound, relegated to serving tea.

Eleanor Roosevelt needed someone outside the circle of her family to see her through this time—and Lorena Hickok became the friend who helped her reconfigure her future and reshape the role of first lady.

When they met, Lorena was a newspaper reporter for the Associated Press assigned to cover the first lady shortly after Franklin Delano Roosevelt was elected president of the United States. They became fast friends; indeed, Rodger Streitmatter, editor of a collection of letters between the two women, goes so far as to describe Hickok as "the woman behind the woman."

Lorena did more than empathize with Eleanor's depression, although that was enough in an era when few could understand why life in the White House would fail to be the fulfillment of her dreams. In Streitmatter's words, Lorena "recognized that ER was poised to do great things." She believed in her.

Historians today debate whether these two women who had such profound affection for each other ever had a romance. Whether they did or not, there is no doubt that Lorena became a critical catalyst for change in Eleanor's life. She took her to the West Virginia coal fields in 1933 and was the person who persuaded her to hold weekly press conferences and to take on writing the syndicated national column that made hers a nationally influential voice. With Lorena as both cushion and springboard, confidante and supporter, Eleanor Roosevelt reinvented her life. And in the process, invented a new vision of what a first lady could do and be.

A generation later, women in politics still depend on friends to give them courage as well as comfort, friends who sometimes encourage them to take a chance and who stick with them. This has been especially true as women muster the courage to run for increasingly important political jobs. There are more and more of these stories of mutual empowerment and risk taking, and they all have one key ingredient: a woman "goes" for it—but not alone. This was how it happened for Mary Landrieu and Norma Jane Sabiston.

These two New Orleans women have lived their lives in tandem from the time they met as teenagers. Mary's father was Moon Landrieu, the charismatic mayor of New Orleans, and Norma Jane Sabiston's mother was his receptionist. Theirs was a friendship forged in the traditional male world of Louisiana politics that has taken them finally—and together—to the U.S. Senate: Mary as a Democratic senator from Louisiana, and Norma Jane as her chief of staff.

They met in the early 1970s on Tulane Avenue in New Orleans at the Greyhound bus station as the two of them, both class presidents at their separate high schools, were boarding a bus to attend a Louisiana Youth Seminar in Natchitoches. This was a seminar for the best and the brightest of teenagers, young people already showing leadership capabilities, and Mary and Norma Jane gravitated to each other immediately.

"I didn't know a soul, and I looked around and I saw Norma Jane and she looked like the friendliest person. So I just went and sat right next to her. I mean, I could see, she had the most spirited manner of the whole group," Mary said with a Southern lilt to her voice.

The four of us were sitting in her new office on Capitol Hill shortly after her swearing-in. The usual pictures of the current senator were securely anchored on the walls, but the frantic atmosphere of the place betrayed the newness of Senator Landrieu's tenure.

"What I remember most about Mary on that trip was just how smart she was," said Norma Jane, leaning forward with wired intensity, short blond hair bobbing, almost prototypically perky. She's the more gregarious of the two women and yet has the watchful air of the always-on-duty aide. "I just knew this young woman was going someplace. And I watched her at the seminar, even though I was totally caught up in what I was doing, and so was she. I kept my eye on her the whole time. And actually, I've kind of done that throughout our friendship."

They realized they liked each other and, from the outset, politics was part of it. They talked as much as they could. "Mary insists that I did the talking," says Norma Jane. And then they went back to their separate high schools.

They saw each other more frequently as they grew older, their lives touching, their careers leapfrogging. They were two women among the men, and at times it could be awfully lonely. When Mary first won a seat as a twenty-three-year-old in the Lousiana State Legislature, male col-

At the swearing-in ceremony.
Senator Mary Landrieu and Norma Jane Sabiston.

(© *Janella Rachal*)

leagues whistled, mocked her from the microphone, and—like schoolboys rather than legislators—put a rubber snake in her desk. But in time, she ran successfully for state treasurer, and Norma Jane, who describes herself as too squeamish to be a candidate, became an aide to Congressman Billy Tauzin. They weren't chatting-on-the-phone friends, but they had an eye on each other. Politics was keeping them on a similar track.

Yet when Mary ran for governor in 1995 and asked Norma Jane to be her campaign manager, Norma Jane turned her down. Very reluctantly. "I struggled with it a lot, but it just wasn't right for me at the time," she said. "The hardest thing for me was to tell Mary that I couldn't do it."

Mary lost that campaign. Then came an opportunity a year later that Norma Jane was convinced Mary shouldn't pass up. Senator J. Bennett Johnston had decided not to seek a fifth term, and Norma Jane, by then a top aide to Senator John Breaux, wanted Mary to run for the seat.

So one night in Breaux's home, over a hot gumbo dinner, Norma Jane tried to persuade Mary to go for it. Mary was wounded from that bruising gubernatorial loss. She stalled. She was questioning herself; questioning whether she had it in her to try again for high office so soon. "I'd been running very hard for two years. I had a small child. My husband had given up his job and everything to help," she said. "I told my dad it was like getting up to Mt. Everest and getting ten feet from the top and then falling down . . . and then somebody comes and knocks on your door and says you gotta do it again."

Other friends were gathered there that night, but the one Mary was listening to the hardest was Norma Jane. She said she wouldn't do it unless Norma Jane ran her campaign. "I wouldn't have done it without her," said Mary. "I just couldn't go through a race again without somebody that I absolutely, totally trusted."

Norma Jane gave up her job and took on the challenge out of loyalty to Mary. After all, she had helped talk her into taking on what could be another losing campaign. How could she not share that grinding, fast-moving, life-crunching experience? Mary took an early lead in the race. Then, in the last week before the election, the retired Catholic archbishop of New Orleans called a news conference to announce that voting for Mary Landrieu would be a sin because she supported abortion rights. Her lead in the polls slipped. She still managed to eke out a narrow victory—an outcome immediately challenged by her opponent.

By the time the recount was over and Mary could relax, knowing that the Senate seat was hers, she and Norma Jane had fought their way jointly to a single goal. So it was only natural that Mary asked Norma Jane to be her chief of staff. They were a team.

"There's a million things Norma Jane does better than I do, and there are things that I do better than she does . . . we're really a perfect match," said Mary. "I'm more intense and serious. Norma Jane is easier." She doesn't mean just a political match. Norma Jane is godmother to Mary's baby; Mary brings sale suits from Lord and Taylor's that fit perfectly on Norma Jane's small frame. They consult on lipstick—"I should give you that color; it looks better on you," says Norma Jane—as well as legislation.

"I think we'll be together for a very long, long time," Mary says. Norma Jane answered quickly, with a grin. "I'll be at your funeral, and you'll be at mine."

We thought afterward about that night they shared the pot of gumbo. Another friend might have been more protective of Mary. She might have said: "You've been through a lot, your family needs you, you don't have to do this." Even, "I know how you feel."

But Norma Jane knew deep in her gut the extent of Mary's ambitions. The core of their mutual understanding was political as well as personal, and she knew that for Mary's career, it might well be now or never. Mary in turn trusted both Norma Jane's instincts—and her friendship. If she was climbing back up Mt. Everest, Norma Jane would come with her. Indeed, Norma Jane did more than advise Mary to run; she ran with her, all the way, taking the heat, reflecting it, sharing it.

When two friends take chances together, go to that next chapter or that next campaign, the balance of the relationship may also be at stake. When Mary Landrieu and Norma Jane decided to join their political fates, it was right for both of them.

In any long-term connection, there is an interplay between the two "I's" and the "we." What do I want for myself? What do you want? What's right for us as individuals, as connected friends? Sometimes one person's needs take precedence over the other's. But when the interplay gets out of balance, the results can be devastating.

Lorena Hickok uprooted herself from her career, giving up her profession and her independence to be with her friend during the critical White House years. She was losing her own identity as Eleanor was finding hers, and the friendship ceased to be a voyage of two equals. Years later, they would debate who was responsible for the cooling of their friendship, and each would loyally claim to be at fault. But it was never the same.

There are many ways friends can change each other's fate. And when they do, there is always a measure of responsibility. What gets women friends through the ordeal is trust, more than cheerleading.

Certainly that was true for Susan King, the head of public affairs for the Carnegie Corporation. After fruitless efforts to get pregnant, she and her husband tried to resign themselves to being childless, until a friend with a newly adopted child began insisting Susan should do the same thing. "She really kept working on me," Susan says. "She made me do the hard work, to think it through. And she and her husband were so excited about being parents; I was sort of transformed by how they were transformed. I think I never would have been a mother if it wasn't for her." Her friend stuck with Susan through those first parenting years, helping her with advice and outgrown baby clothes. "It's brought us even closer, because we're both old moms."

Composing a life, moving from one scene to another, and not always smoothly, you're putting your life into play. Sometimes it happens dramatically, as it did in Mary and Maureen's run for freedom and Mary and Norma Jane's run for the Senate. Sometimes it comes with crisis, through divorce or widowhood.

The older we grow, the more likely that every change will entail some loss—and the balance sheet may be a tough one to calculate in advance. As Mary Gordon says, "Tears are at the heart of things." Somewhere in the meaning of the word *trust* is the assumption that a friend has your best interest at heart; a belief that she knows you well enough, indeed, to have a decent idea of what those best interests are. And that she in turn trusts you to take final responsibility for the decision.

Pat's move to Washington brought us geographically closer—but our friendship could have foundered on its shoals. The change might have put a wedge between us rather than a bridge. But no amount of cheerleading or slaps on the back could have made the decision to move right for Pat unless she both trusted Ellen *and* had the confidence to make the decision herself. We found ourselves with a fundamentally deepened friendship. We—like the friends we have written about—discovered more about responsibility and trust than we had known before.

Pat

Those first few months were tumultuous. The job was great. I had my own column and supportive colleagues, but I was on an intense learning curve in a strange city. My children missed their father, and I felt I was running around with a pulled-up anchor in my hands and nothing to sink it into. I kept driving the wrong way on the Beltway and ending up in Virginia, which irritated the kids when we were headed for Maryland. Not only were there new schools and neighborhoods to figure out, but I was still commuting back to Chicago every other week to host a television show. I felt excited, overwhelmed, worried, out of breath, guilty. Homesick. Definitely homesick.

But the truth was, I never seriously considered going back.

One night I sat alone in the living room after the children were in bed. It had been a day when a slight dusting of snow had paralyzed the capital and traumatized Washingtonians, and I was especially tired. Sitting there, I let myself wonder if I had done the right thing in making this move. I thought of my mother at the age of twenty spying a sign at the Belfast docks offering cheap passage to Canada; how she leaped at the chance to leave Ireland for a better future, leaving her family and all that was familiar. She must have had her moments of wondering—but I knew she never looked back. Was I agonizing too much? Did I have her grit?

But I also thought of what I had found with this move: my sister, Mary, now lived only a few miles away, the first time we had been in the same city together since we were in high school. The night I arrived at our newly rented and unfamiliar house after driving from Chicago with a cat and a parakeet in the car, and my daughter, Marianna, sitting next to me, giving stalwart support, I had been cheered enormously by a bouquet of flowers from Mary, waiting just inside the screen door.

I was also, in one of those strange serendipities of life, already bonding deeply with my friend, Babs Joseph, back in Evanston. When I told her I would be going back and forth to Chicago to do a television show, she handed me a key to her house: "Come stay here anytime," she said. And I did. Many times, sharing many conversations and good food, sitting on the swing on her welcoming, shady porch. Babs was to become a true "friend of the heart," and ironically we might never have developed an intimate relationship if I hadn't left.

So there it was, good mixed with bad. But underneath all my mulling was one true thing: if I had not left, I would always have wondered What did I miss? For I was staring not just at a dusting of snow in a strange city but at a range of possibilities for my life, possibilities that had been closed off in Chicago. I didn't know all of what was ahead—many good things, some not so good—but I had opened the door and walked through it, and by God, it was going to work.

Enough. I reached for the phone to call Ellen.

"How's it going?" she asked, and I heard the thread of anxiety in her voice.

"It's fine," I answered. "It was the right move."

5

Playtime

Pat

So *this* was the glamour of Washington. It was Jimmy Carter's 1977 inaugural, and Ellen and I were off to the city's biggest combination of party and circus, the Presidential Inaugural Ball. There we were, tripping over long skirts (we both still have them; mine was black chiffon and Ellen's was a black $39.95 crepe number from Filene's Basement), running around with our notebooks and with our press credentials hanging around our necks, trying to get quotes. It was bitter cold, and we'd brought our outfits to the office and changed in the cramped bathroom of the Knight-Ridder bureau in the National Press Building, giggling a little self-consciously while enjoying immensely the fact that we were going to cover the nation's splashiest party night together.

Ellen, a veteran of such affairs, was wearing sensible flat shoes; I, on the other hand, wouldn't have dreamed of going to a ball in anything other than high heels (a decision I would soon regret). I had been warned by my friend that a party where many thousands of people would be crammed into several hotels and public buildings would not be quite the glittering event I thought, but I secretly harbored in my mind the image of Jackie Kennedy, elegantly clad in a white satin gown, stepping down snow-covered steps on her way to the 1961 Inaugural Ball. I tend to like fairy-tale images, and that was one of my favorites.

We did see one woman in white satin. She was standing stock still in the midst of a horrible crowd at the Washington Hilton, tears streaming down her face. I couldn't figure out what was wrong until I edged closer and saw that the poor woman was nailed to the floor. Her dress had a train, and every time she tried to yank it free of people's feet, somebody walked over it again. I looked at Ellen, and she looked at me, her expression saying, "I told you so." Scribble, scribble, the vignette went into my notebook, and off we went to the next party.

"ARE YOU HAVING A GOOD TIME?" I'd yell over the roar of the crowd and the music at somebody who looked important, always keeping an ear out for the Significant Quote.

"YES, ISN'T IT WONDERFUL?" some perspiring campaign donor from Chicago or Los Angeles would bellow back.

The absurdity of it all became more apparent—and more humorous— as the evening wore on. Ellen and I nudged each other when a really silly-looking dress came into range and exchanged approving nods when the truly glamorous ones floated by. Vaguely, from time to time, we would hear a band we couldn't see trying to play dance music (not that anyone ever found room to actually dance at an inaugural ball). We were technically working (our professionalism protected by those plastic credentials flapping around our necks), but in truth we were having a wonderful time.

We ended the evening back at my rented house in Bethesda, finally hooked up with my daughter Marianna (who had given up trying to find us and enjoyed the balls with friends), laughing and swapping impressions. I had gone forth secretly starry-eyed and come back a "hardened" veteran. And the whole thing—shared with my fellow working stiff—had been pure play.

Ellen

"Will you be four?" the maître d' asked ever so politely as we stood before him, dressed in raincoats and carrying briefcases that indelibly marked us as ladies who do not lunch. "Just two," we answered with just the right touch of insouciance for the most elegant expense account restaurant of that time, the Sans Souci.

We got that look so often reserved for two women dining alone back in the days when Jimmy Carter was still president. Surely they had a table for two, said Pat, charmingly. Had I tried it, it would have sound like an EEOC complaint. But he offered us—well, her—a table on the discreetly expressed provision that we would vacate it by 7:30. No problem, we assured him as we were led to a corner table that was blissfully not within eavesdropping distance of its neighbors.

The wine came, the menus came. We drank the wine, got engrossed in conversation, and left the menus unopened. The waiter gently suggested we take a peek. We did. The radicchio and endive salads arrived as we had barely begun the list of subjects that needed to be discussed in anthropological and physiological detail. We were, let me confess, freewheeling enough to catch the eye of the lobbyists who were no doubt trying to convince the senator sitting with them of the wisdom of tobacco subsidies. Two women? Eating dinner at the Sans Souci circa 1978? Alone?

Seven-thirty came and went. Eight o'clock came and went. The waiter came and went. We developed the absolute, hilarious determination to hold on to this raft in the inhospitable sea of this snobbish restaurant, and no one could stop us. Could he bring us the check, the waiter asked with that edge poised between Sans Souci politesse and desperation. What about dessert, we responded. We hadn't, after all, decided the fate of the two and a half men in our lives. Or was it the UN?

It was 9:00, then 9:45. Could he bring us our coats, asked the maître d' himself with a barely contained hostility. (Two of them—through two sittings?) We told him we'd love some more decaf, please. It wasn't the first time we'd laughed our way through three hours of dinner, but this time, in enemy territory, we were going for the gold.

By 11:00 we had finished off both the boy talk and the dinner with as much precision as if it had been coffee and doughnuts. Then we amortized the bill at roughly $10 an hour. Not bad for the dinner that went down in our private history as The Night Two Women Closed the Sans Souci.

We were in the same time zone again, at either end of the much-traveled eastern corridor, the megalopolis that ranges from Boston to Washington, from area code 617 to 202. Our phone calls, the checkups and long talks, were now punctuated regularly with visits. Ellen found more than a few reasons to visit her syndicate at *The Washington Post,* more than a few columns to write with a Washington dateline and—curiously—without a single hotel bill. Pat, for her part, remembers an editor peering thoughtfully at her, saying, "Funny how many of your good story ideas seem to be in Boston."

We had turned work into play at the inauguration, and now we could turn to play at the end of a workday by closing the Sans Souci or Hamburger Hamlet, or more often by relaxing with pizza boxes or Chinese food cartons at home. We took long walks. We stopped for coffee, ice cream, shopping. Friendship was our recess, the time out, the time we reserved for us. We had children to raise, deadlines to meet, households to run, but when we were together, we allowed ourselves "playtime."

It's a funny thing about adult play. It's somehow difficult for women to allow themselves "officially" to indulge, especially in a world as time-crunched as ours. In the mid-'80s, *Psychology Today* reported that 25 percent of adults said they always felt "rushed." A decade later, that figure had jumped to 40 percent and was rising.

So it is no surprise that much of the time women spend together is squeezed around work and family—the serious stuff. Play has to have a purpose. Do we say we are going out to "play" with a friend? That's for children. Do we describe each other as "playful"? That's a term used for the family dog. "We function as though there are pleasure police out there," the director of a women's health spa told *The Washington Post.* "If we take an afternoon off and sit out on the porch and read or don't do anything for a whole afternoon, they'll find out and drive up to the house with the sirens blaring."

When we searched the Web for references to women and play, you can imagine what we found. We were scrolling through a virtual wonderland of soft porn. We came up with such offerings as "adult playgrounds," "adult playpens," and "play couples"—not what we had in mind. As for playmates? They were meant for playboys.

For something so obvious, play seems remarkably elusive, hard to define. After all, it is a magic thing at one level, something children know very well. Historian Johan Huizinga, an expert on children at play, highlights the importance of this magic with the story of a four-year-old boy sitting in front of a row of chairs playing trains, when his father swoops down and gives him a quick hug. "Don't kiss the engine, Daddy," the little boy said, annoyed, "or the carriages won't think it's real."

One definition we like, offered by Edward Norbeck of Rice University, defines play as "an upside-downing of behavior, during which the social hierarchy is inverted and customary rules of conduct are suspended." To allow oneself "an upside-downing of behavior" is a delightful way of describing some of the fun we have had together.

Research on play emphasizes how much the entire concept has been corrupted. People are earnestly told they play too earnestly, that they've been caught in the trap of purposeful play, an oxymoron if there ever was one. "We no longer simply 'go for a walk,'" reports *Psychology Today.* "Instead we try to keep our heart rate to within sixty percent of maximum. . . . We focus not on the play, but on the benefits play can provide us and we consciously play for them. We end up playing because we feel we should be playing. It is, ultimately, a doomed endeavor."

Well, we have seen that too. But female friendship is not study hall, and if after all these years, someone asks why we are still friends, it is because of the pleasure of each other's company. And by pleasure, we mean the talk, the intimacy . . . and the sundaes. As one woman we know put it, looking happily around a table of her friends, "This is the very opposite of a cocktail party."

"We have fun together." It's what we hear when we are talking about friendship with other women. This shared "fun" is as ephemeral as the bubbles in a glass of Perrier—or champagne for that matter. Yet the pleasure of each other's company, the fun we have had together, is what has drawn us onto planes, trains, phone lines, even to the writing of this book. Friends, after all, make each other laugh, they build up a core of stories that keep them connected—moments when they step out of duty and obligation and touch the child inside, if only for a short while.

And yes, we've been running out for recess whenever we can.

For instance, to the cosmetics counter . . .

Ellen

I round the corner of the Lancôme counter to find my friend innocently fingering one of the white bottles with the gray caps that explain their virtues in bilingual boasts. "*Anti-rides,*" reads the one in her hand. "*Progrès Plus*" says the other. Pat does not know French, but she knows creams.

"What do you use for night cream?" she asks all too casually. I sniff a trap. "Oh, Lubriderm," I answer in an offhand voice. "Loooo-bri-derm?" she responds, stretching it out to sound as horrified as if I had just said,

"Petrooooleeum" or perhaps "peeeenut butter." I hear a lifetime of information within that drawn-out word. Pushing forty and you use LOOOO-bri-derm? Have you no pride? Is this what forty looks like?

She is stocking up. She is also looking very antiwrinkle, excuse me, very *"anti-rides."* I check the price of the eye cream, note that it is slightly less per gram than caviar, and say nothing. "Do you have a small jar?" Pat asks the saleswoman, who knows a customer when she sees one. My friend then buys a small jar for herself and benignly cons the saleswoman out of an impressive handful of samples, which she places kindly in my hands. Thank you, I say, knowing with absolute certainty that I have just been hooked by my friend, the cream dealer: the first one is always free.

Pat

God, I finally got her to the cosmetic counter! Yes, creams; how can we do without them? (I have a standing order with my friends: if I'm ever in a plane crash that strands me on a desert island somewhere, and the rescue planes are coming in to drop food, please tell them to drop the face cream first.) But creams are serious; the real fun is lipstick and eye makeup. The first time I got Ellen onto one of those tall stools at the cosmetics counter, trying different colors of eye shadow, I knew I had her semi-hooked when she turned to me, semi-embarrassed, and said, "Which is better? Tangerine Tango or Petal Blue?" She even bought some. It was like having your best friend climb into your sandbox.

Not to mention the things we put up with . . .

Ellen

Have I mentioned the cat? Ginger. Or, rather, "Poor Ginger," as Pat tends to refer to anyone more vulnerable than, say, Arnold Schwarzenegger. I have no idea why her children named a black cat Ginger, but then I named a female dog Sam. I have no idea why she thought Poor Ginger was more vulnerable than Arnold Swarzenegger either, but then Poor Ginger and I had a rather difficult relationship.

Ginger hung out in the guest room on the bottom floor of the town-house—only Ginger did not consider this a guest room; she considered it Ginger's room. I, on the other hand, considered it a guest room, and since

I was the primary guest, we had what you might call a turf battle. On her turf. During the wee small hours of the morning.

Let me put it this way. One of the teeny-weeny disadvantages of sleeping at Pat's during the early Washington years was a nightmare that recurred sometime after about 3 A.M. I know the time because of the godforsaken grandfather clock——excuse me, the Poor Grandfather Clock—that Pat regarded as a kindly sentry, gently marking the hours of our life. I, however, regarded it as something akin to a Big Ben boom box on my pillow.

At some point after my 3 A.M. wake-up call, just about the time I had fallen back into deep REMs, I had this nightmare titled: THERE'S A CAT STANDING ON MY FACE.

No door could close tightly enough to keep Ginger out. No admonition could keep her away. She stood, paws placed, uh, gingerly, on my hair. I yelped. Occasionally she would change her mind and sit on my face instead. Occasionally I would shriek.

Are there other non-cat-owners, non-feline-devotees who have ever awakened with an alien pair of green eyes staring into your own? It is a testimony to our friendship that Ginger lived to a ripe old age instead of dying in my custody. It is more remarkable that when she finally died, I thought—for the very first time—Poor Ginger.

Pat

It's a good thing it never came down to a choice between Ellen and the cat, because Ginger, who weighed about a ton and a half and couldn't find her way out of a paper bag, needed love. She was unfortunately looking for it in all the wrong places, probably because I hadn't given her much myself in her earlier, friskier years. You might think my friend would understand her deprived state *just a little bit*. She didn't care, at least not enough to resign herself to being Ginger's Fatal Attraction.

But excuse me, have I mentioned the dog? Every time I walked in the front door of Ellen's house, I had to brace myself for a slobbering onslaught from this ridiculously huge black poodle who had the idea somehow that I was a friend. Paws on the shoulders, wet, slurping tongue on my face. Yuk. This dog was a poodle? It seemed against nature. I have never liked dogs who look me in the eye when I am standing up, and Sam was no exception. I learned to come in the door sideways, the way you do when you're walking into a heavy surf. At least I pretended to appreciate Sam's greetings, mostly for the sake of Ellen's daughter, Katie.

But Sam wins paws down for stupidity (and it takes something to top a cat who gets stuck in a paper bag). One day that huge overgrown puppy jumped happily out of the second-floor window of Ellen's sister's house, almost landing in the pet cemetery. Poor Sam. But that awesome leap gave me new appreciation of Sam's exuberant spirit, and I was glad she survived, even if it was to jump on me again.

Given my charitable approach, why couldn't Ellen put up with a cat in her face every now and then?

———

And then, of course, one of the old-standby pleasures . . .

Pat

Ellen and I go shopping. My first craft show with her was more a politely shared experience than actual fun (like trying to pay attention to the difference between arugula and asparagus in her garden). To my conservative eye, the jewelry looked like squashed roadkill. Ellen would hold up some luridly colored pin with squiggles and nodules poking out and exclaim, "Isn't this beautiful?" and I'd try to think of something positive to say. She would fall in love with vases shaped like twisted bananas wearing beanie caps while I poked at chenille sweaters that I thought might look good lining the cat's box. So what do you say when your friend is about to spend her hard-earned money on something you think looks bizarre? If it was something she was wearing and I thought it looked terrible, I'd say, it's not for you (or for any other human being, only I wouldn't say that part). If it was something she thought would be perfect on the mantel or the coffee table, I'd try to look at it with her eyes. Maybe that vase didn't look like a twisted banana; maybe it was more like artfully twined—um, shapes. I had to figure out how to respond because she actually listened to my opinions about these things.

So guess what happened next? I began seeing things I liked—sort of—in those shapes. I could see how the pin looked good on Ellen's suit, and actually in my mind's eye could put the vase on her coffee table and realize, hmm . . . a certain symmetry here. After about the fourth craft show, something else began happening. I was picking through earrings displayed at one counter when I saw a pair that intrigued me. Nice shape, beautiful workmanship . . . "Aren't these beautiful?" I said, holding them up before I could catch myself.

I saw the gleam in Ellen's eyes. She had me.

Ellen

Pat and I go shopping. This is, I hasten to add, different from saying we go out to buy something. I am talking about leisure shopping, window and street and discount shopping. In its pure, distilled Pat-and-Me form, shopping is not the purposeful search for a pair of sneakers. We shop as a moving background for spending time together. And as an act of trust.

We have been to the dressing room together—the female equivalent of a locker room. I am no more likely to come out of such a room in the wrong size in front of a mere acquaintance than to sleep with a man on a first date. In a dressing room, friends enact a ritual of mutual disclosure, the sharing of flaws and imperfections. It's not to be taken lightly, but . . .

Consider this fact of friendship breakthroughs. Pat has just seen me in a bathing suit. In February. Under fluorescent lights. A bathing suit I *didn't* buy. A bathing suit she wouldn't let me buy. Her words of discouragement were delivered gently, of course.

"Who on earth do they make these things for?" she says with the proper mix of outrage and defensiveness. A good friend refuses to blame the fashion victim. A good friend does not mention Cindy Crawford or the annual *Sports Illustrated* bathing suit issue.

We leave behind the suit and the store, decide that any business worth its net profit would light the swimsuit dressing room with candlelabras.

Where to next? Hot fudge sundaes? Well, hold the whipped cream.

Cats and eyeliner. Long walks and good talks. A favorite story—remember the craft show in Philadelphia where you almost bought that clock made entirely of old bottle caps?—that can make either of us smile or dissolve into a classic seventh-grade giggle fit. We go back to that wonderful word the women from Wellesley College's Stone Center use in naming the good things that come out of relationships: "zest."

Zest. Why has it been relegated to a brand name for soap? It touches on the very best of what friendship is all about: the heightened joy, the lighthearted laughter that comes with a friend who shares the same goofy moment, the same sense of irony, the same humor and perspective.

Women's friendships depend on other words on that Stone Center list, words like *empathy* and *empowerment*. We talk each other out of a crisis or into a new city. But a friendship that is all intensity, all communication, all sharing of innermost thoughts, all problems, can feel more like therapy than play. The richest friendships that we have encountered are light as well as strong, bound by laughter as well as serious talk. If you can't hoot at something together, the relationship loses its bounce.

When friends, young and old, tell us why they stay friends, what they come back for time and again, they always mention fun. Like what? we would ask. More often than not the stories are delightful, detailed episodes of their history together. Maddie and Nadia confess to their Saturday afternoon boy-watching habits: Nadia picks out a true dork of a candidate and announces: "That's your husband." Maddie insists: "No, he's yours." Melba and Linda can even make a funny story of the day they outraced a tornado: "The plate glass windows are coming out of the hotel and *she* decides she's going to park the car!" We have sat back in our chairs, laughing with them, and yet found ourselves nodding when one shrugs and says, "You had to have been there."

We have felt the same way. And we know that friends can find a submerged funny soul inside of themselves through their contact with each other that they never knew existed. Something inside relaxes. Friends can throw away the script.

Why is it hard to talk about adult play? In childhood, having a friend *means* having someone to play with. What is it that small kids say mournfully to their parents on a long rainy afternoon? "I have nobody to play with. I can't play alone."

Having a friend to play with is the first way you feel accepted. Someone will sit next to you and shovel sand out of the pail; someone will holler just as loud as you when you're pulled apart. In the early school years, friendships are begun with no deeper connection than the mutual desire to spend afternoons doing back flips or playing a computer game from Purple Moon. Children choose friends who share their fascination with *Star Wars* or with soccer or the ant farm Grandma sent for a birthday. Friends are even the ones who teach each other to play—introducing the wonders of Pokémon or make-believe—"This time *I'll* be Princess Leia."

Yet as adults, it's true, women often think they need a reason to take time out. Adults do not call each other up on the phone and ask, "Will you come out and play with me?" In adult life, as author Jay Teital once wrote, "Play, like crime, requires both opportunity and motive." But even women whose days are eaten up by work and family grab the "opportunity" to get together in some structure that is a personal—and fun—reponsibility-free zone.

They form book clubs—"Somebody else must want to read a real book on Princess Di"—and lunch groups—"every third Wednesday of the month, guaranteed"—or even, as one group of delighted women reported to us, a Website quilting bee. It's not an accident that *The Divine Secrets of the Ya-Ya Sisterhood,* a novel about a group of four friends united since childhood, has spun off dozens of Ya-Ya groups.

For a long time, women's groups were as serious as consciousness-raising and as professional as networking. But now women are often looking for some respite, a place to go AWOL, absent without leave, from the obligations of daily life. That upside-downness? Try a beauty parlor night in the East Village of New York. Once the idea was about as hip as a Tupperware party. Now a new genre of women's groups—if that isn't too somber a phrase—is emerging, described by *The New York Times* as "part career networking and romance therapy, part retro kaffeeklatsch."

These are gatherings held by women looking for downtime, girl talk, a place where, as one said, you aren't a worker or a wife or a mother. They're small, nourishing retreats. "It's an educated return to those girlie gatherings of our adolescence," said Nikol Lore, the editor-in-chief of magazines *Smile* and *Act Nice.* "As we get older, women get away from that kind of bonding."

In Washington, Pat has been part of a circle of friends who don't want to get away from it. Twenty years ago, they dubbed themselves "the ladies' lunch," and made their monthly gathering a must in their datebooks. In the competitive, all-too-serious, public-policy-wonk world of the capital, this was a place to relax. The lunch group set only one rule: "No shop talk allowed; just gossip."

There is even a campsite in West Virginia that deliberately encourages women to go AWOL, at least for one August weekend each year. Camp A.W.O.L. stands for Athletic Women on Leave and some of the women who come really are athletes, but most are not. They play volleyball and tennis—sometimes they keep score and sometimes they don't—but friendship is the main event. Or, as one thirty-seven-year-old camper told *The Washington Post,* "I'm here to relive my childhood. It's easier now, without the angst of puberty."

Women are also playing when they book a breezy "all-girl" vacation trip or show up for a slightly risqué gathering for a prewedding "spinster party" at—gulp—a male stripper club. Who didn't notice the delight of the all-female audience's reaction to the grand in-the-buff finale to the British movie *The Full Monty*?

Over the past few years, we've begun noticing all sorts of reunions, those annual or occasional times when old friends reconnect without even the pretense of agenda—except fun. We met a group of high school friends on a ferry in Maine, heading off—time out, no husbands or kids—for a retreat to an island . . . and a dose of old times. We heard from five women who met each other in a Delaware church in the late 1980s. For ten years, these women, mostly single and scattered from Seattle to Chicago, have gathered for a week at beach towns between Maine and Virginia. They bring more than sunblock and beach towels. "We bring the latest 'fad' to try," says Tracy Cooper. She ticks off their stuff: "One year Susan brought that hot wax stuff to take hair off your legs. Dianna contributed a 'Korean facial' that she got from an international student, complete with seaweed. Yvonne has become the bead queen, and brought her boxes of beads to make earrings and necklaces. I usually bring some 'exotic' food from the Northwest." They share the fads as a kick, a tradition, along with dinners and long talks.

These reunions with old friends, those women who knew you "back when," are times when women let their hair down—or put it up in big, fat retro curlers and laugh at each other.

Pat's sister, Mary, reconnected with her high school friends—and their high spirits—at a fortieth reunion that turned into a full-fledged celebration. There they were, women whose bonds had loosened over the years, all together on a docked ocean liner, *The Queen Mary*, in Long Beach. "Everybody just took on the personality she had in high school," said Mary. "And within a couple of hours, the years didn't matter. We weren't seeing each other as middle-aged women, we were seeing what we were back then—the one who is always joking, the one who giggles all the time, the one who tops everybody's else's story—it was all dead-on."

Remember pajama parties? There is one group of high school friends in Nebraska that has been gathering every year for an actual, real-live, back-to-the-future pajama party. The 1998 reunion was a Big One, because all the women were turning fifty, and *People* magazine was invited to attend. There they were, in full color in the magazine, thirteen grown women in their pajamas and nightshirts, painting each other's toenails, singing "Be Kind to Your Web-Footed Friends," taking a count of how many of them went out with the cutest guy in the class (seven hands went up), and whooping their way back to a time when life and friendship were both simple and fun. "You move to California, start a new life, think you're a whole different person," said Sandy Koepke, an interior designer. "Then you come back to this group and realize, 'Naah, you're the same girl.'"

"Here we are, these old women, talking about when we lost our virginity," said Kathy Joseph, a kindergarten teacher. "It's like we revert to being kids when we're together." What these women are sharing is an exuberant freedom, the kind that we often tuck away with our memories of childhood.

"Play groups" cement these friendships; they become the highs, the escape clauses. The same sense of euphoria comes through when pals describe a private adventure when they felt free together.

The classic duo, the friends who gave our culture a rare look at grown-up women at play, were television's Lucy and Ethel: the queens of sitcom play, the masters of wacky adventures. Back in the '50s, the nation tuned in every Monday night to catch the latest episode of *I Love Lucy* to see these two—friends offstage as well as on—scheme and plot, keeping millions delighted with their escapades. Is there anyone of a certain age in this country who can't still hear in their heads the sound of Lucy Ricardo's raucous exchanges with Ethel Mertz when she got into trouble?

Our children and our grandchildren continue to watch reruns of this 1950s sitcom with all its politically incorrect plots, but we are especially fond of what it tells us about friends having fun. Lucy and Ethel get into scrapes—stealing John Wayne's footprint from the sidewalk outside Hollywood's Mann's (formerly Grauman's) Chinese Theater, getting overwhelmed by assembly-line candy—and devise crazy plans to get their husbands to do what they want. They bail each other out, cover for each other—and then, one week later, start the whole thing all over again.

Why do these friends have such enduring attraction? We think it's because they convey to other women a sense of freedom: there they are on the television screen, letting go of social constraints, egging each other on.

Lucy and Ethel were looking for loopholes from the confining female roles of their era; they always had an edge of the outlaw about them. We remember our night at the Sans Souci with such amusement because it too was a small act of cultural defiance, a sit-in of its own sort—and neither one of us would have dreamed of doing it alone.

Another generation of sitcom friends came along in the 1990s to echo and update the Lucy and Ethel escapades. In one of these shows, *Cybill,* the two best friends are in their forties, divorced, with teenage and grown children. Cybill, an actress, and Maryann also egg each other on, encouraging wild fantasies of revenge against one's ex-husband, the other's director, and all the expectations of society.

In one episode, an irate Cybill sees herself on a Hollywood Hills billboard. Only it doesn't quite look like her; some advertising whiz kid had airbrushed away her hips! The *real* woman wasn't good enough for the billboard? She and Maryann climb up onto the billboard in the dark of night and paint the hips back in.

For the most part, women haven't grown up with heroes like Huckleberry Finn and Jim floating off to adventure down the river on a raft. And even though little girls like Pat's granddaughters, Sophie and Charlotte, adore Pippi Longstocking, few of their literary heroines are as daring. Fun? Adventure stories are more likely to star boys; men have palship stories and buddy films. As for women, when they get out of hand, on an adventurous roll, they're likely to end up like Thelma and Louise, driving over a cliff.

Adult women have to reach way back into childhood to come up with the kind of innocent and rakish escapades—sneaking out of the house, skipping school, and never mind—that have few grown-up equivalents. They love sharing those memories with the friends who were there.

For Anne Watson, a lanky brown-haired Smith graduate and thirtysomething television producer, it goes back to the days of camp and to Janelle Farris. Anne was from Utah, Janelle from Washington State: Anne was white and Janelle was African-American, and they met as self-described outsiders at summer camp. But Anne says, "We connected on a level of humor. We just found each other funny." When they rediscovered each other a dozen years later, living only blocks apart in Manhattan, they also rediscovered the kids they were. With Janelle, Anne found she could still be absolutely silly, even raucous. "It's connected to our childhood. There's a certain freedom that comes from our having been girls together. When we are childish it's okay, because we *were* children," she says.

Maybe that's part of the enduring sense of play we found among several pairs of friends, including Mary Gordon and Maureen Strafford. From the moment they met, Mary was the serious instigator, Maureen the more lighthearted escape artist. Long before their Great Escape from Queens to Barnard, while still in the Catholic high school where they were supposed to be learning to be "good" girls, Mary and Maureen knew they weren't headed for sainthood. No matter, they decided to have fun anyway by recreating the lives of all the pious people who had made it. They called their counterculture theatrical effort "The Alternative Lives of the Saints." First up for revisionist history was the gentle, animal-loving St. Francis.

As Maureen remembers the script, still delighted with it, "The true story was that he didn't *like* the birds. He was extremely irritated by their waking him up." Worse than that, their St. Francis discovered that his real name was Mimi. Or was it Fifi? Yes, Fifi. In any case, they had the goods on St. Francis: His sainthood had been created as a moneymaking scheme. Needless to say, this dramatization didn't make it onto the school stage.

In the private counterculture of friends from adolescence on, there is a delicious moment when you become a company of two or more against the world. We can do anything! Or, sometimes even better, one can cajole the other into breaking new ground . . . just for fun.

When the two of us hit the cosmetic counter, Ellen stepped out of her own reticence and onto Pat's turf. There was something in that moment that seemed almost out-of-body. Friends can do that, push open that door to another room, even if the eyeliner never gets out of the drawer again.

Patricia Williams, an African-American law professor, described in *The New Yorker* magazine the experience of finding herself sitting in front of a mirror, having makeup carefully applied for a ball by her "best white friend." She stared at herself while her friend busily turned her into Cinderella. All through this private makeover she grumbed to herself, hanging on to the self-image that lurked under several layers of applied glamour. "I'm prickly as all getout, I dress down instead of up and my hair is a complete disaster," she broods. She relaxes—still dubious—only when her friend finally faces her and protests: "Get a grip, it's just a party."

Isn't that just what we need? Who doesn't value a friend who helps you get out of your own skin and reminds you, "it's just a party"?

Most friends, and we are no exception, have ongoing jokes, dusty with history, little pre-scripted exchanges that make us laugh at the familiarity, the predictability. Our stories and moments require only the smallest headline: remember the woman at the inauguration? Remember closing the Sans Souci? How come you never wore that eye shadow? And how come a nice Irish girl can't say one lousy little word in Yiddish?

Pat

"Pat, listen." I watch Ellen put her upper teeth against her lower lip, pushing it out. "Kvetch," she says.

"Kavech."

"No, no." She pushes down on her lower lip again, sliding it out, somewhere in her throat blending the letters into a single syllable.

Inexplicable. What is she doing? I watch closely and make another stab at mangling the word.

"Kivech."

Ellen giggles. "I can't believe it! Ten years and you can't do it yet!"

"How the hell do you turn a *k* and a *v* into one sound? Who would ever come up with such an unpronounceable word?"

"What's so hard about it?"

"It's diabolical. You don't WANT a shiksa to speak Yiddish!"

So on we go, laughing, complaining, playing, poking fun, *having* fun. The fun that exists both in the moment and in the memory, feeling known and understood. The whole elusive thing.

As we've said before, as many friends have said with a laugh and a shrug—well, you just had to be there.

Here's to that birthday: Ann, Pat, Ellen, Lynn and Otile sharing Ellen's 50th.

6

What's a Little Competition
Between Friends?

Ellen

I tend to think of this as a Betty and Veronica moment. Not that we were teenagers the year that Ronald Reagan came into office. In fact, Pat was the mother of teenagers. In fact, her eldest, Marianna, was twenty-three. In fact, any time Pat was called upon to state this fact in my presence, some jaw-dropper would exclaim with utter predictability: "My God, you have a twenty-three-year-old daughter?"

It got to the point where I could lip-synch this response. No one, you see, ever dropped a jaw when I mentioned the age of my daughter. No one ever said, "Impossible—you look much too young!" Not that I noticed.

Pat insisted that it made her feel like the Picture of Dorian Gray, as if somewhere there was a portrait of her falling apart. This was a worry for which I expressed absolutely no sympathy.

But let me go back to Betty and Veronica, the comic strip friends and rivals, or at least to the cultural Rolodex of images of female sidekicks and stars, pals and prom queens. From the beginning of our friendship, I had these occasional sudden, awkward moments when I felt like I was best friends with the most popular girl in high school. Whatever pheromones it is that men pick up from women with their hormonal radar, Pat had them. I didn't.

I remember the first time I had the Betty "clong" of recognition. It was when my friend Otile remarked rather matter-of-factly that while she and I could shine up pretty well—buffed and polished for special occasions—Pat was a knockout. Well, right, I thought at the time. That's right. It was the cheerleader thing and the California thing and, to put it bluntly, she was one terrific-looking woman. Never mind, sniff, that she could give tours of the cosmetics counter.

This was a difference between us. By every cultural calculus, she was more feminine. At the end of our Nieman year, we said good-bye at the Amsterdam airport; I was heading to Copenhagen, and Pat was heading to Rome. But her plane was canceled, and she was left alone in a foreign airport, not knowing the language, trying to get an Italian hotel operator to hold her hotel reservation in Rome until she could get on another plane.

Because it was Pat, a handsome Milanese businessman suddenly appeared, gently offering his help. He straightened the reservation out and, because it was Pat, they ended up on the next plane together—indeed, on half a dozen planes over the span of a short transcontinental affair.

We have laughed about it over the years. What if I had been the one bereft in the Amsterdam airport? What if Signóre Right had offered to help me? There is no doubt what I would have said—brusquely, independently, falsely: "No, thank you, I'm just fine." End of affair. But, of course, Signóre Right wouldn't even have asked me.

Grown men developed crushes on Pat—old-fashioned crushes. I saw it happen a dozen times. She had a certain glow, a way of listening, paying attention, and maybe inviting adventure. Her intensity and her empathy— the characteristics that I valued and depended on in her—were also, of course, attractive to men. But I always knew another secret: under that initial aroma of womanly accommodation, go-along ease and empathy, there was a juicier and tougher woman. At the core, Pat wasn't nearly as malleable or as ladylike as she appeared on the surface.

I remember one night at a different D.C. restaurant (not the Sans Souci; we had worn out our welcome and our credit cards there) when we were engrossed in catch-up conversation. Suddenly a bottle of wine appeared at our table uninvited. It was followed shortly by a little note. No man had ever sent a bottle of wine to me. No man had ever put an admiring note on my tablecloth. Not unless I was with Pat. This time, as before, it was delivered to her side of the table.

What am I, chopped liver? Leaning sweetly over the table, I reminded Pat that she was not the only one who got presents from men. Why, not long ago, I had received a romantic gift from a boyfriend: my very own green metal toolbox, complete with an adjustable wrench. So there. She laughed and poured me a glass of the wine.

How many times have friendships stumbled as women compare themselves to the other? When two girlfriends go to the same dance and one is invited onto the floor time and time again while the other sits out the evening, what happens to their relationship? The possibility that best friends can split into the prom queen and the wallflower exists, and the resulting imbalance can open up a heart of darkness in the light of friendship.

For the first decade of our friendship, Pat and I were both single. The possibility of smarmy feelings of competition—she's up, I'm down—was there, lingering around the edges. I had not purged myself of the memory of myself as the 5-foot, 8-inch girl with 4-foot, 8-inch legs, towering over the eighth-grade boys, lingering on the sidelines at summer camp dances, praying they would soon be over, dreading the next one. It was the girl from another bunk, the one with breasts and the right green shorts, who got the boys.

Can a best friend also be the person who makes you feel most conscious—by comparison—of your own shortfalls?

In our friendship, it didn't work that way. Pat was always one of the smartest kids in the class, and I wasn't sitting home by the telephone, BUT . . . a twinge of envy, jealousy, competitiveness can strike the most solid relationship at anywhere between 2.3 and 6.9 on the Richter scale. The differences between us became part of our repertoire of shared jokes, and made for some good stories over the years.

A long time later, I was sharing a high-spirited dinner in Paris with my older niece, a Parisian, and my daughter, when a tableful of Italian men sent us over a bottle of wine. Point One: Neither Jacqueline nor Katie could believe that I—of all people—accepted it. *"Aunt Ellie???" "Mom???"* Point Two: It was a Pat Moment. Even if they meant the Rhône as a charming tip of the hat to this giggling table of American women in Paris, I accepted it silently in Pat's name.

Pat

There I was, talking with someone at a party about a welfare conference Ellen and I had covered together, when I mentioned something she had said to me about one of the speakers. I saw an expression flicker over the man's face (bemusement? what?), saw a tiny twist of the lips, a polite tilt of the head. What was it? The conversation ended, I moved away, and then—somewhere between the bar and the canapé table—it hit me. The guy thought I was name-dropping.

My first impulse was to laugh. My second one was to go back and collar him and say something smooth like, "Look, you jerk, don't patronize ME. I'm not boasting about who I know! She just happens to be my best friend!"

Except that would be boasting about who I know.

And that made me feel—well, weird.

Soon after I moved to Washington, Ellen was well on her way to becoming one of the best-known columnists in America. Everybody was reading her. Everybody was quoting her. It had happened somewhere outside of our friendship, on the periphery, sort of like nice scenery whizzing by outside the window, but not intrinsic to what was going on inside. We were then, as now, reading each other's work, making suggestions, editing on occasion; we were then, as now, interested in many of the same topics and writing separately about them.

Except that Ellen was famous, and I was not.

Did this eat away at my innards, chew at my soul? No. Did I want to be just as famous as she was? Well, sure. You bet. Did I want to be making the extra money that success was producing for her? Absolutely. Did I want any of this at her expense? You must be kidding.

None of this was very complicated, when considered in a vacuum. But I didn't live in a vacuum, I lived as a journalist in a competitive world. And after that night when I realized that there would be people who thought I was dropping Ellen's name every time I mentioned her, I felt—well, I already said it. Weird. Uncomfortable. Self-conscious. Onstage and offstage. Inside and outside, at the same time.

When Ellen won the Pulitzer, I was thrilled down to my toes. (And I loved her comment, "Now I know the first line of my obituary.") But later a Knight-Ridder editor blithely asked me, "How does it feel to have a best friend more famous than you are?" I don't remember what I said, but I remember the feeling. I was expected to say cheerfully that I didn't care, and he would assume that I cared very, very much. No way would I be able to open my mouth and convince him otherwise.

Ellen's success could have been a problem for us. If she had changed, become more self-absorbed, cared less about my work, I would have been put off. If she had tipped the balance of our internal sense of equality with each other, I might have begun to brood seriously.

Anne Lamott tells a wonderful story on herself in her book *Bird by Bird,* about the time when a friend and fellow writer suddenly became more successful and she found herself unequivocally jealous. "You get all caught up in such fantasies because you feel, once again, like the kid outside the candy-store window, and you believe that this friend, this friend whom you now hate, has all the candy," she writes.

At first she felt like an awful person. How smarmy can you be, to begrudge a friend her success? "You are so supportive," the friend would say. "Some of my other friends are having trouble with this." Well, Lamott was having trouble with it. She was crying when she got off the phone.

Now, if Ellen had regaled me with her successes, if she had thanked me for being "supportive," I would have cried, too. It would have meant she didn't need a friend anymore, she needed an audience. And I would not have been willing to be that audience.

The real struggle was outwardly imposed. I sensed on more than one occasion the curious probing from people who would—not as flat-footedly as the editor I mentioned—bring the conversation around to the fact that, in those early years, I was doing much the same kind of journalism that Ellen was, and getting fewer of the perks and rewards. I was *supposed* to feel competitive. (Either that or a source of information for other people about her, which is another issue.)

What if we had been in the same city, doing the same thing? Or if we had been vying for a place with the same syndicate? I think we both would have been decidedly nervous. And I must say, I'm glad we weren't.

We realized recently that we never actually talked about competition between us until we started writing this book. And we asked ourselves, was it because we didn't want to acknowledge that anything could be detrimental to our friendship? The answer is obvious, now that we are really thinking about it. The answer is: yes.

Wait a minute. The two of us who talked about everything from orgasms to arthritis didn't talk about competition? We dealt with it by not talking about it? That very fact made us pause, and pay some attention to the power of competition and the denial of it. We clearly hadn't talked about our own competitive feelings, other than the periodic glancing joke, because they made us nervous; even surprised us at some level. We realized this topic was probably the least examined aspect of our shared lives as friends. And if that could be true for us, who truly feel a root equality with each other, what about other friends? This needed exploring. How much do women fear all the overlapping emotions wrapped in the word *competition?* How much do women fear the wedge of competition?

We want to make it clear that we are talking about competition between friends—women who really care for each other, who want to stay close and maintain a balance in their relationship. Friendship is after all about feeling safe, connected, trusting, open.

The voice of connection says, "I know just what you mean," but the voice of competition asks, "Which one of you is better?"

Not long ago, the National Collegiate Athletic Association trumpeted the women's basketball "final four" with a female-friendly motto: "There's nothing like a little competition to bring us closer together." Was that wishful thinking? In fact, most women believe that competition doesn't bring people closer together. It separates them.

What friends feel most comfortable with is equality; call it symmetry if you prefer. They talk about what they have in common; they consider themselves on the same side.

No, none of the women we talked with described themselves as precisely equal, if by equal we mean the same. We are surely not the same. These friends often enjoyed their differences: one was serious, the other blithe; one was good on details, the other on the big picture. But they also saw and sought a certain kind of balance. Not a phony balance (let's see, you have the boyfriend, but I have the Ferrari) but a real balance.

Competition, though, is about inequality. It's about asymmetry, about ranking up and down a hierarchy. It's about winning and losing, not about harmony and empathy.

And what most friends know is that there are strong currents—call them what we will, competition, envy, jealousy—that can upset the best of relationships and cast a shadow over the warmest feelings.

We won't get into the debate about whether competition is mostly innate or mostly learned; it simply exists. Competition is a given in our lives. Women experience it on all the playing fields—competition for love, for work, and, of course, literally in sports.

The famed child researcher Jean Piaget once interviewed small children at play and asked these friends, "Who won?" The children responded, "We both won." But Piaget, offering up the voice of the world, persisted, "But who won the most?"

How do friends stay close, when the world asks: "Who won the most? Which one of you is better?" How do they deal with the dividing force of competitive feelings and stay on the same side in a competitive atmosphere?

The cultural messages about competition—is it good, bad, neutral?—are more than mixed; they are Cuisinarted. The Latin root of the word means literally to "strive together," sharing the same root as the word *competence*. There's the kind of competition that makes two scientists work harder and better. There's the kind of competition that brings out the best, breaks the records, unites the fans in the stands. And there's the kind of competition that Gore Vidal described when he said, "It's not enough to succeed; your friends must fail."

For women there is an added edge. Even today, if a man is called competitive, he's usually being praised; if a woman is called competitive, she's often being criticized. With this aura of disapproval, women have difficulty facing their "dark" feelings of interpersonal competitiveness, especially with someone they value deeply. And yet these feelings exist.

From childhood to adulthood, women measure themselves, their achievements, their progress, their lives, against those of their friends. Who got the first bra or MBA? Who got the lead in the play? Whose child was reading first? Friends don't live in an isolation tank. We measure ourselves and the world ranks us all, up and down, by class, success, income, skills, by everything from the size of a house to the score on the SAT.

In a long life, the ups and downs may flow with the tide, the balance sheet may be adjusted and readjusted. But how do you stay close if one is up and the other is down?

Men seem to handle this conflict between friendship and competition by peppering conversations with that ritual exchange of insults and one-upsmanships. But women? They greet each other with connecting compliments: "You look wonderful!" "I love your scarf!" "Have you lost weight?"

Two women friends will stand at the mirror and insist that the other has the better hair, that theirs is hopeless. They go to great lengths to insist that the other is the same or perhaps just a tad better.

The two of us confess now to a ritual exchange that we never even identified until we started to think about this. The subject is weight—and we are, as we have been for more than twenty-six years, within a pound or five of each other.

Pat: Yeah, but you're an inch taller than I, so you can weigh more.

Ellen: But I'm the short-waisted one. You can carry more on the body than on the legs.

Pat: That's ridiculous, look at my hips.

Ellen: Are you kidding? I'm the one with the arms.

We furiously debate how evenly the pounds are distributed. But we know that scale talk is part of a balancing act, one we now acknowledge— if a bit sheepishly.

To protect closeness, women's feelings of interpersonal competition go underground. Differences are ignored or smoothed over, and the strong contradictory heart of competition is denied. We have seen the lengths to which women will go to wave away the smallest whiff of this trouble. Once, interviewing a half dozen women who have formed a close circle for the forty years since they met as young pregnant suburbanites, we asked, "Did you ever feel envious, jealous, competitive?" There was a chorus of nos. Never? We persisted. Not about your kids? Not when one husband was elevated over another? One woman spoke up and said firmly, "Friends wish each other well." In other words, by her definition, friends can't be both competitive *and* wish each other well.

Way back in 1915, Charlotte Perkins Gilman wrote an earnest depiction of a noncompetitive feminist utopia, entitled *Herland,* and inhabited it with women who didn't have the smallest stirring of competitive feelings. "They were sisters and as they grew, they grew together—not by competition, but by united action," she wrote. Eventually in this novel some men discover Herland, and they are bewildered at how the women can make anything work without competition. The women, in turn, are bewildered by their bewilderment.

The heirs to Perkins, the second-wave feminists of the 1970s, also tried to deny the existence of competition. They wanted women to succeed, but not by competing against each other. Sisterhood was powerful. There were attempts to define men as inherently competitive (bad) and women as cooperative (good) that simply didn't ring true.

How much of the reticence about admitting to competitive feelings comes from the cultural image of women, the relentless negative celluloid and literary images of relationships between women that have been served up over the years? Women have long been depicted in the culture as essentially jealous, petty, backbiting, and untrustworthy—especially when it comes to competing for the big prize: a man.

In the classic *All About Eve,* a young actress played by Anne Baxter coolly and calculatedly manages to replace the aging Bette Davis as Broadway's biggest star, and along the way ruthlessly tries to steal her benefactor's husband. Many lesser films and television shows have been variations on the theme of the classic "catfight" of two women scratching each other's eyes out over a man.

In *My Best Friend's Wedding,* Julia Roberts was cast as a desperate woman trying to derail the coming marriage of the man she loves. In one television sweeps week, the producers of television's popular *Ally McBeal* pulled out the surefire I'm-out-for-your-man theme by choosing to have this spacey, short-skirted, young lawyer kiss her old boyfriend Billy, and then be torn with guilt when Billy's wife finds out.

This is still the most tenacious image of female competition. It's the staple of soap operas and the center-ring circus act in the daytime talk shows of a Jerry Springer or Jenny Jones. It is also one of the longest-running jokes of our culture. A lighthearted Visa commercial has Shirley MacLaine and a best friend greeting each other in one reincarnation after another through history. They hug in one century, they kiss in another, and meet again in a third. Finally the two of them run into each other in a modern-day shop. They embrace enthusiastically. Then the friend coos sweetly: "You know, Caesar liked me better."

From adolescence on, women talk about two friends vying for the same man as an absolute taboo, a kind of incest taboo. Nothing is as unforgivable as having your best friend "go after" your boyfriend, your husband—even a man you haven't met but have "your heart set on." Competition for love is the most primal rivalry and source of a lot of pain.

Look through any teen magazine today. "I adore my best friend's boyfriend," writes one girl to *Mademoiselle* magazine, "but she's been acting weird lately when the three of us hang out. What can I do?"

There's nothing weird going on, replies the advice giver. "Her radar has scanned the room, and it's found an incoming missile: You."

In *'Teen* Magazine, two teenagers describing themselves as "Confused Girls," write and ask: "My friend and I have a crush on the same guy. He knows about it and is sending us mixed signals. What should we do?"

Whenever we brought up the subject of competition for men, we got a certain nervous dancing around the edges of the topic. But when asked to describe what they mean by trust, one circle of high school teenagers went right to it: "You trust someone you know wouldn't go after your boyfriend."

Even Jenn and Eileen, the college students who denied adamantly they ever competed for anything, had one small story. Said Eileen, "The only thing that comes to my mind . . . but I wouldn't even call it competing, though . . . would be like . . . Alexander." It turned out they once both had a crush on the same exchange student. But they had a rule they never violated, Jenn said quickly. "If one of us said, I like so-and-so, we don't go for it. That's the rule. And I would never date anyone she's dated. And vice versa. We just don't do that."

This firm declaration of loyalty is an acknowledgment of how deeply important and dangerous vying for a man can be for two friends. As the writer offering advice to the teenager in *'Teen* Magazine said flatly, "For God's sake, even if it's just for the fun, don't flirt with her guy. Best friends are much harder to replace than guys, and believe me, you'll be looking for a new friend if you keep it up."

At the scrambled heart of this competition for love are the dark feelings that psychiatrist Jean Baker Miller taps into when she describes the root pain: "It's the fear of being left out. The fear you won't be chosen, that you won't be the one who is wanted."

Which one of you is better? That question resonates through the competitive air of the workplace and even the culture of celebrity. Women who understand the need to be competitive on the job can be in for painful times when they begin to weigh their accomplishments, success, and celebrity against those of a friend. We talked with many women whose friendships have stumbled over differences, relationships that didn't make it for the long run when one woman became more professionally successful than the other.

But we wanted to get inside one that did endure, a friendship in which two women remained connected even while the world polarized them—and while all the dividing forces were in operation. We wanted to know exactly how a friendship could survive—no, more than survive, *grow*—when the whole world sees them as Star and Sidekick, superstar and gal pal. So we went to the top.

———

A plain brown flower box had just been plunked on top of Gayle King's de-cidedly unstarlike office in the Hartford television station. Casually, she opened it up, revealing a froth of green tissue paper—but no long-stemmed red roses were in this box. Instead Gayle pulled out something far glitzier, and it didn't come from a secret admirer. It came from Gayle's best friend.

It was an engraved invitation to Oprah Winfrey's party for Maya An-gelou's seventieth birthday. "Maya is turning seventy in April, so Oprah chartered a cruise ship," Gayle said, as if it were the most ordinary thing in the world. She pulled out several more cards, all engraved: one said Gayle's stateroom would be on Deck 6, Suite 3, right next to Oprah in Suite 4; an-other was a list of questions about what drinks she might want in her room and whether she would prefer a queen-size bed or two twin beds. And the invitation was addressed to "Gayle King and Guest."

"I guess I gotta find a boyfriend by April. I gotta meet him today," this di-vorced mother juggling kids and a day job as a news anchor said with a laugh. Gayle is a woman who moves in a swirl of activity, a small cyclone unto her-self. She hopped on one foot, pulled on a pair of black panty hose as she talked, filled out a passport application, and opened the box. Gayle is warm and intense, a woman for whom multitasking was in-vented, a contender for first prize in the contest of fast talkers.

Gayle King and Oprah Winfrey.
(© *Harpo Productions, Inc. All Rights Reserved. Photo by Craig Collins*)

That day, Gayle King had more on her mind than a luxury cruise. She had just launched a national talk show of her own, and those who knew she was Oprah Winfrey's best friend were buzzing with the implications. Here they go, head to head, went the speculation. They were competitors now. A fight coming up.

Gayle had a casual response for the snipers. "People say, oh, she's an Oprah-wanna-be. She talks like her, she walks like her, she has the same mannerisms. So I called Oprah up and I said, people think I'm copping off of you, and *you've* taken *my* best stuff. And she goes, 'I know, ain't it a shame? And I already got a show. Good luck!'"

Joking aside, Gayle knew exactly what was at stake. "I don't think that anyone is better at what Oprah does than she is, myself included, so I don't feel a need to compete," she said at the time. "In fact I don't ever want to compete against her anywhere in the country. That's because I don't ever want to get my butt kicked—but mainly I don't want this to be best friend competing against best friend."

Just in case, Gayle made sure she had a no-compete clause in her new contract that precluded her show from ever airing in Oprah's time slot. Which goes to the heart of this unusual friendship: what might look like competition from the outside has nothing to do with the equality on the inside.

That party invitation, for example.

"Oprah was *obsessed* about this damn invitation," Gayle said. "She said, 'I want it to be called "Song of Maya." Should the birdcage on the invitation be square or round? Should it be gold or silver? Should the bird be singing? Should the bird's mouth be closed? Should the bird's mouth be open? And if the bird's mouth is open, should there be those little musical notes coming out of it?' I mean, this is how detail-oriented she is! I mean, I would hear this stuff every day!" She laughed with the ease of a pal who knows what her friend really needed from her on this occasion was reassurance and support.

Reassurance and support? For Oprah?

Real life isn't Hollywood typecasting. Nor are "equal" friends identical. What Oprah and Gayle offer each other is the ability to switch between neediness and strength, the ability to seek help from each other and to give it. And they have been doing this for each other for over twenty years, since the time they first met in 1976, when Oprah was an anchor at WJZ-TV in Baltimore and Gayle was a production assistant. From that first snowy night when Gayle stayed with Oprah, borrowing underwear but not a toothbrush, they have been inseparable.

Oprah sums up what that means for her. "When you are in the public eye, you need a friend you can trust," she told us. "Gayle is a mirror of my-self—a mirror of myself from the interior of who I was when life was a lot simpler, when I didn't have a lot of outside forces affecting me."

Oprah lost that long-ago anchor job at the station in Baltimore—had it yanked out from under her. Gayle was in the newsroom that day, at her desk, when Oprah came out of her boss's office, reeling from the news that the job she wanted to keep was being taken away.

Hearing Oprah talk about it now is like hearing about something that happened yesterday. "I walked right to Gayle, and said, 'Meet me in the bathroom,'" she remembers. "It was my first major demotion. I was the an-chorwoman and they called me in and said, 'That's not going to happen anymore.' I felt like a failure. I felt terrible."

"I was sitting there typing my stuff and she says, 'In the bathroom, *now*,'" Gayle says. "It was so traumatic for her, I mean, that was sort of the most traumatic thing in her life." The two friends spent the entire night talking it through. The demotion, as it turned out, was probably the best thing that could have happened, because within a short time Oprah was as-signed to host a new local show called "People Are Talking." The rest is, as they say, history.

One of the great benefits for Oprah is the fact that Gayle is the one per-son with whom she has been connected through the length of her high-profile career, without self-consciousness, without having to "play down" her spiraling celebrity or bank account. "You don't wake up one morning and say, 'Gosh, my life will be different from my friend's,'" Oprah says. "It just evolved and got bigger and bigger."

There was that moment over a decade ago in Racine, Wisconsin—that astonishing moment when Gayle first realized what a celebrity her best friend had become. The two women were chattering away as Oprah was being driven to the place where she was scheduled to make a speech, when Gayle suddenly looked out the window and saw long lines of people, police everywhere, and a jam of traffic.

"Who's coming?" she asked.

"I am," said Oprah.

"No, no, I mean, who is *really* coming? Besides you? Who are all these policemen for?"

"Me," Oprah replied, starting to laugh.

And as she tells it, at that point Gayle turned toward her friend, and in total astonishment, blurted, "Oh my goodness, what is *becoming of you?*"

This is one of Oprah's favorite stories, a turning-point story. She couldn't have enjoyed this moment of success around someone who might see it as a Big Ego opportunity—only someone who understood what fun the moment was.

And then there are the two bookend moments that frame their twenty years of play.

"The day after Gayle spent the night at my house for the first time, we went to Casual Corner the next morning and saw these sweaters," Oprah remembers. They were $19.95 each. Gayle bought one; Oprah bought two. "My God, you can buy *two?*" Gayle asked.

Fast-forward, twenty years later. It was Oprah's forty-second birthday and she and Gayle, in Florida together, decided to head for the mall. "I was thinking maybe I'd buy myself a watch for my birthday," Oprah says. As they sped down the highway, they caught a glimpse of a great-looking car in the window of an auto dealership.

"Wow," said Oprah, "What kind of car is *that?*" She turned into the parking lot. She and Gayle went the showroom and were knocked out by the gleaming black Bentley sports coupe on display there. Oprah didn't hesitate for a minute. She decided to buy the car. For cash.

"My God, you can pay *cash?*" asked Gayle. "You can't do that, you have to *negotiate.*" Gayle began to bargain with the salesman, asking him to take $5,000 off the price, or at least—how about throwing in the floor mats for free?

But Oprah stood there and laughed. "Gayle, I don't have to negotiate. Gayle, remember? *This is a Casual Corner moment!*"

Having a friend you trust means having a friend who doesn't just clap when you succeed, but who is authentically there for you when you slip. Oprah was there to cheer on Gayle's new show. And she was there when it was canceled—a piece of news delivered, ironically, while she was on the Maya Angelou birthday cruise.

This was a blow that Gayle bounced back from quickly. "I have no complaints," she told us at the time. "It would be different if I was unhappy with my life or felt I didn't bring something to the table, but I've been in television for a long time. I've been nominated for six Emmys, and I won three." And she laughed. "But who's counting? Not me."

"I thought she handled the cancellation of her show with supreme grace. Inside, you always think, you can make it," said Oprah.

Perhaps inevitably, the *New York Daily News* ran a story reporting the demise of the show with this lead: "In the cold, hard world of television, sometimes who you know just isn't enough."

Success has not shielded Oprah from her own professional disappointments. Her film *Beloved,* a serious drama on slavery, opened amidst great publicity and high expectations. How could it fail? Oprah had the Midas touch; everything she was involved in turned to gold. There was a torrent of national publicity, including Oprah on the cover of *Vanity Fair* magazine.

The two friends made sure they were together the weekend the movie opened. They waited nervously that first night for the numbers to come in, the numbers that, in the bizarre world of Hollywood, would tell them within hours whether *Beloved* would be a success.

The results were a shock. People did not flock to the theaters to see *Beloved,* they flocked to the theaters to see a horror movie: *Bride of Chuckie* was the top movie in the country.

"We couldn't believe it," says Oprah. "We were sitting together and saying, 'What happened?'" This wasn't a humiliation that could be endured anonymously for someone as much in the public eye as Oprah. She admits now she felt "a great sense of rejection."

"Bride of Chuckie??" remembers Gayle, shaking her head, still appalled. "We thought we were at least going to the Oscars, and instead nobody liked the movie."

"I can't say that Gayle comforted me," Oprah adds. "We were both totally shocked." Instead, they sought comfort from another direction, sitting down together and polishing off large plates of macaroni and cheese, what Gayle calls "our drug of choice."

Trust is the glue that holds them together, but there is more to what keeps this friendship equal.

"She's my constant reality check," says Oprah. "Gayle helps me maintain my stability and gives me a sense of being grounded." By way of illustration, she tells the story of what happened on a leisurely vacation at her luxury home in Telluride, a high-scale ski resort in Colorado. She had just come back to the house after a hike through the magnificent surrounding mountains, totally enjoying her affluent life, when she got a phone call from Gayle back in Hartford. Gayle was unimpressed with how Oprah was spending her day. Her air-conditioning was busted.

"She said, 'Let me tell you what real people are doing. Real people have busted generators, real people are sitting in one-hundred-two-degree temperatures waiting for some guy to come fix the generator, *that's* what real people are doing,'" Oprah recounts, laughing. "I said to her, 'you should have bought a more expensive generator,' and she said, 'I bought the most expensive one I could!' It's moments like these that she keeps me in touch."

Gayle counters the insular pull of celebrity for this friend who happens to be at the helm of a multibillion-dollar enterprise with total frankness. Oprah can count on her never to be too impressed—and always to be loyal.

"I never feel far from Oprah, no matter where she is," Gayle says. "I'd cut out my tongue before I'd say anything that I think would hurt her. I know that I can always count on her, and that's a very powerful thing. I knew her before my husband and I've known her after my husband. I've always felt very connected to her. I know I can depend on her, and she knows the same is true for me."

That trust doesn't come easily to someone like Oprah. There are too many people in her world who want something from her, too many people who see her as a conduit for their own ambitions.

"Gayle genuinely—and I could cry when I say this—I have never met a human being more genuinely excited about my success than she is," Oprah says. "There has never been one moment of jealousy." She pauses before adding more slowly: "I don't know—if our roles were reversed—if I could have given my entire open heart to someone I saw whose career was blasting off from the earth, and say, 'You go, girl, go to the moon.' I don't know if I could do that."

Gayle and Oprah, who haven't lived in the same city since their Baltimore days, meet as often as they can. Mostly they use the friendship lifeline of the telephone. They are on the phone with each other every day and sometimes spend their evenings "together" watching the same television show with an open phone line.

"We watched the whole O. J. Simpson car chase, me in Chicago, her in Hartford, together on the phone," Oprah says. "She watches TV and I don't, so she keeps up for me. She'll call and say, 'Such and such just happened, I don't want you to be ignorant of what's going on.'"

"I'm a walking *TV Guide*," Gayle boasts. "Oprah called once and said 'My producers are telling me about this show called *Friends,* and they think we should do the cast,' and she goes, 'Have you heard of it?' and I say, 'Have I heard of it? Oprah, it's huge! If you can get those guys, you should do it,' and she says, 'Well, I don't know . . .' and I say, 'I'm telling you, it's huge! Do it!'" Gayle shakes her head at the obtuse quirkiness of her friend.

Sharing lives doesn't go all one way. Oprah, who delivered the eulogy at the funeral of Gayle's mother, is also connected to Gayle's children and is, in fact, their godmother. "I feel I have their trust and I'm their friend," she says. Which brings her to another story that tickles her. When Gayle's daughter's summer camp friends found out her mother was a familiar local television personality, she was mortified. What kid wants to be singled out as different? But she told her mother it could have been worse. "At least they haven't made the Auntie O association, then I'd have *real* problems," she said.

These two women have a way of putting themselves together as part of a whole: the worldly-wise Oprah and the idealistic Gayle; or, as Oprah parses it, the not-so-nice Oprah and the nice Gayle.

"Gayle is far more traditional than I am and a great believer in the American Dream," Oprah says. "She believes in the Kodak moment. I'm not like that." Gayle is her reality check, but she plays the same role for her friend. "She projects her own ideas and ideals on other people, and I'm always saying, 'Come on, get real.' She's one of these people who wants to believe the best about everybody, which can be frustrating to me."

But it is because of Gayle that Oprah feels she can at least "entertain the idea of idealism." And she considers herself blessed to have as a friend "the nicest person I know."

She tells the story of trying one day to do three things at one time, getting frustrated, complaining to her boyfriend, Stedman Graham, that she had too much to do. "And he said, 'So why are you doing it all?' and I said, 'So people will know I'm nice.' And he said, 'You're not nice.' And I said, '*What?*' and he said, 'Gayle is nice.'"

There were earlier points in Gayle's life when Oprah wanted to bring her friend into her own far-flung enterprises. But Gayle was newly divorced and reluctant to take her kids away from the town where their father lived. And she meant it.

"Do you realize what I'm offering?" Oprah demanded on one occasion.

"Yeah, of course I do, but I can't do it," Gayle responded.

"Well, that just doesn't make any sense," Oprah said.

Couldn't it also be because she was uneasy about working for her best friend? Wouldn't a lot of people understand that?

"Not at all," Gayle insists. "I don't have that hang-up. If there was a way I could have accepted that offer, I would have been there yesterday."

Oprah thinks Gayle's great strength—and what she most respects—is her common-sense ability to set priorities. "I marvel at it, really," Oprah says. "I'll say, 'Come to Italy with us,' or, 'We're going to Spain,' and she'll say, 'No, I want to be with my kids.' She's changed my idea of what parenthood can be."

The time came when Gayle could take one of Oprah's offers, signing on to be editor-at-large of Oprah's latest venture, a magazine focused on personal and spiritual growth. "She'll be my voice for the magazine," Oprah said in the announcement. "She'll be there to make decisions and judgments when I can't be there." Gayle will continue to live in Hartford, and commute two or three times a week to New York City.

However simplistically the world tries to define their relationship—Oprah up, Gayle down; Oprah star, Gayle sidekick—the internal reality is very different. They value and enjoy each other's strengths and treat each other as equals with different strengths and weaknesses.

"The hardest part of success is to find somebody who is happy for you," actress Bette Midler once observed. Sometimes "the winner" loses too. She will curb her own spirit—not just because she is sensitive to the feelings of her friend—but because she fears that, at some level, her friend may be lessened by her good fortune.

A few years ago, Midler starred in *Beaches,* a movie about friendship that explores the struggles women have with competition. It is the story of two unlikely friends—one rich, one poor—who meet as children under the boardwalk at Atlantic City and go on to different lives: Hillary becomes a wealthy socialite and CiCi becomes a Broadway star. They continue a long and edgy relationship, alternately envying and faulting each other for bad life choices. In their final competition, a dying Hillary is jealous of CiCi's easy rapport with her daughter, but Hillary still entrusts the care of that daughter to her friend. For once, an alternative message is that a friendship can survive even a lifelong history of competition. Even when you fail each other, you can find a way back.

The truth is somewhat more ambiguous, even in Hollywood. When actress Vivian Vance was selected to play the frumpy Ethel Mertz in the *I Love Lucy* sitcom, she found a lifelong friendship with Lucille Ball—and a lifelong frustration with her role as second banana. Vance wanted to be a star too. Instead she became famous as Ball's sidekick, and the inequality reportedly gnawed at her, sparking frequent feuds with Ball. After the demise of *I Love Lucy* she signed on for a second series with Ball, but only after insisting that her character be named Vivian. When it came time to renew her contract for the show, Vance insisted on and failed to get financial parity with her friend. She backed out of the series, closing it down. Yet, when Vance died, Ball fervently and emotionally described her as "one of the best and dearest friends I've ever had."

We keep thinking about the "noncompete clause" that Gayle King wrote into her television contract. A promise not to compete? It sounds like something corporations force on executives when they leave for a new job and are in a position to take the company secrets. But this was Gayle's choice. For one thing, there were just too many gleeful tabloid writers—the same ones who were always hyping stories about the breakups and break-downs, and making a saga of Oprah's weight loss–weight gain struggle—eager to make up a catfight story. Which would it be: Oprah Wipes out Gayle, Leaving Her in Tears? Gayle Knocks Off Superstar Gal Pal in Ratings War? Oprah and Gayle Duke It Out? Who needs that?

At the same time, what friends wouldn't be wary about going head to head in direct competition? Few friends literally sign a legal paper swearing off competition. Instead they have unwritten documents, unspoken rules by which they covertly pledge to avoid the possibilities of conflict by avoiding competition, as if competition and conflict were inseparable. They make those tacit pledges not to date each other's boyfriends. They may also avoid opportunities for conflict in work as if they were occasions for sin.

There is no easy mix for friendship and competition, and women have struggled with trying to find a balance in many ways. Earlier in this century, Katherine Mansfield and Virginia Woolf were friends, rivals, and catalysts, seen by the world as competitors for the title of best woman novelist of the era. After Mansfield's early death from tuberculosis, in a letter to Vita Sackville-West, Woolf tried to face the mix of jealousy and love she felt on hearing the news.

"At that one feels—what? A shock of relief—a rival the less?" she wrote. "Then confusion at feeling so little—then, gradually, blankness and disappointment; then a depression which I could not rouse myself from all that day. When I began to write, it seemed to me there was no point in writing. Katherine won't read it. Katherine's my rival no longer."

Friendship and rivalry do coexist in all sorts of professions. A woman we know in the movie industry set herself early on a rather flinty rule that she says has served her well: she actively avoids making friends in her particular line of work, at times regretfully. "If I do, if I become close to someone, almost inevitably at some point we will be vying for the same job," she says. "In this town, that's the end of the friendship."

This is a conundrum for many women. Work is where many make friends; it's where they share the neighborly, daily camaraderie. Women gravitate to friends with whom they can share confidences and not censor themselves, but doing that on the job can be risky. Confiding to a friend that you are angling for a promotion may only elicit the news that she wants the same job, compromising you both. Friends in the workplace must sometimes painfully work out new rules for themselves. They live within a hierarchical structure, whether they like it or not. Even when women aren't in direct competition with each other, they are in a competitive atmosphere.

Arlie Hochschild observes that women bring their own relationship styles to the office, "doing friendship" in small moments all day long. This works best for women at the same level. But we heard, again and again, the wistful complaints of women whose friendships were wrecked on the shoals of everyday workplace competition. The woman who gained a promotion lamented that her friend couldn't be happy for her. The woman left behind felt like the "loser." There were real strains between what one woman wanted for herself—a better job—and her friendship.

We received one memorable series of e-mails that came with the sizzling header "Blonde Ambition in the Naked City." They told the angry story of a woman whose "best, best, closest buddy" was transformed by a promotion into her awkward, distant, critical boss. We also interviewed a high-ranking executive who had to fire a friend. The friend, whom she had also hired, was now undermining *her* ability to succeed in a competitive environment.

In sum, a lot of women are learning—not always happily—that they can't mix intimacy and work. They are learning to do friendship "lite," to mimic the male style—just short of intimacy. Some are learning as well how to take competition, winning and losing, less "personally."

There is one area of life, however, in which there is no "noncompete" clause, and that is competitive sports. As Mariah Burton Nelson, a pro basketball player turned author, has said, "In most American sports—the pervasive metaphor for so much of life—a game cannot end in a tie." In sports, there is no leeway for the ritual dialogue of comfort and denial that friends often use to reassure each other that they are the same or at least roughly equal—"Oh, I wish I could get things done as quickly as you." "What do you mean? You think things through so much more *thoroughly.*"

At the conclusion of a match, someone wins and someone loses and each knows it. In individual sports, someone ends up with the cup, the gold medal, the title of Number One. This is where the reality of competition comes to the surface in the most direct, but potentially most honest, way.

Women enter this arena at a linguistic disadvantage. The language of the sports pages is unrelentingly male. Sports metaphors overlap with war metaphors. One person or team "beats," "clobbers," "wipes out" another. Winner takes all. The rest are losers.

Professional women athletes can be as up front about their passion for winning as the legendary Mildred "Babe" Didrikson. Upon entering the 1932 Olympic trials she said flat out, "I came out here to beat everybody in sight and that's just what I'm going to do." They can also be as treacherous as the skater Tonya Harding, who was accused of plotting to club her competition, ice-skating queen Nancy Kerrigan, before the 1994 Olympic trials.

This is sports culture in transition. In sports lingo, the "killer instinct" may be a compliment to a male athlete, but it has a different ring when applied to a woman. And a far, far different ring when applied to a friend.

The two of us have very different life experiences with sports. In high school, Pat played tennis almost every day with a high school friend who was on the school varsity team. This friend constantly told her she was better than she thought she was—she just needed more confidence. Pat vividly remembers the day she missed a baseline shot and called out to her friend for the fourth time that afternoon, "I'm sorry!" The girl on the other side of the net threw her racket to the ground and glared at Pat. "Will you stop saying you're sorry!" she yelled. *"You missed a shot! That's all!"*

Pat's immediate response, she remembers to this day, was, "Oh God, I'm sorry!" Later, when she didn't make varsity, she drifted away from the game.

But for Ellen, sports have always been a playing field for the complexity of friendship and competition. Even at midlife, playing tennis with a friend in Maine has all sorts of echoes of the past.

Ellen

Susan has arrived on the island for her summer stay and we are ready to open what I have come to think of as our Advil Tournament. This "tournament" is something that we both look forward to over the long winter and so we greet each other eagerly as we head for the court together on Saturday morning. As is our habit, we allow each other a set of pregame excuses: our bad knees, how little we've played this year.

We spin our rackets and begin the game. She sweeps ahead of me, returning my specialty shot, a deep backhand, far too easily. I miss my first serve with appalling regularity and then drop a second wimpy one that she returns with a tough and accurate crosscourt. We are off. Soon the score is

5-2, Susan, and then something shifts in the air. I settle down and focus and catch up to 5-all.

There is no tennis match without its muscle memories for me. Those memories go back to summer camp when I played every day with my friend Rona, who took home the tennis prize every year. The summer I turned fourteen, Rona didn't come back and this time, I was absolutely certain, the coveted tennis cup would be mine. I easily made it to the finals and was matched against a sloppier but tenacious player. But at some point, in front of the entire camp, her persistence, her ungraceful ability to keep getting the ball back over the net broke my confidence. To this day, I remember the sinking, salty feeling as the cup slipped away.

Winning and losing. Make no mistake about it, I like to win. If I am playing with someone who can wipe me off the court, I'll fight hard to get a game. But even those who want to win often carry along in the memory bank the experience of losing. Could that be incorporated however subconsciously into a reluctance to make a friend feel like a "loser"?

In the Advil Tournament, Susan and I are now dead even: it's 6-6 and then we go through the overtime scoring that neither of us has quite mastered. The overtime goes over and over overtime until—damn it—there is that crosscourt shot again. She wins the first set.

In the second set, my serve returns from the Land of Lost Serves and again the seesaw balancing act that typifies our games returns to its familiar pattern.

This time, Susan will win the Advil Tournament. The next day, I will. If I stay a week, we will turn up, overall, more or less, even. Or at least that is how we will both remember it.

We have wondered at times whether both of us prefer to play as equals. We don't seem to go for the jugular and on a day when one of us has simply wiped out the other, the winner offers up some excuse for the disparity of score. We each want to win. It's just that we want more to remain partners. Is there some set point of difference beyond which we wouldn't enjoy this part of our friendship? If there were too enormous a gap between us, would the pleasure leak out of it?

As for my friend Pat, who boasts little interest in sports, watching or participating, is it any wonder that the sport we choose is walking?

W e know that young women—the Title IX generation—are coming to the playing field with different expectations than we had—and thank goodness. There has been an enormous generational change. Girls are pouring into team sports and competitive sports in greater numbers than even Babe Didrikson could have dreamed. Pat's seven-year-old granddaughter, Sophie, exults in the fact that she has what her baseball coach calls "a nice pitching arm," and is determined to become the first woman player for the Seattle Mariners. And who could not have been thrilled watching—along with hundreds of thousands of TV viewers—the U.S. women's soccer team win the World Cup? Seeing these women athletes move across a field, so comfortable in their skins and in their skills?

But that motto of the young women's basketball tournament—"There's nothing like a little competition to bring us all closer together!" Is it that simple for younger women who are friends? Or does sports competition still come with a Siamese twin of conflict?

On a steel gray January weekend, we drove down to Brown University to talk to two star hockey players back for an Alumni Day game: Katie King and Danielle Solari. Two years after graduation, they have reached almost mythic status as athletes at this university. Just off the Brown ice rink, in a hallway, we saw a wallful of plaques and poster-size, full-color photos of the pair, barely distinguishable in their gear, helmets, and mouth guards. Along with Becky Kellar, another star player whose picture hangs next to theirs, they were "tri-captains" of their team—a careful decision made to honor them as equals—sweeping up Ivy League titles throughout their time at Brown.

They were best friends. Together they won twenty-eight straight games. Together they won the Ivy championship. But now they are not teammates.

One is coaching their old school team: Danielle.

One went on to win the Olympic gold: Katie.

They are sitting together on a sofa, their hair still wet from postgame showers, mellow with memories, laughing about what it was like for them during those glory years at Brown. Best friends, rooming together, eating together, playing together, racking up victory after victory.

"We were together all the time," Danielle volunteers. She is a lean woman with long dark hair, dressed in khaki pants and a cream turtleneck sweater, and is clearly at ease within her strong, muscular body.

"Right," Katie chimes in with a grin. "If someone would see us and we weren't together, they'd be like, 'Where's your other half?'" Katie is taller, wearing a taupe sweater and jeans, with three gold earrings in one ear and two in the other—which she jokes about, a bit abashedly. She keeps restlessly undoing her light brown hair from its ponytail, combing it with her fingers, and then looping it up again in an elastic band. On the ice she moves with power and grace, but here there is a note of awkwardness in her body language.

Both are public school kids who made the pricey Ivy League; both loved ice hockey since they were children. Danielle is the daughter of a retired sheet metal worker; Katie's father is a computer service technician. Both of them had brothers who paved the way for them, who let them see the possibility that they could be all-out athletes. They already had a lot in common when they met as freshmen at Brown in 1993, the day Katie looked at Danielle's cowboy boots and decided *that* was weird.

At first we hear all their favorite stories: the big wins, the heartbreakers, the last home game as seniors when they won and the song "Time of My Life" came pouring from the loudspeakers. In the sheer exuberance of the moment, Katie "did the lift," hoisting her friend Danielle up from the ice. . . . They love remembering this.

Then there's the "girlie" story they tell on themselves: the night during their sophomore year when the bat flew into Katie's room. "That was so scary," Katie says. "Our telephone cord was superlong, and I started screaming, ran into the hall, freaking out, and she's, like, a *bat?*" They laugh at the memory. These two who look so formidable suited up for a game on the ice delight in the funny, off-rink memories they share.

And they like conjuring up the differences between them.

Danielle Solari and Katie King.

"You're more talkative if we meet someone new," says Katie.

"Yeah, I'm the one who brings Katie out to meet people," says Danielle.

"She'd tell me how to dress," Katie offers. "I was a plain Jane."

"You were sort of a clean slate," Danielle replies.

"But Danielle would be more crazy."

"I probably dragged her more into things," Danielle admits.

"You were with me when I had my first alcoholic drink, remember?" Katie says.

And how old was she?

"Oh, um, twenty-one. Definitely twenty-one."

They laugh, communicating in their own shorthand.

"Our last year was almost like a fantasy," says Danielle. "The season was so phenomenal and everything was—I don't know, it was our senior year, we had close friendships—and like, it was a very emotional year."

And when it ended, it was as if the curtain came down with a heavy, deadening thump. "We weren't ready," Danielle says.

Katie nods wistfully. The elastic band is coming out; she snaps it around her wrist and begins combing her hair with her fingers again. It is more awkward to talk about what came next, when they went from being two of the "tri-captains" sharing the school's "hall of fame" wall—to something else.

That summer, the two friends were invited to try out for the Olympics at Lake Placid. (Becky, a Canadian citizen, would try out for and win a place on the Canadian team.) Katie, who had been in training, was asked first. Danielle got her invitation after she'd already begun working for an accounting firm. She was thrilled. She and Katie would be vying for spots on the U.S. team.

Katie says she and Danielle traveled to Lake Placid together, and Danielle corrects her. "I don't think so, because you drove up, didn't you?"

Katie looks puzzled.

"You drove up, and I took the bus from Boston."

"Did I drive up?" Katie seems to want amnesia. "I don't know why."

"Yeah, I remember I was bummed," Danielle says matter-of-factly. "I felt like, where's Kinger? I need her. I don't know why, either."

They are both now fiddling with their hair. They have not spoken about this before, and the memory, the knowledge, that they didn't travel together on the biggest adventure of their lives is simply a fact that sits between them. But it is Danielle who seems the most calm. She's faced this one down already.

The tryouts at Lake Placid were grueling. They all trained hard and questions were being asked of all of them that made the Olympics seem so provocatively possible: What size do you wear, so we can order ahead for the official U.S.A. uniform for the opening ceremonies?

Finally, on the last day, all the young hockey players were gathered into one room. Danielle and Katie were sitting next to each other; the quiet room was filled with tension. Nobody wanted to display their eagerness to be chosen. No one wanted to look as if she cared too much, was too confident, too vulnerable, too victorious, too devastated.

Then Katie's name was called out. Danielle reached for her friend's hand. "Made it, good job," she whispered. One by one, the others chosen for the team were read off. Danielle's name was not on the list—and there they were.

"It's hard, it's a hard situation to be in," says Katie, and the words tumble out. "I knew she was happy for me." She turns to Danielle. "You know, I knew that." She turns back to us. "And I also knew she hadn't been skating and then she got the letter, she was like, 'Oh my God, I can't even believe it,' and I was like, 'That's so awesome.' And I was psyched, and she had to sacrifice a lot to even go to the tryout and be in that situation and I think, you know, that yeah, definitely it's hard when it's your best friend, and at the same time, you're like, oh my God, *I just made the team!*" She stops for breath.

Danielle has her head resting on her hand, and is looking soberly at her friend. She's too much of a pro not to know exactly how Katie felt, and anyhow, it isn't the act of not being chosen that hurt most. It was how quickly the glamorous new world of Olympic competition would distance the two of them. Katie was immediately swept up into training, meeting new friends—and then came the glory of the gold.

Danielle, working for Putnam Investments back home, was thrilled for her friend. But there she was, in a suburban office, an entry-level accountant, and when she heard from Katie at all it would be a euphoric Katie, a world away, in more ways than one. "I'd be just getting into work in the morning, and I'd hear from her—the time difference is twelve hours? Fourteen hours? So, anyway, I guess I sort of lived vicariously through her for a while," she says.

Danielle has thought a lot about that Olympic summer. In an earlier interview, she told us, "It was really hard. And I'm kind of stubborn. But I was like, she hasn't called me. She's too busy. She knows where I am. She was my best friend and then all of a sudden, I don't have a gold. I'm not good enough now." It was a brooding thought that might have eaten away at their friendship, if she had let it.

Danielle is clearly the one more able, even eager, to get this subject into the crisp air of this alumni weekend. That may just be the difference in their personalities, but among women, sometimes it is perversely easier for the "loser" to talk than it is for the "winner." The winner may be reluctant to acknowledge that her moment of glory could also have a painful fallout. She may resent anything less than a full-throated cheering squad. At the same time, it takes a generous soul to celebrate a victory that she would have loved to call her own.

We are struck by how different their relationship seems from the one we had expected. Before meeting them together, we unconsciously assumed Katie would be the stronger personality. If anything, Danielle seems to be the one taking the lead, pushing Katie to be braver, at least off the ice.

Danielle and Katie acknowledge that they don't have the opportunity to get together very often anymore. "She's in her world, I'm in my world," says Danielle, "She has to be very focused on what she is doing." Katie travels, making public appearances in other countries, and was expecting to be training in Helsinki for the next Olympic games. Danielle, having escaped accounting, is back in the world of hockey, back at Brown, this time as a coach.

We ask how they see the future. Katie says she thinks that maybe someday she'd like to coach a team, too.

"We might be competing against each other," Danielle teases.

It is Katie who says immediately: "You'll be head coach and I'll be assistant coach."

It is time for them to go. Katie and Danielle rise from the sofa and stretch, joking with each other, assuring each other they won't let so much time go by before they get together again. They are eager now to go join their other friends and teammates who have come back for the reunion game. We walk out of the office, past the large color photos of these young women up on the wall in their Brown uniforms. Suddenly Danielle grabs Katie's arm.

"Listen," she says, a grin breaking out on her face. "Recognize that?" Katie listens; they both laugh. A song is pouring from the sound system into an almost empty rink as the Zamboni machine sweeps the ice, which has for the moment a pure and perfect clarity.

"That's what they played after every game!" Danielle shouted back to us over the beat. "Hey, yeah!" Katie shouts back.

The two friends laughed again, threading their way through the rows of benches surrounding the large oval rink, the benches that for four terrific years of their lives were filled with cheering fans as they played and gloried in a game they love.

What was the song? "Simply the Best."

7

Are We Traveling in Different Directions?

Ellen

"Welcome," he lied.

Oh, maybe that's a bit too harsh, let me try again.

I arrived at David's doorstep lugging my garment bag over my shoulder. This was my first visit since Pat and her youngest daughter, Monica, had moved into his brick Georgian house with the circular driveway. For the occasion I had packed all sorts of things that I had never needed when we hung out together at her rented house in Chevy Chase. This visit required a bathrobe.

There was David, the host, leading me on the tour through his house. "This is the living room," he said expansively as he waved me into the long narrow room that contained two black leather sofas, a steel bookcase, a glass and metal coffee table, and an Eames chair. "It's lovely," I said politely to the tall, attractive man who had wooed my friend under this roof. I lifted a photo of his daughter from the end table, praised her, and put the frame back down. Standing beside me, David discreetly moved the picture an inch or two back into its original place.

Of course the house *was* lovely, in a subdued, sterile, divorced-male sort of way, all glass, steel and leather. It looked like a lawyer's office. It just didn't look like Pat. David's home was black and white and walnut all over; Pat was yellow, blue, green, peach, and cushioned all over.

But that wasn't the point. Pat's house had always seemed like a second home. Here I suddenly felt like a guest—a nervous guest. Instead of dropping my bag in the bedroom and making myself a cup of coffee in the kitchen, I waited for David to lead the way to the room and then offer a drink. For the first time I actually, fully unpacked. Neatly.

Pat had met the man I call David six months earlier when she was the reporter and he was the expert on a story about a bill wending its way through Congress. David was smart, handsome, articulate, smitten. I had first met him in one of those awkward events—hello, boyfriend; meet best friend; check each other out—in the National Press Club half a dozen floors above Pat's office. I felt her twitching with the anxious hope that we would like each other.

At the time, Bob and I were in stage two of our relationship, which was not by any stretch of the imagination a whirlwind courtship. In our long stage two, somewhere between love and marriage, the word *commitment* had been run up the flagpole and we were dancing around it.

Sitting in the Press Club with Pat and David, I remember distinctly thinking, my God, look how easy relationships can be. You meet a nice guy, you fall in love, he wants to get married, you move in together. You live happily ever after. Boy, did Pat make it look easy. Boy, was Pat lucky.

Of course, I heard all the little edges of ambivalence in the voice of my friend who was looking for love but also, I suspected, a place to reknit a family life that had been shaken by divorce and the family-splintering move to the capital city. But in that moment, I wondered why it wasn't that easy for me and Bob. We were moving toward commitment at glacial speed.

But on April 1—was this an ominous date?—they had moved in together after much soul-searching on Pat's part. Lock, stock, barrel, and kids. I was on my maiden visit. Not to Pat's house this time, but to Pat and David's house. After the years when we'd led parallel lives—divorced, single, dating—now she was Pat of Pat and David.

Three was not exactly a crowd, but David's larger house seemed more cramped to me than Pat's old digs. There were all those relationships under one roof. Pat was trying to keep the water smooth; David and I were trying to like each other. But why all those possessive gestures from him that seemed to be for my benefit? Yes, I know, David, you are a couple. And why did I drop those references to the time when . . . before he existed in her life?

There was just a touch of tension in the house. When Pat came into the leather and steel living room to settle in for a long talk, I realized that David was joining us. Carefully, he took a paper napkin and put it under the coffee cup—*my* coffee cup—which was leaving a ring on the glass tabletop.

I thought back to the time a month earlier when they had visited in Boston. After Pat's gentle reminder ("he's a bit of a neat freak") I had gone through a frenzy of housecleaning. Neatness Aren't Us, but for the weekend, my daughter's stuffed animals that spilled over into the guest room were exiled to the basement. The dog was banned from the sofa, window ledges were washed, and rugs vacuumed within an inch of their lives. When Pat and David arrived, I saw the fleeting shock on Pat's face, followed by a silent appreciative laugh.

Now here we were in David's very neat living room late at night, all three of us. Was this it, from now on? A three-way party line? I had the fleeting thought that from now on, Pat and I would only talk—really talk—on the phone. I had the sudden and distinct impression that David didn't want to leave us alone to talk about him. David was trying to nail down this relationship and I was a loose tack. The tension surely had more to do with the strains that had already settled under this roof than with me, but I started to squirm, wondering if I would be more welcomed by the desk clerk at the Motel 6.

Mind you, this was a decent guy, smart, great on paper, but whoa. When I came down to the kitchen in the morning, there was David standing at the open refrigerator door, saying, "There's no orange juice!" as if the great juice-delivery system in the sky had failed him. There was David at the closet door, persistent about the jacket that needed to be taken to the cleaners today. By Pat. And there was David—the same David who had fallen for a woman not noted for her culinary skills—wondering what was for dinner. This was the man who once asked in a discussion of why she didn't like to cook, "What do you think went wrong in your childhood?"

When David went off to work, I took one look at Pat's narrowed eyes, saw her quietly fuming. I wondered: Whom should I be loyal to? The Pat who wants it to work? Or the Pat who is ready to pack the car and pull out of the driveway? I was worried about who she would become in this relationship. And if she would change or get out and whether being a good friend meant saying what you think or keeping your mouth shut and your ears open.

I prayed to the many household gods that govern human relationships, and made sure that I put my cereal bowl in the dishwasher. But later that day, when I was stewing over the visit, I said to our mutual friend, Ann: What on earth am I going to do? How am I going to stay at that house again?

So we had come to the most familiar, routine, absolutely predictable turning point in a friendship; a caricature of a turning point. This one was called David. But it was one of the many moments when a friend's life is changing and all her other relationships are in flux. It's one of the moments when the familiar expectations, the comfortable routines are all up for grabs.

Friendship is just one leg of the three-legged stool of a life that includes work and love. But adult women are often juggling a number of worlds and priorities as they compose their lives. What they value is the balance that friendship adds to life—yet totally normal transitions can challenge that balance in ways that are as common as they are unexplored.

Women who make connections through commonality, who comfort each other by saying "I know just what you mean," have to deal with differences. "The unspoken bargain between women is that we must all stay the same," wrote Luise Eichenbaum and Susie Orbach in *Between Women*. "If we act on a want, if we differentiate, if we dare to be psychologically separate, we break ranks. We are disrupting the known: the merged attachment."

And yet again and again, in dating, in marriage, in motherhood, in divorce, even in changing career paths, the decisions that a woman makes for herself can separate her from the people to whom she is closest. And those friends who have grown in connection with her may fear she will now grow . . . away.

How do women who value their friendships handle these transitions? Not always well. There's no structure for riding out the changes. The very voluntary nature of friendship—one of its great strengths—is also a weakness. We can "choose" to leave. We can "choose" to end old friendships as well as make new ones.

The two of us met as divorced mothers with growing children, as journalists with time off, as two women thrown into the exact same milieu. We were in "it" together—working, dating, worrying, juggling. We had brought others with us into our friendship—children, family, friends. We never thought of friendship as a closed corporation, and we both wanted love, sex, intimacy with men with whom we would share our lives.

So we wished each other love. But we had never really considered the effect that the proverbial "right" man could have on our friendship. Would one relationship that we both valued—love and marriage—diminish another—friendship? Does love take precedence over friendship? Does it have to be either/or? Do we have just so much room, time, energy on the pie plate of our lives?

Remembering the life transition that we call "David" makes us think about these turning points, in part because it is so common a story. Friends and lovers, friendship and marriage. In the hierarchy of relationships, love is supposed to trump friendship, and when a woman moves in with her new lover and his leather sofas, more than one friend wonders, will there be any room left for me? More than one friend wonders in return whether she can move into a new relationship without putting a treasured friendship in jeopardy.

This "triangle" of friends and lovers carries all sorts of memories. One day your high school girlfriend is infatuated with the boy who has the locker down the hallway, and then suddenly she is unavailable. The next minute, they've broken up—and she's back on the phone. Nearly all of the women we talked to have gone through the revolving door from boyfriend to girlfriend, infatuation to friendship.

For teenage friends, the memories of being dropped by a best friend for the new boy are particularly raw. In Lynn Johnston's knowing comic strip, "For Better or for Worse," the family teenager, Liz, is so mesmerized by her crush on Anthony, she is oblivious to her friends. In one strip, Liz is putting clothes in her locker, looking a little glassy-eyed, as her girlfriend tries to talk to her.

"Elizabeth, what's happening? We used to do all kinds of stuff together—An' now, all you wanna do is be with Anthony."

There is no response from Liz, so her friend tries again: "You were so jealous when I started to hang out with Candace and Shawna-Marie—an' now you hardly talk to ME anymore!" Still no response. The two girls start walking down the hall, and her friend makes one last try: "I know what it's like to be in love, but you're cutting yourself off from all your friends. . . . Liz?"

Liz is alert now, but not to her friend—Anthony is walking by. He and Liz smile, lock eyes, wave. And inside the balloon over the friend's head, we read the words that sum it up for so many young women who have felt closed out: "Love isn't just blind—it's deaf, too."

These days, girls disapprove and criticize each other for a lack of loyalty. Breaking a date with a girlfriend for a guy—a given in the days when we were teenagers—comes up against a revised teenage etiquette. Even the Spice Girls warn the guys that friends count in their hit "Wannabe," when they sing, "If you wanna be my lover, you gotta get with my friends."

Yet the powerful pull of love is as overwhelming as ever, and the stories of disappointment and abandonment are as common as ever. In *Just Friends,* Lillian Rubin described how vividly women remember their feelings in teenage years and early adulthood. "Repeatedly, people recalled feeling betrayed and abandoned during those years, speaking of being 'set on the shelf,' 'put on hold,' 'expected to sit around and wait,' or just plain 'dumped' when a romantic interest entered the life of a friend. . . . Whether we are forsaken or forsake another, the message is driven home: Friends take second place."

The hierarchy of relationships with love and marriage at the top isn't just the product of some biological instinct to mate. It includes the deeply ingrained cultural assumption that it is natural to move from friendship to marriage. The perfectly matched, properly bonded husband and wife are supposed to find everything they need in each other's arms. They are not just sexually monogamous but emotionally monogamous. It's the romantic notion behind every happily-ever-after story, which heightens the tension of real-life couples who try to fit their relationship into the lives they already have, lives full of kin and friends. Even as far back as 1662, this change was lamented by a writer named Katherine Philips: "We may generally conclude the Marriage of a Friend to be the Funeral of a Friendship," she said.

Even in our times, suddenly a friend is unavailable for dinner—it's just lunch now. Suddenly, a woman no longer feels free to pick up the phone and call her best friend because she's with "him." When this happens, it is hard for friends not to feel a sense of loss. And sometimes equally hard to acknowledge that loss, as if they were ashamed of challenging the assumption.

In the whole genre of romance movies, we found only a handful that focus on this "triangle" of friendship and love. In one of them, *Walking and Talking,* two twentysomething friends wrestle over a mix of feelings when one is getting married.

Laura (played by Anne Heche) feels guilty almost immediately when she decides to marry Frank. We see her friend Amelia (Catherine Keener) moaning to her therapist: "They make me sick, it's like they're glued together. They eat the same thing, they go on diets together. I mean, I think they're beginning to look alike, like people and their dogs." It's the monologue a real-life friend would never voice, but one with which many could empathize.

In the film's climactic scene, it all spills out:

"My problem, Laura, is you're different," says Amelia to the bride-to-be. "Okay, we used to talk about things, you used to need me, for chrissakes. When something happens to me, good or bad, I tell you. When something happens to you, you tell Frank. It feels unfair."

"Amelia, I need you," Laura pleads.

"Not in the same way," Amelia retorts.

"You're right! I don't call you ten times a day, and I don't tell you every single thing that happens to me because I DO have Frank. But does that make me a bad friend because I don't need you when you need me to need you? . . . You know when I do call you, it's not enough. And if I do see you, it's not enough, nothing is ever enough for you. It's like when Frank and I got engaged you decided that I don't care about you anymore and that's just not true!"

"Stop for a minute and think what it's like for me! That's all I want."

"What's it like for you?" Laura asks.

"Hard. Sad. I miss you. What is it like for you?" says Amelia.

"It's lonely."

There is no scriptwriter to help real women articulate the feelings of exclusion and loss, the fear that your best friend has just joined a new club from which you are barred. These conflicts are not aired and resolved in one climactic scene. But that sense of abandonment can ricochet in either direction.

Our friend Lesley Stahl of CBS's *60 Minutes,* has never forgotten what happened to her at Wheaton College after her roommate and best friend Judy stopped speaking to her. This was not just for a day, a week, or a month but for their entire sophomore year. It is a story she tried to write about in her recent autobiography, and decided was too painful to include.

"I was nervous and scared when I got to Wheaton, and you know, you really want to get along with your roommate. Luckily, Judy and I got along famously. I loved her, and we became inseparable during our freshman year," she remembers.

The two friends would spend every weekend together, getting in the car and driving to Boston, going to museums, plays, concerts. Lesley adored

Judy, describing her as an intellectual mentor. "I admired her so much," she says.

But Lesley came back to school in her sophomore year with a new boyfriend and began spending weekends with him. She was no longer available for those outings with her friend. Everything changed.

"Judy simply stopped talking to me. We lived in a tiny space, and she wouldn't tell me what the problem was. She just wouldn't talk to me at all."

The two roommates spent a year in complete silence—getting up in the morning and going off to breakfast, sitting at separate tables, going to separate classes, coming home to the room in the evening—with never a word exchanged.

"It was a devastating experience," Lesley says. "She was physically there, but it was as if a door had been slammed in my face. I ended up spending almost every night crying on the telephone to my mother."

Judy left Wheaton a year later, and Lesley heard nothing about her—or from her—for twenty years. Then one night a few years ago she had a phone call from a friend who had been a classmate. "Judy wants to talk to you," the friend said. "She has lung cancer, and she's dying."

For Lesley, the years melted away. "My heart almost stopped," she says. "This was someone I had loved who rejected me." She eagerly told her friend she wanted that conversation very much.

The next day, at a prearranged time, Judy called. When Lesley heard her voice, she thought it sounded stronger than she had expected. They chatted easily about family, work, their parents, about Judy's illness. But "the elephant was sitting in the corner," Lesley says.

In the middle of the conversation, Lesley finally asked the question that had been on her mind for twenty years. "Judy, why did you stop talking to me?"

"I couldn't help myself," Judy answered.

"You really hurt me," Lesley said.

Judy apologized. She said she knew Lesley had suffered, and she was sorry; that she had a history of "pushing people away."

But why?

Judy wouldn't say why, but Lesley does. "I'm convinced it was the boyfriend," she says. "She and I had an intense, very intense, friendship, and I think she felt I betrayed her."

They talked for a very long time that day, closing the circle, reconnecting—but not quite getting rid of the elephant in the corner. Only weeks later, Lesley had another call: Judy was dead.

Lesley—who is known among her friends for her generous spirit—has never since had a "best" friend. "That experience changed my pattern of friendship," she says matter-of-factly. "Even telling this story, I remember in a physical way how it hurt."

If, as Lesley believes, Judy simply could not accept the friendship on any other than its original exclusive terms, it was a sad and significant loss for both of them.

Women who grew up with one-on-one friendships, forever testing—who is your best friend?—and ranking relationships by who is the closest, who the most distant, may find making a transition to "second place" very hard to accept—or talk about. Few women want to sound like the blunt friend of writer Carolyn See who told her, "I can't stand your happiness. I can't stand that you've found a man that you really like." But some can't help harboring resentments, or may even feel their friendship claims are il-legitimate. It may not be until—or unless—both are mated that two friends "get back on the same page."

Single women, in turn, may remain connected to their married friends, but they frequently gravitate to circles of friends who are also single. As the years go on, these women truly become each other's chosen kin; they spend their holidays with each other, travel together. Single women at all stages of life tell us quite simply, "I don't know what I would do without my other single friends."

It is in transitions that we find out if friendship has elasticity. Can it ex-pand to allow change? Is there room for individual change? Can one accept another's relationship and, conversely, can the other—does she want to—stay connected?

Of course in the triangles of friends and lovers, there is another player. Many men have a garden-variety unease about the old friends, classmates, work friends, single pals of their girlfriend. They may suspect, as David did, that he was the subject of discussion, or even dissection. Or they may feel in some competition for intimacy: "What can you say to her that you can't say to me?"

When Gayle King was trying to decide whether or not to attempt a rec-onciliation with her estranged husband, Oprah flatly advised against it.

Oprah had never felt Gayle's husband was the right person for her. "When she first met him, she told me it was like hugging a board," Gayle says.

Oprah argued against the reconciliation, and then, finally, backed off.

"When Gayle said, 'I want to try,' I said, 'Okay, I give up, do what you have to do,'" Oprah told us. "She said to me, 'If I don't go back to him and try again, I'll always wonder what might have happened if I did.' I understand. Everybody's on their own journey, and I respect that. I gave my sincerest advice, because I believed it wouldn't work. But she was right, she needed to try." And then, dryly: "I wanted her to, so I wouldn't have to hear about it for the rest of my life."

Oprah's wariness proved prophetic, in the end. Especially after the one horrifying moment when Gayle couldn't help comparing her friend and husband—and realizing which one was the keeper.

That moment came when Gayle was on a plane, heading to her high school reunion. The plane developed serious trouble with the landing gear, and the pilot told the passengers to prepare for a crash landing; people were asked to remove their glasses, even their false teeth. They were told the plane would circle for forty-five minutes and dump fuel before attempting to land. In one of those nightmare sequences that any frequent flier can fantasize about, Gayle reached for the airplane phone. "I honestly didn't know if we were going to make it," she says.

First she called her husband at work, then Oprah, then her mother. "I said, guys, I'm really scared, and I said to Oprah, 'You've been a really good friend of mine and I'll never forget you and please, if you could, look in on the kids,' and I was saying to my husband and my mother, 'Oh my God, this is so scary.'" Then she hung up and tried to prepare herself for whatever was coming next.

The minutes that followed seemed unbearably long. Finally, the plane began a normal descent, and then the wheels touched the ground—no injuries, no crash, no disaster. They had landed safely. Gayle could hardly believe it. She ran from the plane to the first phone she could find and quickly dialed her husband's number. "And he's not there! It's unbelievable, he's not by the phone!" she says.

She called her mother, who was waiting anxiously. She called Oprah—and found out her friend had already contacted officials at American Airlines and had been getting a blow-by-blow report on the plane's progress. Shaky with relief, Oprah already knew Gayle was safe.

But her husband wasn't waiting by the phone? Why? How, as she found out, could he have nonchalantly taken the newspaper and headed down to the basement to the bathroom—without telling his friend sitting next to him what had happened—while her fate was still being decided in the air?

"I felt like a fool," said Gayle. "I'm thinking, 'God, he must really not like me.'" She paused in the telling of her tale, then added: "I called my husband first. I should have called Oprah."

Gayle and her husband are now divorced.

Says Oprah with a rueful sigh: "I went through her divorce with her, and I feel as if I've been through it myself."

In the hopscotch of life—first one is mated and then the other—these two have always stayed connected. "No pullbacks. Ever," says Oprah. In fact, they talk freely about how Oprah's relationship with Stedman Graham has enriched, not divided, their own friendship.

Oprah, Gayle, and Stedman have a very relaxed way of including each other. When Gayle visits, she often curls up at the end of their bed and talks to the two of them until three in the morning. And it is a relationship where Girlfriend and Boyfriend feel comfortable enough to tease. "I better go," Gayle will say. Stedman, rolling his eyes, will say sarcastically, "No, stay another hour. You gotta go now?"

And there is another story that Gayle tells about the weekend after her divorce was finalized when she flew to Chicago to see Oprah. She was feeling sad, missing her kids, and in need of a place to feel safe. She came out of her bedroom one afternoon and found a small figurine outside her door, a doll playing a guitar. And with it there was a note: "Dear Gayle, may the music play in your life again. Don't worry. Love, Stedman."

Gayle is fully aware of where Oprah fits in the continuum of her life. And she sees the irony of how differently the men in their lives have played a part in their friendship. Stedman has accepted her totally. And her former husband? "She was my friend before I met my husband, and she was my friend after I divorced my husband. It's the friendship that lasted."

Pat

Okay, it was the friendship that lasted for me too. One morning during the time I was living with David, I awoke sweaty from an awful dream. In it, I had been sitting at a long rectangular table with people lining both sides, and a judge sitting next to David, directly across from me. I realized to my horror he was about to marry us and I had no say about it. I let my sleeping self know the truth: NO—I don't want to marry him. What am I doing here? In my dream, as the judge was intoning, I slithered slowly down in my seat, lower and lower, hoping nobody would notice, until I was under the table. Then as carefully as I could, I began to crawl away, trying not to touch anybody's feet.

I awoke. To the truth.

Very shortly after, I said good-bye and moved out. He was a good man, and would make a good partner for someone else, but the two of us had been trying to nail down the wrong relationship.

Ellen had come back to stay in David's house several times, and she did not trumpet her misgivings. She made no declarations that could have put me in a compromised position. She did not point out to me how unsuited he and I were for each other, nor did she make jokes about the orange juice or his determination to fit me into his neat framework of habits.

I didn't like acknowledging to myself that, as charming and likable a person as David could be, he also represented a safe haven. He had almost literally fallen into my life, an instant romance with no backlog of friendship. He worked out perfectly on paper, and he was pressing me to get married. But I was deeply ambivalent, on many fronts, and that ambivalence was finally resolved in the subconscious.

If this relationship didn't chill our friendship, I suppose it's because we never fell into a stiff silence about David—the silence of distance. This was not a mute time for us. I certainly talked plenty about my own concerns. I was figuring things out as we talked about them. But I knew Ellen wanted to follow my lead, to be loyal and discreet, a combination we'd never had to factor into our friendship before. She knew how much of a leap it had been to move in with this man. And once the decision was made, she was there to support me—as I would have been for her. Unless it was somebody really awful.

So, yes, the transition to marriage can easily become the wedge that drives two friends apart. But then what about the longing to have children? Nothing changes a woman's life more than having a child. And nothing can be as divisive as watching your best friend sail away from you on a sea of baby shower gifts, diapers, and formula, leaving you behind on the shore, waving good-bye. She's taking up residence in a foreign country; the two of you hardly speak the same language anymore.

When Pat's youngest daughter, Monica, was still yearning for a child, hoping each month that she would become pregnant, her two closest friends both found themselves expecting. It was what they too had been hoping for; in fact, there had been a running joke among the three over which one would succeed first. Suddenly, two of them had done it. They were naturally delighted, and the conversation at their regular lunches could easily have turned from, oh, will this happen, to buying cribs, choosing hospitals, talking morning sickness. But it didn't. Out of deference to Monica, the two friends were trying to edit themselves, to channel conversation away from what so truly and totally engrossed them to safer, more generic topics.

Finally Monica, unable to stand the new awkwardness anymore, burst out at lunch one day, "Don't do this. If you don't talk about what you're really interested in right now, we won't be able to stay friends. You gotta trust me to be able to enjoy with you." That broke the tension, but it had not been easy.

What happens when there is no simple way to cut through this experience of disappointment and separation? What happens when two friends want, more than anything in the world, to have a child—and only one succeeds?

––––

It wasn't until Tineke Vandegrift, a low-key woman with a slender, angular face and long blond hair, was in a crowded maternity shop buying her first maternity bra, surrounded by salesclerks busy with other mothers-to-be, everybody chattering and laughing, that the full reality hit her. She was pregnant. It was real. Finally.

"I was a member of the club," she says. "It was a great feeling, but . . ." She glances across the table where we are sitting in this small clapboard house in Waltham, Massachusetts, at her close friend, Susan Lee, an equally contained woman, tall, with a moon-shaped face and sleek brown hair and large blue eyes. "I couldn't stop thinking about Susan," Tineke finishes. "I felt in my happiness, I was wounding her."

In their search to conceive, these two friends had formed deep ties as they went through wearying, and sometimes grim, treatments for infertility. They checked in with each other frequently, commiserating, joking together, trying to keep their spirits up through the escalating medical intervention. They even knew to the day when each other's periods were due. As graduate students in psychology, they would often walk together down the hospital corriders during their clinical rotations, feeling like outsiders each time they passed a pregnant woman. But they could turn to each other with the shared lament, "How come she can get pregnant and we can't?"

And now Tineke was a member of the only club both of them wanted to join.

"I almost felt an abandonment," Susan admits.

"And I felt I was trying to take care of Susan from the moment I told her," says Tineke. "I began to resent it. My fantasy was that she could be joyful with me."

"And mine was that we would get pregnant at the same time." Susan folds her hands together and smiles faintly, a small opal pendant around her neck catching the light. "It was really hard, really painful to me, really hard to kind of figure out ways to come together. . . . It felt different now, passing pregnant women in the hall. Once Tineke was pregnant, she was on the inside. I was behind the glass, viewing. They would smile at her, and she would smile at them."

They still find that time hard to talk about. They treat each other and this subject gingerly. Susan, an adopted child, wanted very much to have her own baby, to be related to *someone* by blood. The two friends struggled with what they couldn't share for a long time—and through the first six months of Tineke's baby's life, a winter of blizzard after blizzard, for one reason or another, Susan did not make it by to see the baby.

It took Susan four more years to conceive. But it took somewhat longer to close the distance between them. Tineke acknowledges that, gently: "I thought, I'm happy for her, even though she wasn't happy for me when I was pregnant. It was painful, her raw feelings against mine."

"Maybe it would have helped to talk more about it," Susan says with a tremor of doubt in her voice. "It made me sad that I hadn't been able to go shopping for maternity clothes with Tineke. She was more present for me."

Time has passed, and Tineke now has two children. Susan has a lively, curious three-year-old boy, and is pregnant again. She has what she wanted, a home filled with all the brightly colored toys and paraphernalia of parenthood, including a pet parakeet adding just the right touch of cheerful chaos as it flies around the dining room.

"I thought we would never have the same closeness again," says Tineke. "Something had been ripped." In fact, these two friends who had to struggle through mutual feelings of being abandoned have let time heal the rift, and time has done the job. We had the sense that they were talking to each other, through us, throughout our interview. They know what happened, but for the most part, they chose not to pick the scab.

Did Susan and Tineke stumble over empathy, have too much of a good thing from the start? When a woman talks to a close friend, she anticipates the other person's feelings and, in the process, may begin to preedit her own half of the conversation. This is what Judith Jordan calls "anticipatory empathy." One person knows—or assumes she knows—how another will feel. The mutual empathy can give women wholly satisfying feelings of understanding and being understood, or it can set up stumbling blocks that make it impossible to talk honestly and directly. As Tineke and Susan practiced the skill of reading each other, the desire to protect each other, they were disconnecting. And now they feel grateful relief that they made it through that rough stretch.

If the desire to become a mother can put a strain on one friendship, so can motherhood itself. The full realities set in, usually with a roller derby of clashing emotions. Suddenly you are in charge of a vulnerable, wholly dependent newborn. You are a sleep-deprived, hormone-raging parent, with a new identity, a new role, a new set of tasks to perform from nursing to bathing a baby, a new set of emotions from love to terror.

The most prepared mother—with strollers and portable-cribs and up-to-the-minute diaper-crunching equipment plus a shelf full of baby books—can suddenly find herself panicked. Who knew about belly buttons? Who knows about sleeping, teething? Who can understand why you tiptoe into a room at two in the morning in the irrational belief that the baby isn't breathing? During Rosie O'Donnell's first three months as a new mother, she says she doesn't know what she would have done without her friend, actress Kate Capshaw: "You'd say something to her, like, 'I don't think these are the right size diapers,' and suddenly you'd hear *beep-beep-beep,* and a truck would be pulling up. And a deliveryman would say, 'Here's ninety-five thousand diapers from Ms. Capshaw.'"

Every relationship shifts with motherhood—and a woman quickly realizes that friends who aren't interested in or ready for motherhood know nothing about the things that now matter most. It's at that moment that mothers need, well, other mothers. Somebody else in the same leaky, shaky boat. Somebody who can talk belly buttons. Or diapers.

So what are two friends, on either side of the motherhood dividing line, to do? Give up? In an on-line parenting column, Jahnna Beecham writes about FBCs—Friends Before Children—who come visiting: "FBCs don't know how to integrate children into their universe. They think the baby announcements we sent out were for puppies. And that our 'puppies' can be patted on the head, tossed a Milkbone, and locked in the basement while they are visiting."

On the other hand, a thirty-five-year-old woman quoted in the *Los Angeles Times* laments the loss of leisurely Sunday brunches with her lifelong friend, who is now a mother. In the old days, "We'd talk about families, men, friends, what we did. We'd spend four hours drinking coffee and talk. You'd end up very wired and feeling like someone's listened to you." And now? "I get to her house and sit and wait while she gets the baby ready for an hour. Then we go out. We talk about the baby for a half hour. Then she wanders out to the car or bathroom to change the baby again for another half hour. I'm alone, waiting for her in some fashion, for an hour and a half."

These tensions often separate friends. New mothers begin a search for a fellow traveler, for someone who will know "just what you mean." And they feel estranged from old friends. These old friends do their own drifting away, looking for others who have more time or just interest. Even our own researcher, Laura, a thirty-year-old mother of two babies, let out an e-mail groan on this subject: "If only *one* of my friends would have a baby!"

The loneliness is particularly intense for new mothers at home with small children. The steady, daily support of work, the "play group" of colleagues is gone.

We met Ann Adler at one of the formal meeting grounds for stay-at-home moms trying to remake a community of friends. She had joined FEMALE, an acronym that once stood jocularly for Formerly Employed Mothers at Loose Ends, now rechristened as the more politically correct Formerly Employed Mothers at the Leading Edge.

A small, lively woman dressed that night in a red sweater and black pants, Ann captured our attention with her ability to see some humor in the isolation of motherhood. "In parks I meet people and we'll start talking to the other person's kid," she said. "It's safer than walking up and saying, 'Hi, my name's Ann and I'd like a friend.'" She joked about how the effort to find a friend is like the effort to find a date. "When do you say, oh, she seems cute, I think I'll invite her to lunch?"

But she also seemed most conscious of the transition from one world and identity to the other, and of how hard it is to stay connected to her old friends. Later, she told us why.

Jamie Donahoe, her closest friend, was married, childless, and living in Croatia, a world away from the life Ann, a new mother, was living with her husband. When Jamie came to visit on a trip back to the States, Ann found the differences jarringly obvious.

"She was here for five days, and it was kind of weird. Everything had to be done around Charley's (her newborn son) schedule. It took me two hours to get out of the house in the morning. You feed him, you change him, you feed him again, the whole thing. And it seemed like there was something between us that hadn't been there before. I couldn't figure out whether it was a little jealousy on her part, or a little bit of 'stand back,' or 'this kid bothers me.' There is a still a little kernel there that we haven't discussed."

This distance spilled over into their e-mail relationship as well. "I get on-line, and all I've done all day is take care of Charley. She tells me about her latest trip to Paris or building houses and that's really neat and all I have to talk about is how Charley said his first word. . . . I don't really get responses on that, so I don't talk about it."

We asked Ann and Jamie to let us eavesdrop or e-drop as their e-mail bounced back and forth across an ocean and two worlds. On one side of the ocean was a thoughtful, introspective woman running after an active toddler and on the other an adventurous, outgoing woman building houses in war-torn Croatia. The miles were easy to bridge with technology. We saw, however, how wide the psychic divide had become.

Their friendship had begun in the first few days of their freshman year at Hamilton College and, as it grew, they realized they each brought to the other something new. Once in their senior year, the cautious Ann went rock climbing with Jamie and, to their mutual pleasure, completed the climb. Another time, Jamie took a CPR course that Ann was teaching. Then there was the famous snowball fight. . . .

We asked them to mull over a single question: Why are they friends?

Jamie begins her e-mail in an ordered, thoughtful fashion: "We are alike and share certain common experiences. . . . Since we will always have those things in common, one would presume we will always be friends, despite distance and change and the like. . . . When my mom died, I called you to figure out what to do; when I developed a wild crush on another guy, I called you to figure out what to do. So, we're friends."

Ann reciprocates wholeheartedly: "You've helped me grow, encouraging me to try new things, but holding your tongue or making light in a nice way of my lack of athleticism." She adds with an almost hopeful note: "In some ways, I think our lack of a specific 'thing-in-common' has helped us build a longer-lasting friendship. It insulates us from drifting apart when things change."

Ann's e-mails, often written either late at night or with her son, Charley, playing nearby, inevitably include periodic references to her child ("Even the thought of putting Charley in day care gives me stomachaches.") But Jamie stays distanced from this mother-angst.

Finally Ann ventures a question about what she shared with the women in FEMALE—Jamie's visit the year before that had left her frustrated and troubled. "I feel close to you, regardless of the fact that you are gazillions of miles away. I would love it if we could get together more frequently, but wonder what it would be like to actually spend time together. What did you think of our last visit?"

Jamie's answer is a mix of honesty, denial, and uncertainty. "I think your having Charley is the biggest change yet, and I think the weirdness was possibly reflected in my last visit," she writes—but adds quickly that at least "some of the awkwardness" was probably because she was trying to cram in too many things in a ten-day visit to the States that included touching base in three different places. "Once I have (fingers crossed) a child, we'll be back more on equal footing. I don't think having children should make all that much difference." She concludes by saying e-mail "has definitely helped our relationship" because when you don't speak frequently, "it's hard to know what to talk about, and small daily events are hardly worth making long-distance calls. . . . Maybe we'd chat real-time more if we were in the same town. Will we ever find out?"

This unleashes a flood from a relieved Ann: "It was good to hear you talk about your last visit. . . . It felt strained to me, and in my usual paranoid style, I formed hypotheses. I felt like you were annoyed, and wondered, did you not like Charley? Not approve of how I was as a mom? Not like me anymore? Was I too focused on Charley and not paying enough attention to you and me? I think you're right that things will "even up" (not your quote, I know) when you and Jason are also blessed. . . . I would love it if we were closer, so we could get to know each other now."

It was an open invitation to get to the heart of the matter. But Jamie tiptoes away. She writes about her next planned visit to the States—most of the time will be spent in Colorado with family. She writes about sexism and the weather in Croatia. "Not much 'friendly' conversation here," she concludes with a certain briskness. "What else do you want to talk about and what is the anticipated length of our discussion?"

Ann appears jolted by the abrupt change of tone. Her own reply changes tone as well. It becomes brightly impersonal as she expresses pleasure that her friend will at least "get a trip in"; she goes into detail about her concerns about day care for her son and tells Jamie about an interview she has scheduled for a part-time job. She cheerfully deplores the sexist anecdotes Jamie has shared. She signs off by saying she's off to watch the Academy Awards.

When we hear from Ann again it is to tell us that they have called off the e-mail conversation with us. The terrain was too touchy.

Sometimes in this situation, friends trying to "stay in touch" find themselves stumbling awkwardly to establish the mutual turf of their friendship.

One friend will struggle to keep her stay-at-home pal informed on what's going on back at the office—and out in the world—and hear a clong. The other will try to share all the cute things her toddler is saying, and hear the tinny sound of, well, boredom. These women may be at a loss in finding the new common ground.

In less important, less intimate relationships, it is easy to feign polite social interest in the unshared experience. "And how is the new baby?" may elicit a package of photographs from a proud parent's handbag, which can be skimmed through quickly with a few flattering comments. Nothing more is expected. But two friends who have known what mutuality really is can hear the false notes.

Ellen's stepdaughter, Jenny, is at a stage of life—late thirties—when nearly all of her friends have children. Sure, gaps can open up, she says. It's hard enough to make friends as couples—instead of two people who like each other, there have to be four—let alone as families. Married without children, she's had to convince friends: yes, you can bring the kids, yes, we truly enjoy them, it's okay if there are toys on the floor and no big deal if they watch *Teletubbies* in the living room.

But there's another side, she says. Jenny and her friend Victoria, both artists, have strengthened their ties in the years since Victoria started having her three children. In one sense, they work their talk time around the mother's schedule; Jenny knows the times when to call and the times when her friend will be up to her ears in kids. But in a life filled to the brim with family, Victoria actually looks at her friendship with Jenny as the place where she can be an artist, an individual, not just a mom. On a family reunion trip to Idaho, she sat down to write a long letter. "This was her 'private time,'" says Jenny, "what she did for herself."

The mere fact that two women are not both mothers isn't necessarily a deal breaker. Conversely, the fact that two women *are* both mothers doesn't mean they are on the same page either. Mothers often find themselves choosing up sides—opposing sides—in today's so-called mommy wars, that hostile, prickly conflict, overt and covert, between stay-at-home moms and working moms.

We've been hearing about that "war zone" for over a decade in one frontline report after another. It's not surprising that the military metaphor for this personal-is-political division has become so popular, for it captures the animosity felt by many women on both sides. Women who choose to stay at home may judge mothers who work for neglecting their kids: why have them if you don't want to be with them? Mothers who work may see mothers who stay at home vegetating: what do you do all day?

But there's plenty of unexpressed ambivalence on both sides. A committed stay-at-home mom may worry that the longer she's out of the workforce, the less financial and decision-making power she has over her own life. What is she doing for herself? A committed working mom may admit that she worries about child care or family life in a stress zone.

Women who used to carry briefcases to work each day and now find themselves fixing formula in their bathrobes at eleven in the morning may feel depressed and guilty. Back at the office, women still hurrying to work each morning with those briefcases, the occasional wails of a child following them out the door, will frequently feel just as depressed and guilty. One may envy the other's financial freedom to stay home. The other may envy the paycheck.

The only place that feels "safe" to air this ambivalence is among other women who have made the same decision. This is one of those times when women don't feel comforted by old friends if those old friends have taken a different turn in the road; they feel judged. The uncertainty is real and the fear of making a wrong choice is terrifying. In that climate, when a close friend makes a different decision it can be deeply polarizing.

Nevertheless, the two of us look at these life cycle changes, at the mommy wars and the "friendly enemies" dilemma, from the perspective of how much has changed in our own lives. When we were young mothers, one at home, the other in the office, the gap was huge. Since meeting each other, we have been through many phases ourselves—both single, then one married, then both; one with and one without grandchildren; changing careers.

From our vantage point we see a more complex terrain. Yesterday's single friend may be today's married friend. One woman is absorbed in children and just comes up for air when her best friend dives into motherhood. In the fluid economy, women change sides in the mommy wars, indeed change the combat zone itself, much more frequently than they expect.

We don't want to diminish the real divisions between women, when they head down paths so separate that they can't find their way back. Women friends expect a level of understanding, and those high expectations can be easily disappointed.

We also know from our own lives how deeply divorce can disrupt all the familiar patterns. In some ways, divorce—not marriage, not motherhood—can do the most collateral damage to old friends. The recurring cry of divorced—or widowed—women is that their old friends desert them, drop them off the party list, feel awkward around them. Pat remembers ruefully how depressed she was after her divorce when her name was "mysteriously" dropped one summer from the list for her own neighborhood block party.

One seventy-year-old woman, publicly and humiliatingly "dumped" twenty years ago by her high-powered political husband, still stews over what happened next. "People chose sides and a lot of them thought that it was more fun to be with my ex-husband. You find out a lot. I really learned who my friends were." Even now, after ten years of remarriage, it's the friends who stayed by her whom she trusts the most. She has joined the ranks of women who often say of their friends, "I never would have made it without her."

At the same time, women going back into the world of single people are often the first to pull away. It's a time of great insecurity, when they need someone to share new, strong, and confusing emotions. They also crave a guide—"What does a forty-year-old wear on a first date?"—or a helper. And sometimes old friends don't fill the bill. They don't understand.

———

"She was my oldest friend," says Kathy, fishing a camp photo out of the lower drawer so that we can see the two of them, twelve-year-olds in blue and white uniforms in front of Bunk 11. Kathy's apartment in Los Angeles looks like Single Mom-ville. Her six-year-old son, Peter, comes into the room looking for his *Star Wars* shirt. It's somewhere under the laundry, she says.

Kathy is the buyer for a women's clothing store. But in that camp picture, she's the chunky brown-haired kid holding two fingers over her friend Becky's head, like donkey ears. "We were joined at the hip," she says of their years as campers and then teenagers, when Becky was the adventurous one and she was the sidekick. It was Becky, willowy and redhaired, who got her period first, and Becky who had the first serious boyfriend, and Kathy who covered for her friend one night, sitting by the phone to pick it up before her mom did, praying that Kathy's parents wouldn't call to check up on whether Becky was *really* spending the night.

All that is a long time ago. "I can't believe how far apart we are now," she says, getting up off her knees and brushing Fritos off her skirt. "It seems so dumb."

It's only six years since she and Becky were thrilled to find themselves pregnant at the same time. They lived within jogging distance of each other in Santa Monica, two moms at home, a bit restless, a bit unhappy in their marriages. "I think in retrospect we spent most of the time we weren't running after the kids venting about how pissed off we were about our husbands," says Kathy, who is now forty years old. She asks us not to use her name, for the sake of her son, or maybe Becky, but talks about how they would match stories, comparing notes, assuring each other. "Socks on the floor, our husbands' ability not to hear the kids cry, all that stuff," Kathy repeats it wearily. "Look, I was *already* a single mom."

When Peter turned three and Kathy started a part-time sales job, she shocked Becky by confiding she was tucking away some private money. "I wanted some money of my own," she remembers. "She knew. She said, 'You mean it, don't you? You're going to leave him.'"

Kathy slowly puts the picture back into the drawer. "I think Becky was just terrified. Like divorce was contagious or something. I'd always thought that she was the brave one, so it took me awhile to get it."

Over the first few months after separation, a civil, if cool, marriage became a rancorous divorce. Within a year Kathy had to sell the house—"it was a money pit"—and leave the neighborhood.

"For a while we were pretty tight. The kids would still play together, although I was having trouble handling Peter. She was terrific when I would rail on about my ex; she never liked him." But gradually Becky stopped talking about her own marriage, as if scared by the shadow of divorce.

There is a domino effect to divorce. The old patterns break up. The problems are different. "I started to feel like the odd one out when I did go visit," says Kathy. "You know what it's like. You're sitting with three couples all talking in the first person plural—'we're planning this, we're planning that'—and the only 'we' in my life is a little kid."

At this point, Kathy breaks out the raspberry iced tea ("It's that or chocolate milk") and says directly, "The big thing was when I started to date. Really. I was thirty-five and a little screwed up. I was back in this whole weird thing—'Is he going to call? Should I sleep with him? How do you ask for an AIDS test?' I just couldn't talk about this stuff with my best friend."

Did Becky disapprove? "No—well, she wouldn't say so. But she was clueless and threatened, I think. She was the married lady. She didn't know. But think about it. She's still in a place where she's wondering why he doesn't pick up his socks. I'm saying, the hell with his socks. But I'm in a place where I'm wondering about whether I should call him. We just weren't talking the same language." Kathy was talking the "same language" with a woman she'd known only slightly, but they clicked, laughing over dates and ranting about child support.

The real dividing line came when Kathy started her first long-term relationship. "I mean, we're talking Mr. Wrong." She lowers her voice, remembering her son, Peter, is in the other room, "Mr. Sexy, but Mr. Wrong. He was a buyer too and it was a bad idea, but . . ."

One afternoon, Kathy and Becky found themselves at the same kids' birthday party at a local bowling alley. "There are these three- and four-year-olds dropping balls on the wooden floor and screaming. We go outside for a few minutes and we're just talking. Nothing big. But it was more relaxed than we'd been with each other in a while. And somehow we start talking about birth control pills and wouldn't it maybe be easier just to get your tubes tied. Becky said she was thinking about it, because, she said, kind of casually, 'I just feel weird swallowing a pill every day. What if you don't have sex that month?'"

Kathy takes a swig of her iced tea as if it were a good stiff drink and looks at us. "I was so surprised, it just came out of my mouth. 'That *month?*' I said. Here I am, having sex with Mr. Wrong everywhere but the elevator. I couldn't *believe* she was sleeping with her husband only once a month. Maybe. You should have seen the look on her face; I'm telling you, I could have kicked myself. She clammed up and turned red. That was it."

It wasn't the sex. It wasn't the one wrong sentence. But in that exchange, both of these women had to face how far apart their lives were.

Since then, they've run into each other from time to time. On birthdays, Kathy calls and Becky is friendly and cool. "To be honest, I just don't know a way back. I don't even know if I want to get back. We just don't have much in common anymore. Maybe, someday . . ."

———

The end of the story? Maybe. Or maybe it's just what Maureen Strafford once described as "a time of superficiality." She used that expression to describe a painful period of estrangement between her and Mary Gordon when she decided, in the face of her friend's disdain, to go into medicine and become a doctor. She had to find her own way, separate from her friend. That estrangement lasted for about five or six years. They would talk on the phone every now and then, but it was all quick and polite and not very connected.

One day, Maureen bought a copy of Mary's novel, *Final Payments,* and read it straight through. This was the authentic voice of her friend, the one she knew and loved, and she couldn't wait anymore. "I was overwhelmed with what she had done, it was incredible. She had written about our lives. I couldn't bear to let the separation go on any longer." She called Mary immediately, already crying, and told her the book was beautiful. Mary ignored the dinner party that was going on in her own apartment and also began crying. "It was pure emotion," Mary says. Their friendship rebounded, and they have never faced a "time of superficiality" again.

Speaking of happy endings . . . we heard via e-mail from Ann again, much later, with an update on her transatlantic friendship with Jamie.

"Ta-da! She's pregnant, and expecting in July. Not only was our old connection more visible, but we had current things in common—discussion about the physical and emotional aspects of being pregnant, anticipation of her needs for maternity and baby stuff she needed to pick up or order during this visit . . . as well as enjoying time with and without Charley. I feel like our friendship is back on track! I mentioned before my thought about our friendship being in a kind of cryogenic storage. Well, it felt thawed out."

So we know that women's lives go through a striking number of transitions, none of which may be permanent. It's no surprise that we leave friends scattered by the roadside. But life is long, and the transitions that seem so stark at one point in life may fade. If there is one thing we have seen it's the possibility and importance of allowing differences, keeping the elasticity in the bonds that we don't want to break.

Ellen

Has anyone ever listed weddings as a health hazard? The week before our marriage was a test case of dangers in the prenuptial zone. In November 1982, Bob and I had finally moved into our new home. The renovation from hell—or at least a contender for that hotly contested title—was more or less complete, if you didn't count the missing kitchen cabinets. But who needs kitchen cabinets?

Nervous? Not us. In the countdown to W-Day, I had one car accident on my way to work and Bob was handed two tickets—one for speeding and one for making a U-turn in an illegal place and in an emotional daze. Three days before the wedding—hello, Thomas Edison—I actually used a knife to wrench a plug out of one of our new wall sockets and watched the damn thing go up in sparks. Bob has kept the knife for posterity and for proof that he was one wooden handle away from being a prewed widower.

Finally, on the night before the wedding, my sister prevented further self-destruction. She invited my closest friends to what we did not call a bachelorette party. At the table were the women I had known before and would know after Emil Winkler, J.P., led us through our vows.

This was the trousseau of friends that I brought with me to this second marriage. It was a sample of women composing and recomposing their lives and relationships—but not our friendships.

My sister, Jane, my first best friend, the only one in the room who had been there at my first wedding and every other moment of my life, was at the head of the table: newly divorced.

On my right was Ann. We had met in my early *Globe* days when I was married and she was single. Ann was the one on the other end of the phone when my first marriage was collapsing, and I was there—literally—the day she and Mike fell in love. And the day they were married.

Next to her was Lynn. We had become friends in the early '70s when she offered her apartment as my New York hotel and we had laughingly discovered that our wardrobes were interchangeable. These were the years before Larry came into her life. In a few years—too few years—her wry and handsome and loving husband would leave her widowed.

As for Otile, she had taught me how to sing "Stop, in the Name of Love!" and drink Irish coffee (well, half-strength for me). At her wedding seven years earlier, in between toasts and dancing, I had been overwhelmed by premonitions of loss. But every addition to her life—her husband, Bob, her daughters, Julia and Maggie—added to mine.

And, of course, Helen. We had met in what we liked to call a previous life—first marriage—but became friends over pizza and kids and proximity and single motherhood. Our friendship outlasted the kids' and the Wednesday night pizza fests and even single motherhood. In another year, she and Steve would marry.

Beside me was Pat. Where was she at this moment? In a relationship that bridged the time span from Mr. Wrong, David, to Mr. Right, Frank. On the eve of my wedding, my best friend was single.

There wasn't a woman in this room, friend or sister, who hadn't been through some transition from single to married to divorced or back again. Among us, two had been stay-at-home moms, three working moms, one who had stepchildren. We had been friends through all of these transitions. Now it was my turn again.

I don't know the anthropological meaning of these prenuptial gatherings, or even if they have one. Did men gather together for one last bash before incarceration? Did women gather together to deliver you into marriage?

In the secular-Jewish tradition to which Bob and I haphazardly subscribed, you stomp on a wineglass to symbolize the breaking of an old life—but we were already part of each other's old lives. We came to this wedding fully accessorized for adulthood. I brought with me a sister, daughter, mother, aunt, uncle, nieces, cousins. He brought a daughter, son, aunt, brothers. We also brought friends. Neither of us was looking for a complete break with the past.

Our wedding was a delicious mixture of food and champagne and the heady pleasure of finding our safe harbor with each other. Added to the mix were the endless, humorous toasts about us that Bob encouraged— "More toasts, please"—until the room closed.

But I also remember that mixed in with the nuptial anxiety and its truly "electric" shock, was some nagging worry about change. Especially in my long-distance friendship with my single friend.

Was it something Pat said? Something Bob said? No.

I think it was inside me. Had I looked around and counted the number of changes in that one friendship pod, I might not have been anxious. But Pat tells me that I have an overdeveloped sense of responsibility, as if life were a dinner party and I were the hostess. In truth, I see life less as a dinner party than a jigsaw puzzle. I want all the pieces to fit. I don't want the seams to show—yet they do.

Of course Pat came with me, like the four-poster bed and the dining room table and the fourteen-year-old daughter. I knew that, and so did Bob. But more than Pat, I had moments of worrying how our old friendship would fit under the marital roof. Would it work? What do they have in common except me? Did it matter?

It seems to me now that in lives full of transitions we do learn something. Not just that life takes inevitable and numerous turns. But anyone who has been there—single or married—and done that—made and lost relationships—knows that it can happen again. We resist the centrifugal forces.

Weeks after our wedding, weeks after the night when we tried and failed to convince all our friends to come with us to the bridal suite for a postparty party, Bob and I got back the photos. There in the middle were three rather silly but delightful pictures of Pat and me. Everything about those photos shows her sharing my pleasure and my sharing it with her. I framed them as a triptych and sent them to Pat. It was a simple "wedding gift."

Pat

It was Bob who opened the door first. "Welcome," he said, meaning it. I stepped inside the 150-year-old newly renovated house, feeling just a slight twinge of strangeness. It was, after all, my first visit to the Ellen and Bob home.

I looked around. The hot red walls of the hall in Ellen's old house had been replaced with walls of cool cream, strong evidence of the merger of tastes going on here. I'm more partial to cool cream than to hot red, but I felt another slight twinge—of what? Nostalgia, I think.

But before I could mull that one over, Bob was pulling me into the kitchen to show me the bright yellow faucets and cabinet pulls that were his pride and joy. Then he was pulling me upstairs to see "my" renovated bathroom. Next on the tour was "my" room, a brightly lit space with cheery yellow wallpaper, which Ellen knew was one of my favorite colors. A lamp that worked. A table for magazines. A chest for clothes. I could unpack in this bedroom, instead of rummaging in my suitcase for fresh clothes every morning. I was feeling very comfortable, and definitely less nostalgic for the old place.

Then it was back downstairs, where a bottle of wine was opened and the three of us raised our glasses in a toast to the new Ellen and Bob home. The new Ellen and Bob life. It was so easy and real to wish them the best. And I did like the temporary ownership of bed and bath that Bob had so immediately bequeathed to me.

Yes, things would be different. I would no longer be in the upstairs hall wrapped in a towel yelling down to Ellen that we were out of soap. I wouldn't be using her hair dryer in her bathroom at seven in the morning either (although I noted there was a new hairdryer ensconced in "my" bathroom). And we would no longer be sending out for a small pizza for two—now it would be one large, please, and hold the broccoli. Bob doesn't like broccoli on pizza.

It would take some getting used to, this new male presence that had prevailed when it came to those cream-colored walls. And to hear the unfamiliar sound of a televised football game snaking around the corner (in our separate single-life homes, Ellen and I didn't do televised sports). There was a new zone of privacy, a new dividing line.

We were definitely on an altered course, and nothing here would be quite the same again. When Ellen visited my little post-David, empty-nest townhouse in Washington, we could indulge our own idiosyncratic way of dividing up the sections of *The New York Times* (and God help her if she walked away with my morning *Post*); we could eat what and when we wanted, and stack the dishes in the sink .

But even as I thought about these differences, I also knew that Ellen's upcoming marriage to Bob caused me no problems and no feelings of loss. I had been part of the progression of that relationship for a long time, and I was delighted. She had found what we had both wished for each other since the beginning days of our friendship: love, loyalty, and joy.

And Bob liked our friendship. You can't make it up; you can't fake that. Over the years, he has seen us off to travel together to Martha's Vineyard or Maine, displaying real pleasure at our pleasure. And when I moved in with the two of them to write this book—but that's a story for another chapter.

So I felt for my friend when I heard the anxiety in her voice on the phone a few weeks before her wedding. What are you worried about? I asked her. He's a great guy and he loves you and you love him, and you and I will be fine. He likes me and I like him. Yes, it's a crossroads, but it will be okay.

"Just the same . . ." she murmured.

I couldn't argue that we hadn't reached a major divide. I was single, in a stalemated relationship, and a long time away from finding the combination of love and trust that I wanted for myself. But I had my children, my friends, and my work. Life wasn't lonely and it wasn't emotionally impoverished. Actually, it was pretty darn good.

I was touched that she worried about what was coming next. She is a person who lets few people in close, and when she does, she nurtures those relationships and doesn't want them to change. She checks the gear, fine-tunes the engine, and finally takes off the brake.

So then came that delightful prewedding party of friends, a night that Ann and I, on our own forest walks in Maryland, still talk about with pleasure. And then the wedding, that great splashy party, and there was this happy woman dancing half the night away in her wine-colored velvet wedding dress. Hey, I knew her. And I was up there babbling through what was probably one of the longest toasts in the world about what a great thing was happening, and meaning it, every word.

I thought about that the other night as I stood in the library of my home, staring at a wall of photographs my husband and I put up when we moved in, a wall filled with pictures of our kids and grandkids and other family members. I consider it the linchpin of our home, this wall. We put it together so our grown children could stand here and ask questions and learn about each other and each other's family without feeling crowded or

The triptych from Ellen's wedding.

strange. We wanted to give them an easy way to feel part of what now, with the acquisition of a new stepparent, was to be a shared history.

And on the wall, dead center, is that framed trio of photographs Ellen sent me after her wedding all those years ago. It brought back memories of how I felt the day I pulled the triptych out of its brown wrapping paper and realized what it was. On one of the happiest days of her life, Ellen gave a gift of a memory to me—of us. On the first day of Ellen and Bob, she included Pat.

So when I pulled out a hammer and nail and hung the triptych for the first time that long-ago day, I was feeling a very nice glow. It hangs on the family wall now because that is where it belongs, part of the sustaining and permanent history of this woman's life with her friend.

8

The Bad Stuff

Ellen

Now we brake for the bad stuff. Shit happens, even to the best of friends. I don't mean just the times that Pat and I tiptoed around the edges of competition, or the times that life threatened to take us down different side roads. I mean the bad stuff, the moments of disconnection, when something that happens between us comes, well, between us.

Pat and I are not seamless friends without the rough edges of difference, without strong personalities or opinions. We don't just go along to get along. We disagree, we misunderstand, we get hurt, and we get over it. And we've had to admit it and learn how.

By and large, the friends that we talked with said "we never fight." They swore to it. "No, I don't think we ever fought." In fact, only the women who had known each other as children were willing to acknowledge fighting—but, of course, they put such stuff behind them, like playing with Barbies, like something they outgrew.

Well, Pat and I do not fight either. No fisticuffs. No screaming across the room. But we have had to tell each other, "I'm sorry," and not in the pro forma way that women apologize for everything including the weather. We've had to say it because we hurt each other. And we'd rather say "I'm sorry" than "good-bye."

There was the time Pat doesn't want to write about, so I will. The time when we were having dinner together and on the way back from the ladies' room I passed a star-studded table of acquaintances. I stopped to say hello. The greeting turned into a chat, which turned into a talk. I left Pat sitting alone at the table, wondering who this person was who had just dumped her for the in-crowd in the junior high lunchroom.

In my mind, I thought it was five minutes. In my mind, I thought, why didn't she come join us? In my mind, I was thoughtless. Wildly thoughtless. By her more accurate watch it was thirty minutes. At that point she was contemplating exactly when she would walk out of the restaurant.

There were other moments that neither of us wants to write about—and we won't—because part of trust is not telling tales and part of friendship is forgiveness. Pat and I never betrayed each other. Betrayal can be, after all, the terminal disease of any friendship. But let it be said that at times I wondered whether to tell Pat what I thought she needed to hear. Would telling her kill the good feelings about the messenger? I found a way to tell her anyway.

As I write this, I can hear another little voice saying, "Well, you have trouble with anger." You bet I do. Feeling angry is lousy. Having someone close get mad at you just plain stinks. In my family, anger was regarded as a pretty lethal weapon—don't use it. Marriages crumble under the force of anger, and friendship is even more fragile. Friends don't have to sit across the table from each other at breakfast. There's no guarantee that they will even bother to make up.

My best friend from childhood was, not accidentally, my cousin Judy. We couldn't exactly run out on each other. But all around me were images of girls trusting and betraying each other, breaking up and not necessarily making up. Friendship was never as sturdy as family. The walls of trust were circled around our household.

In my friendships I often exhibited what I suppose you would call pre-emptive understanding. I would "understand" why a friend had been neglectful or thoughtless without, of course, ever actually confronting her. I would figure it out, forgive, protect myself from feeling hurt, and never say a word.

But what if Pat had left that restaurant without a word? What if she hadn't told me how angry she was, and simply, silently, chalked it up against me? What if I hadn't taken it to heart? And what if, at other times, when I was upset, Pat hadn't called with full apologies?

No, you don't have to fight with a friend. You can tamp it down. You can get up and leave. You can pretend to forget about it. How easily you can let all that bad stuff harden around your heart.

Pat

We've sat together thinking about this, turning the pages of our lives back as slowly as we could, looking for the jolts, the disappointments we experienced with each other that qualify as "bad." We haven't found much, which makes it harder to write about the few we did find.

That night when Ellen did not come back to the table and instead joined a group of people I didn't know was not a good moment in our friendship. When the waiter brought me a dessert, ordered for me by "the lady across the room," I couldn't believe it. I was sitting alone in a public place, while my friend was having coffee at another table. Ellen, with whom I felt very safe, had dropped me off her screen. In the framework of a secure friendship, it raised a totally unfamiliar question: How important was I to her?

My first impulse was to call the waiter back, tell him to deliver her the check at the other table, and then walk out. It was a very tempting option.

But underneath the desire to react this way was something steadier. Did I act only on what had just happened, or on the deep reality of the whole friendship? Did I really believe I was suddenly rejected or was I experiencing the nasty surprise of realizing even your best friend can do something dumb?

Instead of walking out, I told the waiter to deliver my dessert to the other table and bring an extra chair. I then went over, introduced myself, was welcomed, and sat down.

Later, when Ellen and I were driving home, it was time to talk. I couldn't store this away or bottle it up, because if I avoided confronting her, she and I might lose something fundamental: our trust in each other to deliver the truth.

It was a strange experience to confront my friend. We had never before needed language to express anger with each other or to search for reconciliation. But we used it that evening. And because we did, we were able to get by a nasty jolt.

My way of dealing with anger is somewhat different from Ellen's. Neither of us goes for the slam-the-door, slam-the-phone-down style. With women friends, I wait a beat or two, and then I carefully try to say what I have to say. But sometimes I brood, particularly when I'm standing in the shower in the morning, a self-indulgence that often only makes a problem bigger.

Anger with a friend is a surprise. Women act as if in a good friendship, there shouldn't be anything to be angry about, that the absence of anger is what makes friendship safe—safer than marriages or family relationships, where there is no easy way to walk out or let relationships simply drift away.

But if you can't get mad at a friend, how do you know whether or not you have a relationship strong enough to get by the anger? If I hadn't confronted Ellen that night—and I hated doing it, it scared me—there would have been a barrier between us.

The fear of confrontation starts in childhood, and I know as a child I was very anxious about being liked and included. To be liked required being "like" the other girls, so differences were abhorred. Everybody had to conform to a homogeneous pattern and heaven help the girl who didn't. Those childhood fears follow women into adulthood, where some limit their expectations of friendship out of the fear of testing it, convinced that confrontation will ruin what they have. So they settle for the safe world of social pleasantry rather than taking a chance.

And yet when two friends allow themselves to express their feelings honestly, even when those feelings include anger, that is itself an act of trust. We certainly feel periodic flashes of anger with each other, especially during this joined-at-the-hip process of writing a book. But we deal with them directly and as quickly as we can, often in the car, bumping over potholes, listening sometimes to criticism we don't want to hear. It's not a big plate of bad stuff. Mostly, they're little things. But they are the kinds of things that can over time corrode a friendship—unless it is strong enough to roll over the psychic potholes.

Everyone has lost friends. Everyone has felt distanced at times, angry, hurt, or betrayed by a friend. But the reality is hard to face. "One of the tricks of the culture is to put forth the illusion that relationships can be always harmonious, kind, loving, good, sweet, tender, gratifying and a great comfort—and then put women in charge of making sure all this happens," Judith Jordan said. "Which is really a way of making women move away from their own anger, their ability to be in conflict and to feel ashamed if they *are* angry."

As we started this chapter, we put a quote on the wall that came from a lecture given by psychologist Janet Surrey. "We want it real, not nice," she said of women in relationships. "Yet it's so hard to stay in the real. And so hard to hear the real. The tension between being nice and being real is profound."

Women want friendship to be "nice" too. In friendships, women tell themselves, relationships can run smoothly. No conflict need apply. But real relationships come with inevitable scrapes, nicks, and middle-sized wounds. They come with disconnection. They come with conflict and hurt and, even, betrayal.

"Real" includes everything from a birthday that's forgotten, a criticism that cuts to the quick, a secret accidentally blown, a piece of gossip believed, a promise unfulfilled, a breach of loyalty. "It's a mistake to believe that intimate friendships will always run smoothly . . ." said psychologist Joel Block. "Long-term friendships have their difficult periods; what makes them endure is not the absence of conflict, but the skill of each friend in handling anger and resolving conflicts constructively."

"All my life I have counted on the compassionate nature of my own sex," playwright Wendy Wasserstein writes. ". . . My most significant others have always been a circle of intimate women friends. What I have constantly been afraid to acknowledge, however, is the difficulty of sustaining these friendships. Perhaps I never speak about soured female relationships because men are always so ready to portray women as competitive, jealous felines."

Working on this project, we heard echoes of two stereotypes of women's relationships. The old view described women as constantly at odds, combatants in that endless Jerry Springer show—backbiting, gossiping, catfighting, untrustworthy. The other view of women was endlessly empathic, supportive, kind, nurturing, understanding, caring. According to these stereotypes, friendship between women is either seamless, without a hint of conflict, or it's impossible.

Clare Booth Luce's classically acerbic play of the 1930s, *The Women,* underscored the former. In the movie version, we see a shot of two pampered little dogs on the ends of leashes fighting each other; two bitches, yipping and yapping. It does effectively set the tone. Later, a mother, speaking presumably from age and wisdom, warns her daughter, "Oh, one more piece of motherly advice—don't confide in your girlfriends. They'll see to it in the name of friendship that you wreck your marriage and lose your home. I'm an old woman and I know my sex."

The other image, the newer, airbrushed, everything's-wonderful image is summed up in the Hallmark phrase, "She's always there for me." But good friends, best friends, are not *always* "there" for women; sometimes they don't like each other's behavior or they let each other down: that doesn't mean they are "bad" friends. It means bad stuff happens.

When writer Nina Burleigh shocked her friends by falling in love with another man while on her honeymoon, they made their disapproval clear. "I'm the one who didn't talk to her for a month," one friend was quoted in *The New York Times* as saying. "She took her husband to Paris on a honeymoon and a month later she was on a date! You're not supposed to do that."

There are not just two sides of the friendship coin—all good or all bad. Most of us have had experiences all across the spectrum. Ann Neel and Pam Smith are two women from Missouri with a passion for family genealogy who shared friendship and research for three years—before they learned that Neel's family had owned Smith's great-great-grandfather, who had been a slave. It was enough of a jolt that, at first, Smith could barely speak to Neel. But when she could, they found that facing the fact of how they were linked by slavery brought them closer as friends. Asked to give an account of their experience at the University of Idaho, they have been giving presentations ever since.

Sometimes when a friendship is irretrievably broken, women find it hard to get over feeling burned. They carry the "bad stuff" they can't forget into new adult relationships; they become wary, unwilling to get "real," and unable to retrieve friendships when they falter.

The trust we have talked about as the basic building block of friendship doesn't emerge full-blown. Women begin to reveal themselves to each other, sharing confidences and feelings and, in the process, opening up. To become known is a delight, but that also means women must allow themselves to become vulnerable—and *that* means they must trust their friends to treat this vulnerability with respect.

We have watched little girls, including our own, fight, make up, fight again, make up again. They often idealize friendship, sure that they will stay close, and they are able to get through angry moments, to holler and yell at each other, and then reconnect. As they grow a little older, some girls have thought through what they value and how to keep it going in a remarkably sophisticated way.

There was a wonderful exchange between best friends Sasha and Hannah, two fifth graders, that Janet Surrey shared with us. What had they learned from their friendship? these girls were asked.

Hannah answered, "You can't just take out your anger, it has to be thought out. You have to be able to hear you have a flaw."

Then Sasha chimed in, "Learning how to fight means learning how to listen and be open to what the other person thinks. You have to be able to forgive."

Hannah and Sasha had a serious, near-friendship-ending fight in the fourth grade. But a year later, with the wisdom of age, Sasha said, "In the end it helped our friendship."

How?

Hannah responded, "We learned you can tell a friend how you feel. We were afraid to say what made us mad. You should be able to tell a friend anything."

Sasha added, "It's not easy. I was wicked nervous. We were afraid it would hurt our friendship but then it kept us apart anyways, so we had to try."

That little piece of dialogue, printed up on a card and tucked up on the bathroom mirror, might be useful to many women. The adult fear that conflict will end a friendship makes many hold back. And in turn, the holding back ends the friendship anyway.

"I couldn't stand the way she refused to discipline her son," said one woman simply. "She was warm and generous, but she never disciplined him and it bugged me. She'd bring him over and he'd wreak havoc, he'd turn my house upside down and get my son into a frenzy. I never saw a way to talk to her about it, so it seemed easier to pull back, because I hated being mad at her. When she'd call to see what I was doing, I told her I was 'swallowed in e-mail,' or 'just heading out the door,' or 'going out of my head with work.' I didn't mean to let it end. But it just dribbled away, and I'm sorry now. I didn't trust myself or her to get to the heart of it."

From the earliest years, as girls learn about trust, they also learn about betrayal. Harvard psychologist Carol Gilligan tells the story of the day she and Lynn Brown, looking through their interviews, were suddenly startled by what they saw. "We started to do what was kind of in the air at that time, that girls were empathic and girls were relational. I remember sitting with Lynn, looking at our interviews, and saying, 'Wait a minute . . .' Girls were telling us about talking behind each other's backs and getting angry," she said. "Plus, there were statements like these: 'She's my best friend. I hate her.' Their relationships felt like the weather—they kept changing."

These are the years when girls begin to practice the familiar and cruel art of inclusion/exclusion. These are the years when cliques are born.

Girls begin to cluster in groups, discovering power in whom they accept—and reject. They can experience both the heartbreak of being excluded and the heady, hurtful power of excluding. And for those excluded, the experience is unforgettable and horrible. Many children write to best-selling children's author Judy Blume, someone they see as understanding their lives, and much of what they pour out in their letters is about the pain of exclusion. Here is one grade-schooler's anguished confession after a girl in her school had led the pack to force her out: "I discovered that all of my old friends were crossing my name off their notebooks. I was horrified. My whole body felt like Jell-O! What had I done to them?"

Or this ten-year-old who summed up so perfectly the power of the clique: "I just lost my best friend," she wrote. "Her name is Carolyn. We used to share secrets, play together and we even had a club! But then Jennifer came along. Jennifer has a clique with some other girls. Me and Carolyn made a vow never to be in that clique because Jennifer, the leader of the pack, tells you what to wear, what to eat, who to like and what labels to buy. But Carolyn went with her anyway and now Carolyn doesn't like me anymore."

For children, betrayal and trust are two sides of a constantly spinning coin. They come with the territory of growing up, so much so that children's literature and films are filled with stories about a friend who humiliates you or makes fun or simply walks away when you need that person most.

It is no accident that the vastly popular children's movie *Harriet the Spy*, based on the book of the same name, mesmerizes girls as young as five years old. Harriet, a would-be writer, keeps a notebook that contains her innermost thoughts, even those about her friends. When her nemesis, the smug and artful Marian, steals the notebook and reads it out loud, Harriet's friends are shocked at her scribblings. They feel betrayed. ("Jamie really freaks me out," reads one entry. "I wonder if she'll grow up to be a total nut case.") They angrily band together with Marian, shutting Harriet out, making her miserable. Harriet retaliates. She gets even. The war and the misery escalate until her much-loved nanny comes through with wise advice: "Good friends are one of life's blessings. Don't give them up without a fight."

What draws children to this tale is its honesty about their complicated struggles with issues of trust and loyalty. They see Harriet reaching out, lashing out, making compromises, and finding a way to grow with those friendships. They see it as real.

But along the way, girls often lose their resilience, or for that matter, the willingness to stay together in and through conflict. Wounds accumulate and memories stay locked in place. Ellen remembers watching as the small circle of girls in her daughter's fourth-grade class routinely cast each other out according to some mysterious and hurtful timetable. To this day, Katie, now thirty and watching this saga replayed as a camp director and drama teacher in Montana, can still remember the first time she found herself "out."

"My visual memory is that I was sitting in one of these circular lofts that looked out over the library. I was reading. I can still picture it. My three friends came over and began imitating me. I didn't understand why they were teasing me. I had a feeling that it was my fault. I had done something wrong. This wasn't an impulsive moment. They had definitely conspired and planned. I remember it feeling mean, not funny."

The ins and outs went on all year. Why did she stick with them? Katie responds with a laugh. "In a small community, who will you hang out with? The losers?"

What she sees now in working with kids this age and older is that this "teasing" leaves many of them with a fear of being ostracized. "I think the feeling carries over into working in groups with adults." It carries over as well in the sense of urgency that many girls feel about getting and staying in a group.

Margaret Atwood's *Cat's Eye,* a story of a tortuous power struggle between childhood friends that has nearly lethal results, is a classic, almost gothic, interpretation of this need. Cordelia, the leader of a small clique, launches a vicious ritual of exclusion against the hapless Elaine, finally abandoning her one icy day in a ravine from which she barely escapes alive. The situations are dramatically reversed by the time the girls reach high school. Elaine flourishes; Cordelia becomes fragile, mentally unraveled. And Elaine's triumph, unmarked by compassion, is described this way: "The person I use my mean mouth on the most is Cordelia. She doesn't even have to provoke me. I use her as target practice."

It is a tale of breathtaking cruelty. "Little girls are cute and small only to adults. To one another, they are not cute. They are life-sized," Atwood observes.

By ages eleven or twelve, the emotional rough and tumble, the struggle to be yourself while still being a friend, starts to change. These are the years when girls begin to go underground, and it is no longer safe to admit anger or jealousy. The imperative to appear "nice," to be "good," settles in. Yet this is also the age when cliques become impenetrable institutions, and it's the age when girls begin to talk of betrayal.

To understand the importance of loyalty, and all the longing for trust, and the fear of betrayal that women bring with them into any friendship, all you have to do is go back into the scrapbook of adolescence. The memories lie there, as fresh as ever, in page after page filled with images of groups of girls, those girlfriends who ruled the female roost of school, deciding who was in and who was out.

Cliques are the adolescent tribes of girls. From middle school on through high school, they are known by their own uniforms, their own codes, their own chiefs. Some of them hold in their hands the power of judge and jury to decide the social fate of their classmates. And many of us who stood before one of these tribunals have never forgotten the experience. The memory of exclusion, of disconnection, being set adrift, wafts over our adulthood like a poisonous cloud. Cliques are powerful because they tell women who is acceptable and who isn't, whether they will be welcomed into the group or cast into some societal Siberia.

When Pat thinks of her high school, St. Mary's Academy, she can still recall the mysterious transfer each year of the prime lunch spot, a cupola shaded from the noonday sun in a grove of trees called Senior Glen, to the next senior class in-group. That transfer was tacitly agreed upon by everyone. The in-group was never challenged. But no one ever knew precisely who wrote the residential permit on that piece of lunchroom property. You transgressed at your peril, at the risk of what was perhaps the worst putdown: the exercise of chilly politeness. If you were invited into the group, your status soared with all the girls clustered around the Senior Glen cupola. If you were new to the school and were rejected, the lesser groups that aspired to the cupola themselves didn't want you, either.

Even if you were an insider, you didn't rest easy, especially if you felt restive in that one group alone. It was important to be very careful when you made friends outside the clique, and not to spend "too" much time with other people—especially if they were linked with slightly "odd" interests, like band or the math club. You risked your ticket to the cupola if you did.

These traits are what Gilligan had in mind when she suggested to us that cliques represent the "herding instinct" of adolescent girls who are keeping each other in line. "They reminded me of sheepdogs," she said. "Any girl who started to stand out, you know, was kind of herded back into the group. And that function was to limit other girls, limit the reach, limit the accomplishment, limit the risk taking and so forth, and label the ones who are out there 'too this.' In that sense there can be a dynamic that's pernicious."

To those inside the cliques, they are a security zone, a tight, in-crowd group of friends. But cliques virtually force the members to act alike, paying a price of individuality in return for belonging. The not-so-subtle message in these friendship circles is that the girls who simply want to be different cannot belong.

We found a tour guide through the labyrinth of high school cliques and their obsessions—boys, looks, status, and clothes—in an almond-eyed, sassy, hip, sixteen-year-old named Sherie.

A self-designated "outsider" at South Portland High School in Maine, Sherie is the live-wire "tough cookie" of a group of teenagers who gathered one morning around a table and a tape recorder. While proudly asserting her independence, she raced through an assessment of the cliques at South Portland that would have done an anthropologist proud. She had them all tagged: the cool kids, the preppie kids, the hippies, the skaters, the Park Rats, the Hoochee Mamas—all nailed down to the last pair of Doc Martens and Gap T-shirts.

"When I was a freshman, everybody stood around in little groups," Sherie said. "You had to know people just to stand, like, in the breezeway. If you didn't, people would look at you and say, 'Who is this kid?'"

She described a high school saga of moving from one clique to another, trying them on like costumes. "The first clique, they were all smiling, happy, at the cool lunch table. I was the stray, not knowing where my place was. I went over to sit down and they said, 'Oh yeah, She—ree, we don't have any more seats for you.' I was like, okay, that's cool. But I learned. Cliques stick to their own. You're either in or out."

The preppie girls? "They have to have the right money, the right clothes, the right talk to be in. They like to gossip. They wear the cute little stuff, jeans not too baggy, not too tight, a Gap shirt, sweater. The more clothes you have the more you show them off. It gives you a higher rank in the clique."

The Hippies or Park Rats who hang in the park? "They're like intimidating. Grungy looking, hair in braids, tough."

The Hoochee Mamas? How would she describe them?

A sudden spark of delight flashed in Sherie's eyes. Her body in its tight navy shirt began to undulate and her voice went up half an octave as she gave her Hoochee Mama Rap: "Tight clothing, lots of hair, gotta have the nails, gotta have the walk, gotta have the strut." She raised her arms over her head in mock horror. Suddenly she WAS a Hoochee Mama checking out another girl: 'Oh my *God*,' she screeched, 'like, we should take her shopping, she doesn't even know, oh my *God*, whatever, I know, what's up, okay? You best check yourself!'"

You could have set it to music. Sherie knew how to speak the language of *that* secret society.

She also had a dead-on assessment of the heart of a clique. "It isn't all sweetness and calm. They make each other mad, pick each other off inside, too. They go out with each other's boyfriends. Make fun of someone else . . . Nobody has their own personality. It's kind of like just what looks good." When asked why these groups are so defined by clothes, she figures, "See, you have to represent where you come from. Clothes express what kind of background you're coming from. It's attitudes."

While that may seem weird when one group is identified by tongue rings and another by cargo pants, how different is it really from the way adult women friends type each other? Women know instantly that Anne Klein II goes with Ellen Tracy, that a Land's End type also shops L.L. Bean. They can judge a woman by how she dresses. What she likes, what she values, whether she's in style or hopeless. They can make snap judgments straight from high school about whether she's worth knowing—or not.

Sherie proudly insisted she had outgrown the world of cliques. "I've wandered in and out of different circles for a long time. You gain information, you learn things. They made me who I am. Now, all of a sudden, I don't need a clique anymore. I know who I am." This person who now declares that she knows who she is, who is now clique free, isn't alone in the world, though. "I have a tight circle of friends who are real and open-minded and not freaked out by who I am."

Not a clique? Laurie Wood, an astute teacher, prodded Sherie and her friends to acknowledge that the other students might see them as a clique too. They disagreed; they are friends only, not a clique. They protect each other, give each other a place. They are the insiders. The preppies and the Hoochie Mamas are the outsiders.

Not a clique?

"Cliques are an invasive and permanent part of the school structure," says a resigned Laurie Wood afterward. "They are necessary, more so all the time, because so many of these kids have no sense of belonging. Cliques, like gangs, provide a certain security. . . . Basically they keep out anyone who threatens the values which that clique holds dear. If someone does not toe that party line, they will be excluded." She also talked about the poignancy of kids who come to the world of high school, still liking and hanging out with friends they've known from as far back as the third or fourth or fifth grade. "They must now figure out which crowd they will be allowed to hang out with," she said.

Like it or not, cliques are the female equivalent of bullies. In the hierarchy of the world of boys, it's bullies who keep the order of who's "up" and who's "down." In the hierarchy of the world of girls, it's the cliques who keep the order of who's "in" and who's "out." Both are the autocrats of adolescence, and no one has anything good to say about them. "People say that bullying is part of normal childhood development," says Gilligan. "Boys have to learn to make it in a world where there are bullies. And girls have to learn to make it in a world of inclusion and exclusion. I'm not sure what 'normal childhood development' is, but I don't think this is it."

Women never quite grow out of the clique mentality. In college, they jockey for acceptance at the right sorority or the right table in the right dormitory. As adults, there is an in-crowd in many a club and town. And a class structure as well. As a contrite Holly Hunter told Queen Latifah in the movie, *Living Out Loud,* "I dumped all my old friends because their husbands didn't make as much money as mine."

Even an office may have an unofficial social admission committee of one or two or three, drawing up the A-list, deciding whom to include or exclude. All of these are "bad stuff" opportunities, times and places for slights and omissions, for the small betrayals that women experience. Cliques that offer security to those who conform, and cause insecurity in those who don't, are powerful influences, informing women that conflict means exclusion, that to be "yourself," to differ, to disagree, may mean isolation. These are reminders to keep it "nice," and it doesn't matter that "nice" may not be "real."

Keeping it "nice"? What about gossip?

Sometimes gossip gets a bad rap. "Telling what's happening in your life and the lives of those you talk to is a grown-up version of telling secrets, the essence of girls' and women's friendships," says Deborah Tannen. It is, after all, a way of exchanging the daily news bulletins of life, and men frequently enjoy it as much as women—even as they criticize women for enjoying it too much.

In her book *Secrets,* ethicist Sissela Bok points out that everyone is interested in personal information about other people. "If we knew about people only what they wished to reveal, we would be subjected to ceaseless manipulation; and we would be deprived of the pleasure and suspense that comes from trying to understand them."

Gossip can indeed be lighthearted, the work of true friends, a relief from the serious business of life. But there is a major difference between gossip and revealing a friend's secrets. When a woman offers a piece of information confided by a friend and puts it on the public table, that is a violation of friendship. And the route from gossip to betrayal can get slippery, even treacherous, in our "who's in, who's out" society. The hunger for acceptance, the desire to appear "in the know," all grease the slide.

Pat was once at a gathering where a stranger suddenly tossed in a bit of tasty gossip about Ellen and Bob's romance, without knowing of her friendship with Ellen. The gossip was dead wrong, and Pat said so, which put a pall on the conversation. It also underscored for her how the temptation to pass on tidbits can look very different if you know, and care for, the person being talked about.

"Those whose casual talk stops at no boundaries, leaves no secrets untouched, may therefore shut themselves off from the understanding they seem to seek," writes Bok. "Gossip can be the means whereby they distance themselves from all those about whom they speak with such seeming familiarity, and they may achieve but spurious intimacy with those *with whom* they speak."

The message is clear: inside information doesn't automatically get you on the A list.

So these are some of the venues of the "bad stuff." Secrets revealed, a child's name scratched off a friend's notebook. Friends who hurt and betray. Among smaller children this may be of the Harriet-the-Spy variety, but in the world of adolescent girls, the word *betrayal* is used more frequently and fervently.

This is, as we've discussed, the time when girls shift their sights toward boys—the age where betrayal means "stealing" a boyfriend. Want a nightmare image of betrayal? In the movie *Hope Floats,* Sandra Bullock is conned into appearing on a television show for a "makeover," and instead is confronted by her husband and her best friend announcing to the nation that they are having an affair. More than a few women must have squirmed as they watched the camera catch her utter humiliation.

It would be nice if it only happened in the movies. But much as women want to feel safe with friends, there are the *true* stories hovering around the edges, warning of danger. Like Letty's story.

It was a rare afternoon off for Letty. A single mother and Web page designer, she had driven up from San Jose to San Francisco on business and was standing in Union Square in front of Macy's, staring at the shoes in the window. She glanced up and suddenly saw the reflection of a woman standing next to her. For one long moment, as Letty told us the tale, the two of them stared at each other.

Letty registered everything. The streaked hair, the same gold love-knot earrings, the good navy suit. In the first shock of recognition, Letty even remembered her shoe size. 7½AA. At that point she wheeled around, turned her back, and walked away as fast as possible from the best friend who had slept with her husband.

"There was nothing else I could do," she says now, running her hand through short, gray-flecked brown hair. "Part of me wanted to reach out to her and part of me was paralyzed. I was scared. I don't know why. What else could she do to me?"

Letty is not her real name. She agreed to tell us her story of a friend's betrayal only if she were not identified.

Six years earlier, Letty and the woman we will call Joan were best friends. They had known each other since college; in fact, they had married men from the same fraternity. They knew each other's secrets, and they trusted each other. Back in their freshman year, Letty had found herself pregnant, and it was Joan who came with her and held her hand when she had an abortion that no one else would ever know about.

In their thirties, they moved to the same Silicon Valley community, shopped together, carpooled together. They gave each other honorary-aunt status. On no-school days, Joan would take care of Letty's kids. Letty remembers the day that her daughter broke her leg in the playground and Joan stayed with the child in the emergency room until Letty could get there from work.

Then Joan's marriage began to falter. She confided to Letty that she was ready to leave her husband, but with her part-time paycheck, she was frightened about what would happen. She was sure he would try to pay her as little child support as possible, and what could she do?

Letty wasn't surprised; but both she and Fred, her husband, were concerned about Joan's future. "So I called my uncle, who owned a small store, and he said he could use another clerk," remembers Letty. She felt good; she was helping her friend.

Joan's husband moved out soon after, and the scene was painful and ugly. Letty and Fred saw how hard Joan was trying to ease the transition for her kids, and they began seeing more of her—inviting her over for dinner, sharing a baby-sitter so the three of them could go out every now and then to a movie. Gradually, the intimacy of Letty and Joan's relationship began to include Fred. When Joan one night started to cry in the car over the latest battle in her fight for child support, it was Fred who put his arm around her and consoled her.

Letty describes the moment: "I was sitting in the backseat and feeling for my friend, really feeling for her. And I was glad that Fred was paying attention. I wanted him to understand why I cared about her so much, and why I was willing to do a lot to help her out. I felt proud in a way that he wasn't like other husbands, the kind of jerks who never want a friend around. And then suddenly she had her head on his shoulder and he had an arm around her and—and I had the oddest sensation. There was something in the car that hadn't been there. It was a kind of electricity—and I sat there, feeling like an outsider. A stranger. I didn't know what to think."

She hurries by what came next. A series of evenings when Fred had to work "late." A series of phone messages left for Joan that were not returned. She would stand in the kitchen cooking dinner and not believe what her brain was telling her—something was going on between her husband and her best friend. "I was devastated that Fred might be having an affair, that was bad enough. But with Joan? How could Joan do that to me? How could she possibly do that?"

As we talk to her, Letty still seems more shocked by her friend's betrayal than by her husband's. But the double whammy was both stunning and banal. "The weird part was that I kept wanting to tell my best friend that my husband was cheating on me. I needed a friend to talk to—badly. But my best friend was the one he was sleeping with. It was so lonely. I can't even tell you how lonely."

Weeks went by. Letty finally confronted her husband, who admitted everything. He said that he had started out comforting Joan and fallen into something he felt terrible about, and that he would end the affair.

But he didn't. "I was furious with Fred, and I hated Joan. But I still couldn't believe that the woman I knew, who had been my friend, who I trusted, who knew everything about me, would keep this going."

Finally Letty swallowed her pride and went to see Joan. It was late, the kids were asleep, and as Letty tells it, "There I was, sitting on her front steps with her where the two of us had sat so many times before, asking her, 'Why?' Asking her—no, begging her to call a halt. To stop sleeping with my husband. She looked horribly tired and depressed, and she just kept shaking her head, and saying, 'Letty, I'm so sorry. I can't help myself. I'm not as strong as I thought I was.'"

Letty doesn't remember much about getting home that night. She just remembers feeling a yawning sense of loss. She was angry and hurt and terribly confused, because she had seen not only the guilt but the pain in her friend.

Letty's marriage did not survive—nor did the relationship between Joan and Fred. All three went their separate ways. Over the years, Letty would now and then pick up a scrap of information about Joan: a failed second marriage, a move to another state. And still she kept wondering how it could have happened.

"I lost my husband, and I lost my best friend, and even back then, I wasn't sure which was worse," she admits.

Until the morning in front of the window at Macy's.

"You know the strange thing?" Letty says. "When I turned, she was smiling at me. Just this small, sort of half-embarrassed smile. And for just an instant, I think I started to smile back. You know those horrible moments when you've forgotten you hate someone and you start to be friendly?" Letty tries to laugh, but it sounds forced. "I almost opened my mouth to ask her how she was, before I caught myself. But what kind of fool would I be if I had done that? She betrayed me. It was unforgivable."

This classic betrayal set off a cluster bomb in the world of friendship these two women had created for themselves. When Letty failed in her appeal to her husband, why did she go to Joan? Because, she told us, she actually had hoped she could persuade Joan to call a halt to the affair. Would that have made any difference? Probably not, she realizes now. The trust was gone; the fabric of both marriage and friendship was ripped apart.

Often women are quicker to blame "the other woman" than a wandering husband; to forgive him, but never to forgive "her," in part because of the deep family and economic roots of marriage. But when that "other woman" is a close friend, the allocation of blame isn't always so easy.

Letty's story reminded us of something Carolyn See once wrote: "I had a strong friendship once, a ten-year one, that was destroyed because we both loved the same very undeserving man. When she flew off with him to the island of Yap, I was devastated—not because of him, I wanted to *kill* him, but my heart broke for the loss of her."

But we wondered too about Letty's children, who were now all teenagers. After all, these two families had celebrated holidays together and these two women had a storehouse of knowledge about each other's children. They had raised them together, shared all that intimate worrying, the problem solving. One kid's shyness, another kid's bullying. All that history had been wiped out by betrayal.

Ironically, when she was going through her divorce and her kids were rebelling, Letty would catch herself wondering what Joan would tell her to do. Now, watching her daughter as she negotiates the oscillating triangles of boyfriend and girlfriend, love and friendship, she finds herself wary for her.

Wary of what, we ask? Did we expect some echo of the mother in *The Women* who warned her daughter away from members of her own sex?

There is a long pause while Letty tries to figure out if she is more afraid that her daughter will be hurt by her girlfriends or more afraid that she'll hold back from making close friends. Despite the fact that Letty has never talked with the children about what happened, she suspects her daughter knows. It was she who never mentioned Joan's name, she who never asked to see Joan's kids again, who never asked where Joan was.

Not long ago after that encounter in Union Square, her daughter had a fight with her best friend over a guy. Letty sat her down to try to patch it up. "I said, 'Really, it can't be that serious. You guys can work it out.' And she gave me this look and said, 'Mom . . . come on.' That was all she said, but I remember thinking, 'She knows.'"

There are other betrayals that send women running for safety; it is small wonder that some choose not to get too close in the first place. Sometimes, of course, distance is a simple lesson of maturity. You can't trust everyone. Pick and choose. Test carefully. But for others it is part of a lifelong disconnection. It comes with fame (in whom can Chelsea Clinton confide?) and it comes with everyday disappointments, secrets turned into gossip, as well as betrayal.

Betrayal? We can't leave the subject without exploring the betrayal story of absolute mythic proportions for our times, a story that reverberated strongly in the world of girlfriends.

It began as the whole nation eavesdropped on a slice of girl talk. Just two chicks dishing, one calling the other to talk, confess about something as small as a tie and something as deep as a relationship with Mr. Wrong.

"I bought the creep a tie," says the first woman.

"Oh, please," says the second.

"I know," answers the first. "It was twenty bucks at Marshall's."

"Oh good. Who makes it?"

"Calvin Klein . . . Yeah, it's gorgeous. It's real different than all the other ones. So I put a really funny note with it."

You can almost hear the sigh of the second woman, as the first repeats what she wrote to the creep. "'And just think, now you can pay homage to me if you want, by having a work week in which you wear one of my ties every day.'"

The second woman laughs indulgently. "'Cause this will be the fifth one, right? You'll have to give him one for the weekend days."

"No, I think this is it. That's what I want. You know, that's my fantasy, is to have him wear one of my ties every day."

"You're a nut," says the second woman with fond familiarity.

This is the standard stuff of telephone talk between girlfriends: no detail of a relationship is too small to dissect, no text of a letter or pattern on a tie too minor to mull over. It's the grown-up version of friends endlessly dissecting a small exchange in the high school hallway between one of them and a boy. "He said . . . and then, I said . . . and do you think he meant . . . and maybe I should have said . . ."

Except, of course, that in *this* bit of daily dialogue, one friend was Monica Lewinsky and the other was Linda Tripp. We—that is, the entire nation—were able to eavesdrop on their talk about creeps and Calvin Klein ties, courtesy of a tape recording. As everybody knows, that laughing, indulgent pal on the other line taped hour upon hour of her conversations with Monica, and then turned them over to Special Prosecutor Kenneth Starr, who ultimately used them in his unsuccessful effort to get President Clinton removed from office.

Complains Monica, "He hasn't even called me."

Advises Linda, "I think you should sleep on it. Is there any way you can put it out of your mind tonight?"

Even talk about which dress to wear to a party . . .

Monica: "Well, that dress—I don't care about pretty; I care about thin. That's all I care about."

Linda: "Well, okay. And this outfit makes you look thin and beautiful."

As Lucianne Goldberg, Tripp's coconspirator and agent, described the conversations: "A lot of pain, a lot of anguish, a lot of shopping."

Was there any woman who didn't shrink from the horror of the headlines? "Linda Tripp: Backstabber"; or the *Newsweek* line: "With friends like this, who needs assassins?"

What woman couldn't recall similar late-night unloading of tears and details, the nights when we most cherish having a friend on the other line, someone who will hold on and hold on to us, until, like Monica, we say, "Thank God for you! Oh Linda, I don't know what I am going to do."

Who could imagine having every private thought, every secret revealed, read in the papers, every part of your life grist for the gossip mill, available on the Web and broadcast to the world? One of our friends compared the violation to discovering that a man she loved had videotaped sex and handed it over to cable TV.

Small wonder that Monica's last words on the subject were a childish and deeply felt, "I hate Linda Tripp." Or that so many added, "Hear, hear!" The "backstabbing girlfriend" presented the country with nothing less than a modern parable of trust and betrayal. When women heard those tapes, there was an almost visceral defense of female friendships; it was as if the whole country refused to accept betrayal as a norm. A search through the Web with just two words—*Tripp* and *vilified*—brought up hundreds of hits. And when the original Linda Tripp Website asked "Is she a hero or a lousy friend?" the jury ran three to one for "lousy friend."

The universal damnation of Tripp said volumes about the unwritten set of rules for friendship between women. It suggests to us how strong the desire is on the part of many women to protect the safe harbor of friendship. As Margaret Atwood once wrote, "Because friendship is supposed to be unconditional, a free gift of the spirit, its violation is all the more unbearable."

The "bad stuff" of the Tripp variety, of Letty's double-whammy infidelity, is off the charts. We have trouble imagining how anyone could clamber back up over the edge of such a canyon of treason. And we are no more surprised when a friendship ends than when a marriage ends.

But against the background of experiences with the cliques of adolescence, the gossip, the classic betrayals, we do wonder how many women retreat to safety. The safety of superficiality.

Seeing the effect of cliques—the desire for inclusion, the fear of exclusion—we have come to believe that adults should take these adolescent learning circles far more seriously and step in far more readily. Adults sometimes, by ignoring the child's world, leave their children in a state of siege.

How do grown-ups who don't fight—and don't want to—handle trouble when it comes along? What do they do when the imperative to keep it smooth, nice, conflicts with the desire to get real? When they fear that conflict will end a friendship, do they just drift out of it, allowing it to end, anyway?

We have learned something about our own way of dealing with the inevitable misfires and misunderstandings. It's by no means a flawless system. But Ellen resists the temptation to tiptoe, because Pat calls her on it: "What are you saying?" Pat resists the temptation to stew because Ellen hears it: "Are you mad at me?" We listen to what we don't always want to hear. We try to balance care with honesty. When there is an edge, an unsettled question, we call back: "Tell me what you meant." And "Did I miss something?"

We let some things pass—no big deal—and wrestle out others. We don't let things fester. We have built up confidence.

We aren't saying that women who do not "fight" don't get "real." We haven't turned our relationship into therapy where every sentence—God help us—must be understood and every feeling plumbed. And we know how tempting it is to keep it nice.

But stuff, bad stuff, happens. If women could recapture that brief moment in childhood when friends could get mad, go home, and make up—vaulting over all that comes after—maybe they would discover again what is often missing in adult relationships: resilience.

9

We're in It Together

Pat

The goose bumps began on June 12, 1984, the day Fritz Mondale announced that he had chosen Geraldine Ferraro as his running mate. I was standing with a cluster of male colleagues in the Knight-Ridder newsroom, watching the television, hoping none of them would notice how excited I was. A little over a week later, I was in San Francisco, leaving the hotel on the final day of the Democratic National Convention, flying down the street to the Moscone Center in my newly purchased running shoes and business-as-usual suit, feeling for the first time like one of the big-time political reporters who eat up political conventions like pistachio nuts.

For me, it was a special professional moment—my first assignment to a convention, except this was bigger, much bigger than that. For the first time, a woman was on the national ticket. This time women journalists were not just being permitted into the male political world; the editors needed us. We mattered in a new way.

The excitement in the arena on June 16 was palpable. This was the day

Ferraro was to be nominated, and I was determined to shove my way through the narrow hall to the credentials desk to get that precious inner-sanctum floor pass that would allow me to go anywhere. Elbowing in among the Big Foots was wonderful, my apologies to the nice guys. I got the pass, with instructions that it was good for only fifteen minutes; then connected with Ellen, who had her own precious pass. We hung them around our necks, clutched notepads and pens, and plunged into the crowd, not planning to emerge until we felt like it. It was that kind of afternoon.

The speeches rolled on. There would be one spectacular moment when one state—and we were sure it would be New York, Ferraro's home state—would put Ferraro over the top, and we promised each other we'd be together when it happened. "Meet you at the corner of New York and Oregon," we told each other as we went our separate ways. The noise was spectacular—speeches, the music, the raucous delegations—all standard for an American political convention, but it was my first one, the best one I could ever have hoped to cover.

The roll call began. Alaska voted for Ferraro, with one abstention. The outcome was preordained, but the moment when it became real—when Geraldine Ferraro would become the first female vice-presidential nominee in history—was almost upon us. My pen behind my ear, notebook held close, I moved as fast as I could through the crowd, headed toward the corner of New York and Oregon, that wonderfully impossible geographic location that existed only in the delegate seating plan fashioned by the Democratic National Committee.

Arkansas was to vote next, but yielded to New York. It was going to happen fast.

I got there as the head of the New York delegation stood up, and there was Ellen and our friend, Lynn Sherr, who—along with Ann Blackman—would be my twenty-four-hour-a-day pals on the Ferraro campaign. (As the ABC correspondent, Lynn would gain a place in the Women's Hall of Fame for announcing to a crowded campaign plane of macho males that they weren't the only ones covering this campaign anymore, and they should *put the toilet seat down*.) In this sea of people, we found each other as promised, and now we were craning our heads for the best view of what came next.

New York moved that Ferraro's nomination be approved by acclamation, and the crowd exploded. It was official. The music became a roar and balloons showered down from the ceiling. Coming out on the stage with

Fritz Mondale was a candidate in a skirt, a woman, someone who looked like us. It was actually happening. And what really electrified me was how astounded I was at my own astonishment. How could it be that this had never happened before? I felt myself tear up. Horrified, I looked around and saw some women reporters openly crying, tears falling on their scribbled notes, and it didn't seem as if we professionals who had battled our way up in a male business could help ourselves.

I particularly remember one television reporter leaning across several seated delegates, reaching out impulsively to Betty Friedan, the mother of feminism, actually blurting out what many of us felt to be true. "You're the one who made this possible!" she shouted above the din. "It's all because of you!"

And then Ferraro stepped up to the microphone. "Thank you, Vice President Mondale," she said in that Queens accent that was to become so familiar to Americans over the next several months. "Vice President. It has such a nice ring to it."

Speeches, balloons, cheers. By the time we handed in those long-overdue fifteen-minute floor passes, history had been made. And Ellen and I had been part of it.

Ellen

Goose bumps? Journalists don't do goose bumps. But at the same moment Pat, just off the Gary Hart campaign, was watching the announcement in Washington. I was watching in the *Boston Globe* city room.

"American history," said Geraldine Ferraro, "is about doors being opened." I could feel the heady breeze from the doorway.

In my office there was a poster from 1941, the year I was born, of Wonder Woman at a national convention being nominated for president. The caption described it as "A thousand years in the future." But it was only forty-three years later and Ferraro was going to be nominated for vice president. America was ahead of schedule and, like so many other women, I felt a surge.

I sat again that night with my daughter and watched it on the evening news. Maybe every mother and daughter in America, Democrat or Republican, shared the feeling they were invested in Ferraro. And however "unprofessional" it appeared, most of the women in our profession felt part of something. She was the Story and she was Ours.

Pat and I arrived in San Francisco on the eve of what we would forever think of as the Ferraro Convention, forgetting—as, alas, did the country—that it was Fritz Mondale at the head of the ticket. In the past only one woman had been sent by my newspaper to each convention and she was usually expected to cover the parties—"color"—or the candidates' wives. Not this time.

One night we gathered in the bordello-red recesses of Ernie's, the restaurant Lynn Sherr had chosen for the "girls' dinner." Around the table, Pat and I and the "Wellesley College Media Mafia"—Linda Wertheimer, Cokie Roberts, and Lynn—shared gossip and politics and the palpable sense of having arrived.

We were an inner circle now too. How different it was, I thought that night, from my first convention in 1972, when Ann Blackman, then at the Associated Press, and I, as a token cadre of women, had been invited once to join the boys on the bus—the old political boys—but only as an audience to their war stories.

I think in our generation, the women's movement forged all kinds of friendships, and not just among women who marched together or went back to school together. Feminism made friends of women who thought they were "the only one." It made friends of women who got goose bumps together.

In San Francisco, deep in the Moscone Center, Pat and I shared history. So today in our mental scrapbook, along with the weddings attended and the problems shared and the plans hatched, there is also an image of us with press tags hanging from our necks and Nikes on our feet, notepads in our hands, trying not to lose our professional cool and cheering anyway.

On the confetti-littered floor of that deep bunkerlike convention hall in San Francisco, we knew that when we were old and playing "Do You Remember," we would look back on the night we stood together at the corner of New York and Oregon.

Even today, long after Ferraro made her mark in that failed campaign, after her two unsuccessful races for the Senate, after two political wives, Hillary Clinton and Elizabeth Dole, became political candidates, we think of that summer of 1984 as a time when the personal and the political were deeply entwined. This was not just history in the making. It was *our* history.

From our first meeting, the professional and the personal, the public and the private were all mixed together into the dough of our relationship.

Our work and family lives played out against the background of the times. Our conversations would always range from kids to editors, because work was a common thread. It was our community, our language, the ethnic neighborhood that we shared, what brought us together even in the underground recesses of the Moscone Center. It was what this Los Angeles daughter of an Irish immigrant and the Boston daughter of a first-generation Jew initially had in common.

We were also linked by the women's movement. We were not card-carrying members of anything—no journalists need apply—but we were part of the movement in the widest sense of that word. We were our own consciousness-raising or consciousness-reinforcing group. Many of our most intimate conversations came in the heady atmosphere of questioning everything about women's place in the world. Our sense of connection in-cluded the connection to something larger than ourselves.

We take our friendship personally. Over the years we have thought of it as "a private thing," something that is located in the private zone of our lives, where we are tied by no strings except those of good feelings and old times.

Until now, we have talked about women's friendship this way, as an emotional connection, a place where women enjoy each other's company without any other "agenda," a place where they play, a place where they can talk without restraint, a place where they can feel comforted and empow-ered, can work through and work over the issues of their lives. Deep, down-to-the-bone friendship grows out of the intimacy of shared experience and feelings. Even our talk about the strains and pulls of friendship, the transi-tions in life, the inevitable "bad stuff" has been, by and large, in a personal context.

But friendship has also taken us outward. Women do not live just pri-vate lives, nor do they connect solely through sharing their feelings about their jobs, men, child-raising, or the latest movie. Many find the pleasure of friendship in connecting together to something larger, more important, than themselves.

There is an enormous rush of excitement that comes from a shared com-mitment. There are women who, either figuratively or literally, roll up their sleeves and plunge in together to change something or make something happen, women like Jane Addams and her friend Ellen Starr, who—ap-palled by the problems of urban poverty—set out together in 1889 to cre-ate Hull House, in Chicago. They, like so many others, took on the work together as friends who had a goal beyond themselves.

Not all shared commitments take place on a large stage. They may be as close to home as fighting for a neighborhood traffic light or safer water. Pro-choice women find common cause; so do pro-life women. Women involved together in the PTA are as energized by the fight to improve their children's schools as the political women who worked hard to put Ferraro on that podium. There's an added joy in this shared activism. In many ways, friends know they empower each other—and that means they have a better chance to make something happen. Because they are in it together, they'll *get it done.* They have a vested interest in each other's growth—whether they are recording history together, trying to change social policy, or trying to create a work of art. The women who have experienced that sense of collective energy never forget it.

Aristotle believed that a true friendship involved a commitment to the common good. That often seems missing in discussions of women's friendship now. But in fact the reality of women's "civic friendships" is as old as the more romantic view of soul mates. In the nineteenth century, women's clubs were essentially friendship organizations, but as sociologist Ann Swidler says, "that friendship was put to a civic purpose." Women joined together to push for pasteurized milk or widows' pensions long before anybody thought of consciousness-raising circles. As the authors of *Habits of the Heart* remind us, "It is also part of the traditional view that friendship and its virtues are not merely private: they are public, even political, for a civic order, a city is above all a network of friends."

We can't think of a better example of this than Susan B. Anthony and Elizabeth Cady Stanton, the two founding mothers of women's suffrage, whose friendship was created and flourished in the context of shared ideals, and who were jointly dedicated to something larger than themselves.

From the moment they met in 1851 on a street corner in Seneca Falls, New York, when Anthony was thirty-one and Stanton was thirty-five, they fought together for women's suffrage and the rights of working women, the whole panoply of issues known then as the Woman Question. Stanton, who later became "plump and square, with a head of curls lined up like bedrolls and a penchant for naps," was on her way to becoming the mother of seven children. Anthony was unmarried, an angular woman, hair drawn back in a severe bun with "wire spectacles perched on her nose." Stanton was the theorist, Anthony was the organizer.

Stanton wrote of their relationship: "In thought and sympathy we were one, and in the divison of labor we exactly complemented each other. I am the better writer, she the better critic. She supplied the facts and statistics, I the philosophy and rhetoric, and together we have made arguments that have stood unshaken through the storms of long years; arguments that no one has answered."

The two of them, over a friendship spanning fifty years, pushed each other along, helping, exhorting, supporting. "If I get all the time the world has, I can't get up a decent document," Anthony complained in an 1896 letter as she implored her friend to produce a speech to give at the New York State Teachers Convention. "So for the love of me and for the saving of the reputation of womanhood, I beg you, with one baby on your knee and another at your feet and four boys whistling, buzzing, hallooing Ma, Ma, set yourself about the work. It is but of small moment who writes the address, but of vast moment that it be well done. . . . Now will you load my gun, leaving me only to pull the trigger and let fly the powder and ball?"

Sometimes, when Stanton didn't have the breathing room to "load her gun," Anthony made sure she provided it. "Aunt Susan" would frequently come with stacks of documents and baby-sit for those babies and whistling boys while she and Stanton planned. "I forged the thunderbolts, and she fired them," Stanton said, describing their early partnership. Her husband put it differently: "You stir up Susan and she stirs the world."

Late in her life, Anthony acknowledged how much more they had done together than they ever could have done separately. "The one thought I wish to express is how little my friend and I could accomplish alone. . . . I have been a thorn in her side and in that of her family, too, I fear. Mr. Stanton was never jealous of anyone but Susan, and I think my going to that home many times robbed the children of their rights. But I used to take their little wagon and draw them round the garden while Mrs. Stanton wrote speeches, resolutions, petitions, etc., and I never expect to know any joy in this world equal to that of going up and down, getting good editorials written, engaging halls and advertising Mrs. Stanton's speeches. After that is through with, I don't expect any more joy. If I have ever had any inspiration she has given it to me. I want you to understand that I never could have done the work I have if I had not had that woman at my right hand."

In many pursuits, in many different ways, women have felt that sense of gratitude toward the friends who have been in it together with them. As Stanton and Anthony knew, this is especially true in times of change, when women are striving for acceptance.

Consider the pioneer corps of screenwriting women making it against the odds—and in collaboration—in the early days of Hollywood.

"They were friends, but they took their friendship into the professional arena in a way that our more self-conscious and liberated age, with a few notable exceptions, hasn't managed to, at least in the movie business," Marsha McCreadie wrote in her book, *The Women Who Write the Movies*. "They wrote parts for other women. They exchanged jobs and information about jobs. They hired each other when they could, and they often worked on the same projects together."

This hardy group felt a surge of excitement as they tried to find a place in the fledgling industry, and they were delighted at how much consternation their presence caused the men who ran the studios.

"Bess Meredyth, Anita Loos, and I were asked our advice on virtually every script MGM produced during the thirties," wrote Frances Marion in an interview before her death in 1973. "It would have been embarrassing had other writers discovered that the executives asked our opinions about their work and that we were, without credit, making revisions. When we carried the scripts on which we were doing re-writes, we made sure they were in unmarked, plain covers. But we knew male writers were complaining about 'the tyranny of the woman writer' supposedly prevalent at all studios then, and particularly at MGM."

The idea that 'the tyranny of the woman writer' could affect the shaping of movie screenplays is as quaint today as it was in Marion's time. We rarely see a screen image of two women uniting to be part of something larger than themselves. Only the very rare movie, like the vintage *9 to 5*, portrays women rallying together at all. If they join together, it's more likely to be for a private vengeance, like the women in *The First Wives Club*, determined to get back at husbands who left them for trophy wives.

Only occasionally, as in the movie *Julia*, based loosely on Lillian Hellman's life, do we see female friendship and a cause entwined seriously. In that story, against a background of World War II, Lillian has bravely smuggled a package of money to her friend Julia in the Resistance. But as they sit together for their last meeting in a restaurant, Julia, who is under surveillance and knows her fate, tells Lillian: "I want you to know that you've been better than a good friend to me, you've done something important. We can save five hundred people—maybe a thousand, if we can bargain right."

Lillian realizes she and Julia have been joined, with that one delivery, in a higher cause. Her friend's final words include a high accolade: "You've been better than a good friend to me."

In life, off-screen life, there are any number of stories of women who have been "better than a good friend," women who have come together and stayed together, engaged in both public and private life. Such overlapping worlds were at the heart of the friendship between the writers Vera Brittain and Winifred Holtby, two spirited women who met at Oxford after nursing the shattered victims of war on the battlefields of World War I. Brittain achieved fame with a haunting account of the experiences of her war generation in *Testament of Youth.* After Holtby's death, she wrote *Testament of Friendship,* a biography of her friend and a celebration of a friendship founded on a shared view of a world torn by World War I.

Women in political life have in recent years worked hard to bring together their skills and convictions and energy. Senator Mary Landrieu and her friend and chief of staff, Norma Jane Sabiston, have that connection. After her historic nomination, Gerry Ferraro went on to become one of the Washington women of a certain age who call themselves 'The Golden Girls,' a group that also includes Senator Barbara Mikulski, former Representative Barbara Kennelly, and Secretary of State Madeleine Albright, a tight band of political women who vigorously support each other and their "joy of shared missions," as Mikulski puts it. "We have a foxhole friendship," she told Ann Blackman, Albright's biographer. "It started on Gerry's campaign, which was very intense. We'd sit together on planes, trains, buses. You really get to know each other that way."

Women at many levels are in "foxhole friendships," and they learn to fight for each other, and not just in the upper echelons of government. Some are like Dottie Stevens and Diane Dujon, two former welfare mothers who have shared a lifetime of energy from their joint passion for community organizing, a commitment that simply changed their lives.

We first met Dottie and Diane, friends and allies, friends and activists, in Diane's home, an actual house she now owns after a lifetime of living in cramped rental apartments. When she and Dottie met twenty years ago, they had just one thing in common—poverty.

What Diane remembers most was a woman sitting in the classroom every day, wearing a funny floppy hat that she kept pulled down over her eyes like Greta Garbo—except she was actually Dottie, a mother on welfare with four kids who was wondering what she was doing there and frightened to death to open her mouth.

"She was so quiet," said Diane, describing her first impressions of the woman who would become her lifelong friend. "She had bangs that went straight across here, and that's what I remember—that she always wore a hat, almost like she was concealing herself." Not anymore. Today Dottie is a comfortably large woman, her gray hair pulled tightly back. She has a rich laugh and a mind that she speaks without hesitation.

In the 1970s, Diane and Dottie were in an unfamiliar place: a college classroom at the University of Massachusetts, enrolled in a

Dottie Stevens and Diane Dujon.

program constructed to help poor women work toward college degrees. Diane was also a welfare mother back then, with a five-month-old daughter and a monthly check from the welfare department for $314. They were both in decidedly foreign territory, and a lot of time was spent surreptitiously eyeing each other and the other women, wondering what came next.

Diane was one of the lucky ones. She already had a high school education, and she had signed up as fast as she could for the program. Dottie had been married and divorced three times and been given a choice by welfare officials: get a job or go to school so you can get a degree—and then get a job. Otherwise, no money.

For Dottie, there was no choice. As one of five children of Irish and German background in a female-headed household, she was raised on welfare. She had run the streets, shining shoes, selling papers, and even going into taverns with her father and dancing on a bar, so the other drinkers would give them chips and Cokes. With only an eighth-grade education, four kids, and still struggling to end a relationship with a man who battered her, she knew she would never get off welfare without help. So she bought herself four pairs of knee socks and signed up for a course called "Basic Organizing."

"I thought it would help me learn how to run an office," she says with wonder at that naive young self. "What'd I know?"

She soon found out. "Basic Organizing" was a community activist program, and the sparks that came from this group of women, when they began seeing ways to take charge of their own lives by learning the system and making it work for them, would reverberate through many years to come.

Dottie doesn't deny she was trying to hide behind that hat, even as she was peeking out, trying to assess the others. "I remember feeling very, very insecure because I didn't have any background education and I would listen to the rest of the women, especially Diane, and say, 'Wow. I think I'm out of my league here.' But they said, 'No, no, no.'" She was awed by Diane. What she saw was this forceful black woman who was an actual high school graduate, and who was clearly smart. "I would listen to her talk, and I thought she was very learned," Dottie says.

Diane, her ample body clothed in a bright red sweatshirt, her hair in cornrows, starts pouring tea into the cups she has carefully laid out on the yellow oilcloth covering her kitchen table. She is grinning as she tosses back to her friend her own compliment.

"Dottie would have these outbursts every once in a while of terrific ideas," she says. "It was like, 'This sounds great! Yeah! Let's do it! Hey, Dottie, you should go do it!' and she'd say, 'I don't know how to do that.' And we'd say, 'Sure you do.'"

Almost from the beginning they began to intertwine their personal relationship with common goals: to make the poverty programs work better. Gradually poverty became their cause, not their trap. They began to see their private lives in a larger context. The poor women in their class also experienced that connecting insight: I'm not the only one.

Armed with new tools for organizing, they began attending welfare demonstrations, joined housing protests, fought for heating oil for poor families, and lobbied for legislation.

It took a while for Diane to coax Dottie out of her shell. The group would send her to meetings to collect information, but she had to admit to them that her ability to spell was poor. She was embarrassed. She feared she would let them down.

"So we would help her," Diane says. "We said, 'We don't care how you spell it, just do it phonetically. Just bring us back ideas and information.'" She looked at her friend, shaking her head. "It was amazing what she did." Dottie's growing belief that what she was doing was important brought her out from under the brim of that hat.

"We began to do things for each other," Diane remembers. "So a lot of what happened was, we were doing our schoolwork together, and we would do papers together, and we would help Dottie with her writing. She began to get exposure to the world because I kept pushing her out there. 'Yeah, go and sit on the Citizens Energy Corporation.' She'd come back and she'd say, 'I don't know what they were talking about. They asked me to be a chair.' And she didn't even know what that meant, you know. So we had to explain to her, 'No, nobody's going to sit on you.'"

The friendship was in no way unbalanced. "I think I learned how to deal better with people through Dottie," says Diane, "how to look at people in a different way, and to find that everybody has something down inside, no matter how hidden, no matter how buried. Dottie always finds that something. And so she's taught me the patience to look for that, to not give up on people."

They knew each other's practical needs as well. There were the everyday hassles and small humiliations of dealing with the welfare office. Nobody had to be embarrassed about what they didn't have. The women in the class took turns digging into their pockets to buy lunch for whoever was broke that day. They juggled schedules and baby-sat for each other's kids. They helped each other in whatever way was needed, no questions asked.

"The whole group, we really became a sisterhood. I mean, if you could think of a poor woman's sorority, that's what we were," Diane says proudly.

"You bet we did. This lady"—Dottie is pointing at Diane—"can work with anybody to make them feel good about themselves. I learned through her how to look at people in a different way. I never knew what being part of a community meant. Now I know."

At night Dottie and Diane would walk out of the university, ready to go home, to take the T back to nearby neighborhoods. "It was funny to analyze how we would leave school," says Diane. "We would say good-bye at the front door, but she would take the Red Line and I would take the Orange Line. Because she's white and I'm black. She felt more comfortable on the Red Line and I felt more comfortable on the Orange Line. And one day we said, 'Boy, isn't that really weird how we say good-bye at the door?'"

"That's when I decided to buy a car," Diane says, laughing. "Who needed that?"

They widened the lens to see their private struggles as political. "It's why we're friends," says Diane. "We saw they were doing it to both of us, white and black. They want to divide us. But we're the working class."

They also knew exactly how to be there for each other in more demanding personal ways. Dottie's ex-boyfriend, the one with the fast fists, forced himself into the elevator one day with Dottie and several of her teachers and began shouting at her that she should get home and take care of her children. That encounter was humiliating—but the day he came to the school with a gun and demanded that she leave with him was frightening.

Diane was the one who on several occasions would face him down. "He and I would go head to head a lot," she says. "If she was going somewhere with me and he would find out, he would try to stop her, and I would say, 'No, she's going with me.'"

And then came graduation, and one fabulous night when all the women who had made it through held a party and danced in a conga line, singing "Girls Just Wanna Have Fun."

Diane began a new job at the university where she still works. Dottie became active in poor people's campaigns and actually made a quixotic run for the governorship in the late '80s.

Over two decades, Diane has been the one reaching out most often with a helping hand to her friend, whose health has suffered in recent years and who now lives on disability. But Dottie's spirit has stayed buoyant and gritty. Today it's Dottie who fixes chicken soup when her friend comes over on her lunch hour needing a little comfort and relaxation. They know what each other wants and needs. Diane buys practical gifts for her friend, like a garden hose and a kitchen bucket—useful things that can make her life easier. Dottie is the one whose gifts dance—dolls for her friend's collection, a crystal prism with a hummingbird inside.

Dottie offers her house with its precious lawn and fourteen trees for summer barbecues; Diane brings the food. From time to time, when Dottie is in bed with a bad back, Diane is the one who drives over, encouraging her to join another protest. She reenergizes Dottie, coaxes her out of the house. They've stayed committed against the odds and against the current tide.

But even as Diane exults over her new home, she and Dottie launch into an agitated protest of the new state regulations that limit the chances for other poor women to get the education they got. "We've had more than we ever expected," Dottie says earnestly. "And we did it together. If I didn't see Diane for ten years, I would still consider her my friend."

Diane cradles her teacup, staring at the table. She is thinking about the most significant impact of their friendship. "If I hadn't met Dottie," she begins slowly, "my life would have been different. I would have stayed more in my own community, a community of color. She's added dimension to my world."

We say a lot about friends making a difference in our lives, and we also talk about friends making a difference in the wider world. For Dottie and Diane, these two ideas merged, and they have become part of an extended family, built on soldiering together, making a difference together.

When we talk about being in something larger together, we are thinking about work in the broadest sense of the word. There are other, less public, less "civic" ways in which friends take their personal relationship and write it large.

When Pat's daughter, Maureen, a family doctor, was in her first year of residency, one of her closest friends, a second-year resident, asked her to deliver her baby. "I was flattered and stressed when she asked me," Maureen says. The delivery turned out to be very difficult and deeply exhausting for them both. But the experience deepened their friendship in a fundamental way. "I realized she trusted me as much as I trusted her," says Maureen. "We gave each other the confidence to make decisions on what was right."

Women who collaborate together creatively are also testing whether they can be greater than the sum of their separate selves. Is there another canvas on which to test out, to play, to express the good stuff of connection?

We went to talk with two artists, Inga Frick and Gillian Brown, because the work they were doing let us literally see how two friends could create something larger together.

It's fitting that we saw the art before we met the artists. Pat visited a Dupont Circle gallery one day and happened upon a joint show by these two women that intrigued her. Sandy Fitzpatrick, the owner of the gallery, described the artists as two friends engaged in exploring each other's mediums: Gillian was a photographer and conceptual artist, Inga was a painter.

In the art world, they inhabited different camps. But here they were, exhibiting work they billed as "a conversation." The conversation was "art talk" of course, but we could see there was something more. Each woman was willing to risk herself to try something at which the other was very good. Their ideas flowed back and forth—almost, according to one brochure on their work, like "borrowed clothes."

––––––

The two artists who come to talk with us could never literally borrow each other's clothes. Inga, reed-thin, with a Modigliani face, is dressed exuberantly in a rust-colored peasant dress and taupe sweater with fur-lined short boots. Gillian, short and contained, might have stepped out of a Land's End catalog, except for her earrings: tiny, unexpected silver coffee cups.

Gillian Brown and Inga Frick.

Lugging a slide projector and carousel holding a decade's worth of slide shows, they quietly, almost sheepishly, apologize: "We won't be able to explain our collaboration. We'll have to show you through our work." We arrange a towel over the bookcase in Pat's library. They settle in, their voices more eager, their demeanor less self-conscious, as they put the slides up on the wall. Slowly we watch the evolution of two artists in collaboration move from two ends of the spectrum to one stunning moment of fusion.

It would be easy to stereotype these two friends, both now in their forties: Inga is flamboyant, the proud granddaughter of pioneers who settled Oregon; Gillian, the daughter of a British war bride and a veteran, is more reserved. They appear to be polar opposites. And certainly when they met in the 1980s in an artists' studio building in Maryland, their work was as different as their clothing.

Inga was painting large, expansive, abstract expressionist canvases. Gillian was creating installations, heady, intellectual pieces. In one, photographs of family members melted from the floor into a staircase.

Definitely unlikely "conversationalists" in the art world—but they remember hitting it off right away. Inga confesses she had an internal grading system for deciding whether someone was worth spending time with and "Gill had a high rating." Gillian says promptly she knows how she passed that test: "I made Inga laugh."

Right from the beginning, they had a tremendous respect for each other's wholly different work with paint and photographs. Even as they took us through the first slides, they began explaining and praising each other: ("You do detail better than I do." "No, you do it better.")

Gradually, as Gillian remembers it, "The work we did started looking like each other's." They realized they both liked that. As their respect for the other's artistic expression grew, and their influence on that art grew, so did the friendship. Or was it the other way around? No matter.

At the same time, they offered another eye onto their private lives.

Gillian's marriage went through a rocky period and Inga was sent reeling through a second divorce—"I stand on marriage and it turns into a whale that swims away," she says.

The gallery brochure describing them as "borrowing clothes" was apt—but they jokingly refer to their increasingly merging work as "stealing." "It wasn't a decision really," says Gillian. "We felt really free to borrow from each other. Which I don't think you usually feel. You usually feel uptight about borrowing somebody else's work."

In a world in which the artist's vision is expected to be highly personal and individual, they loved the give and take of borrowing, swapping, stealing. Gillian looked at Inga's free-spirited canvases and said to herself, "Gee, I could paint. I don't have to spend all this time in the darkroom." Inga, in turn, began to use photographs.

Soon they were exhibiting together, creating work that was individual, but also part of a running dialogue. It was an artistic conversation they found as nourishing as a long telephone call. Inga was experimenting with collages of tiny photographs that formed a whole portrait. Gillian was playing with work that bore titles like "He Had Nothing Upstairs" and "She Took It to Heart." And just to underscore the conversation between these two girlfriends, they filled the exhibition space with a soundtrack of children yelling and laughing on a school playground.

These two intense women, who care for each other rather like delicate china, began to feel more playful and take more risks. "We actually embolden each other," says Gillian, with a touch of timidity. Inga says they use each other as a reality test, a kind of artistic safety net. If she is headed in the wrong direction, Gillian will tell her so.

The layers of this relationship are painted on as finely as the layers on one of Inga's canvases. They trust both the friendship and the artistic judgment. "I don't know what I would do without her," says Inga, and for a moment we don't know whether she is talking about the friend, the critic, or the collaborator. "When my marriage ended and I thought I wasn't going to be able to cope," she continues, "I just sort of said, Gilly, you have to come save me. Get me through."

Gillian in turn remembers with a deep abiding gratitude the time when she had to go through the grueling process of finding a nursing home for her mother, who was afflicted with Alzheimer's. Inga went with her. They needed all this trust when they took the next step, which was to create a single work. This effort was not to be a conversation, but two artists using one voice. They designed an installation for a New York show they called, not accidentally, "You/Me." It emerged as a soaring, haunting, backlit series of seven-foot screens covered with white gauze depicting shifting human figures that emerge and fade and reemerge through undulating light.

How did they plan it? Gillian uses careful artistic phrasing to describe their intent: "We were interested in watching one person bleed into another. There was a quiet morphing. It speaks to the hunger for oneness." But the work was a challenge, a classic strain between two I's and a We. Two women, each with her own artistic sensibility and style, came together—in what could have been a collision.

Inga and Gillian don't pretend that "You/Me" was seamless. The "hunger for oneness" came with serrated edges. At the very end, a deadline loomed and the final task of installing their work turned out to be a technological nightmare.

"What happened is that we were under so much time constraint, all the nice lubrication of understanding how to work together was—well, was taken away," said Gillian.

Inga grins, tosses a look at Gillian. "We found ourselves having little fits of one kind or another. Behavioral fits. A little childishness, pretty bad."

"It's just, I know how to put things together," Gillian offered. "And we'd have to do things, and we'd have to do them fast, and I would have figured out a way. Well, Inga, being an artist, has the same kind of know-how. And it would drive me nuts that she would refigure out what I had figured out. And I'd say, 'Do it this way,' and Inga would say, 'Well, I don't know.' We were really bent out of shape."

"So it would take us twice as long to do things, because we each had to do it our way and do it over again," Inga said. "We slept together, we got up together, we were together every single minute, and boy, did I ever want to get rid of her!"

The two of them lean back and laugh at the difficulty of two egos producing one installation. "It was quite humbling," Gillian says.

When the work was done, Inga remembers, "We walked into the room with the lights on that night and it was a moment of complete exhilaration." Together they had made something extraordinary that neither could have made alone.

Many friends, knowing of the pitfalls, are afraid to put the weight of collaboration onto the back of a friendship. But Inga and Gillian consciously took care of their friendship even as they were wrestling to bring off their ambitious project.

"We'd get together in the morning after working late the night before and have these long elaborate conversations that are essentially girl talk," said Gillian with a smile. "I labeled them the Women's Fine Feeling News—you know, examining all those areas and fine feelings women do so well. All the drawn-out delicate nuances of every relationship in our lives. This would start the day."

It has a nice sound to it: "Women's Fine Feeling News." It's not yet a newsletter or a Website, but it says a good deal about the practice of friendship. In the corporate world, these kind of exchanges may sound like a waste of time, inefficient and unproductive. But not here.

As Inga and Gillian packed up their slides and prepared to leave, they told us they now trust both their collaboration—and friendship—enough to embark on an even more ambitious work of joint authorship. It is not one they can easily explain—no slides yet. The New York show, they tell us with a laugh, was rather like writing nonfiction together. This time, the work is more akin to joining forces to write a novel. "We are truly in each other's heads," says Inga.

———

To collaborate in creating something larger than yourself does mean staying "on the same page" or the same canvas. But every collaboration also depends on boundaries, on managing distance and closeness, what we refer to as the "I" and the "we." It's the trick of managing difference and sameness, respecting the differences that give friendship its edge and energy, and also valuing the similarities that make friends speak the same language.

Ellen's daughter, Katie, directs an all-women's improv group, Broad Comedy, where the troupe members are like acrobats, passing a line, a scene, from one to another, working without a safety net. "The work really gives us a common vision; you fail in front of each other, you succeed together; the pressure bonds us." Yet along with the collaboration she describes the independent desire to shine, to be *the* star, the one who comes up with the best line, the last laugh. The bottom line? "We absolutely could not have done it without each other."

There is a kind of rhythm and harmony to collaboration. And sometimes we mean that literally. We've heard that rhythm and harmony in the rock-roots music of two women who are known by a shared name ever since their album, "Strange Fire," took off in the late eighties. They are the Indigo Girls, separately named Emily Saliers and Amy Ray. They've known each other since fifth-grader Amy first sat in a darkened school auditorium and listened, fascinated, to the blond sixth-grade Emily playing the guitar and found herself thinking: I want to play like that.

There is an unmistakable distinctiveness to the music of the Indigo Girls, a blend of the raw edginess of Amy and the mellow lyricism of Emily. These are women who have different voices, different styles, different private lives. They share political beliefs, a commitment to out-front lesbian politics, and one solid, shared core: music. They write their songs separately and perform jointly. They maintain independence and connection in a friendship under constant road-trip pressure and public scrutiny. How?

We meet Emily and Amy on the nineteenth floor of the Omni New Haven Hotel, overlooking the quad at Yale University, where they are booked for a concert that night. We'd taken the train to New Haven, prepping for this interview by listening to tapes of our favorite songs, the roiling, poetic songs like "Galileo" and "Closer to Fine."

Emily Saliers and Amy Ray.
(© 1999 Sony Music; Photo by Michael Halsband)

Emily, a relaxed, reserved, strawberry blonde, joins us first. She is wearing no make-up and bearing no pretensions. Amy comes next, the coltish, wired half of this duo, her dark, close-cropped hair wet from the shower.

They've both been working out—separately—in the hotel gym. It is four in the afternoon and we are, with official dispensation from the restaurant, sitting at a table set for dinner, sipping water and coffee. We take turns holding our feet in the air as a hotel employee runs a noisy vacuum around our feet.

So, we ask, when did you guys first become friends? Not in that Georgia grammar school, as it turns out. It was when they both joined the high school chorus, long before they ever dreamed they would be selling five million records together.

"You start talking with somebody, and you realize that you are going to bond. It's hard to explain how that happens or why or exactly when, but that's what happened with us," says Emily, carefully putting down her glass of water so as not to disturb the silverware. Back then, they were listening to James Taylor and Neil Young and Carole King and having long deep discussions about life and music. "We were just a couple of buddies who could talk to each other, and play guitar," she adds.

But these two women who even write lyrics about their attitudes—"You know me / I take everything so ser-i-ously"—also describe those years as "intense . . . really intense."

Emily does a riff on her first impressions of Amy, a younger, more reserved Amy. "She used to wear dress pants and Izod sweaters and just stand with her eyes closed and just play, mostly ballads," she says, glancing at her friend. "Now she's like this rock 'n' roll queen."

But Amy became the driving force behind their joint career. It was Amy who worried that calling themselves Saliers and Ray would typecast them as just two girls playing acoustic guitars. It was Amy who saw that they should be a unit, not just a duo. A unit where their harmony could become a striking, recognizable sound, whether they were doing thoughtful melodic ballads or knock-your-socks-off rock numbers. And so, the Indigo Girls were born.

Over the years, as these women shared a stage and a career and public image, they carefully kept room for separateness, room for a voice of one's own. Part of this separation may come from their sexuality. Though both women are lesbians, they have never been lovers. Not only do they firmly say "we're not each other's type," but they add that their collaboration depends on not being lovers. It helps them maintain two lives and two identities—inside one professional creature.

In a business that keeps them on the road together for grueling weeks at a time, they also need some distance.

"We see each other so much," says Emily. "We're on the road, staying in the same hotels. We used to have to stay in the same hotel room early on, because we just couldn't afford two. At this point, when we go home off tour, we go our separate ways for the most part. You know, we need a certain amount of space. We're more like sisters now—with deep respect for each other."

In Atlanta, Emily, who seems more introspective and careful, is also the gregarious one who socializes with family and friends, while Amy, who is more uninhibited, lives by herself in an isolated rural community outside the city. Says Amy with a shrug, "I don't really understand the need for that kind of social environment, and she doesn't understand how I could spend so much time not seeing friends."

Without ever spelling this out, they've kept their friendship and collaboration strong, by accepting the ways in which they are different. And they've allowed and adapted to—and encouraged—a tremendous amount of individual change.

There are, in the first place, the different musical sensibilities. They write separately; each song has one byline. But then they come together. Emily brings the melodic sound of ballads like their classic "Closer to Fine" to their work. Amy brings the harder, more driving, edgy "Blood Fire." Emily plays delicately on the guitar, Amy with hard, sure strokes. They have different musical vocabularies, different ways of expressing themselves lyrically. But many of their songs have a call-and-answer quality, a point and counterpoint.

To see how the difference works you have to listen to their music. Does it seem these friends exaggerate the differences to bring passion to the shape of a song? In one of our favorite songs, entitled prophetically "The Power of Two," Emily begins sweet and high,

All the shiny little trinkets of temptation
something new instead of something old
all you gotta do is scratch beneath the surface
and it's fool's gold.

Meanwhile, Amy sings a soft and low counterpoint, that is almost a running commentary on their collaboration:

Make new friends
but keep the old
but remember what is gold.

There are other songs, like Amy's "Jonas and Ezekial," in which Emily seems to be trying to soothe the more volatile Amy; as if saying, "it's all right . . . calm down." The music becomes an echo of the theme of what happens when you "multiply life by the power of two."

Like the other friends we've talked to, these two are quick to acknowledge each other's strengths.

"Emily's more of a virtuoso," Amy insists, looking at her friend as if to preempt any disagreement. "What I worry about is, I want it to be a challenge for her. If we're talking about the idea of us being different, with different talents, I don't want to be dragging her down, holding her back. For me, that's important. That compels me sometimes to work harder."

Replies Emily immediately: "There are things that Amy does that I can't do, I'll never be able to do—her delivery of a song, and her passionate performance and her edginess and her rock and roll sensibility." The good news is, as Emily says, "We get to live two musical lives." The tough part is that they are constantly compared in public. They don't brood on this, but they talk about it up front.

Even some of what is true begins to get at them. "Amy's the dark one and Emily's the light one, and Amy's this and I'm that, you know. . . ." says Emily with weary distaste. But what about when the crowds take sides? "Like every now and then, we'll have a crowd that's an Emily crowd, and we take requests, and it's all Emily songs," says Amy, with a grin and a slight shrug of her shoulders. "And I'm sitting over on the other side of the stage going, 'Well, jeez.'"

Remember how the popular singing duo of Simon and Garfunkel broke up? Well, Amy and Emily keep it light, refusing to let fan worship turn corrosive. "It's like a natural push and pull," says Emily, "Think about it. Take a look at us—we're two women, there's bound to be comparisons all the time by fans, by the press."

After all they have something else in common, a shared politics. Over the years, the Indigo Girls have put their stamp on causes, as they give benefits for environmental, Native American, and feminist causes. They put together a high school tour in 1998, hoping to encourage some easy talk about their homosexual lifestyle—and were banned from playing in a high school in Columbia, South Carolina.

In such an intense career, the seams show in even the best of collaborations. A few years back, when Amy was pushing for more concerts, more traveling, Emily complained they were working too hard, taking on too much. They kept going from city to city, from hotel to hotel, from concert to concert.

They finally reached a point in 1995 at the end of their "Honor the Earth" tour when they knew they had to retreat. Go home. Stop performing together. Risk the Indigo Girls, so they could reclaim the individual Emily and Amy.

"I was having nightmares about fans," admits Emily. "I got to a certain point where I felt very exposed and scrutinized and things made me feel insecure and made me want to run away. Anyway, we were just tired. Burned out."

"Burned out in a way that was just so obvious," agrees Amy. So they called a halt.

That year off was a hard one for Amy and yet one of the best. She was getting over the end of an eight-year relationship and used the time out to work on music and start up an independent label. Meanwhile, Emily played the banjo for a change and got her hands down into the earth in her garden.

When they did come back together, they felt the first awkwardness. Amy came back with songs she was used to playing alone, and she wanted to move Emily into them slowly. Emily had songs that weren't exactly right for Amy. Their chemistry felt rusty.

It was one of those times when creative partners either keep each other in the same place, on familiar, maybe *too* familiar, ground—or push each other. They pushed. They began shaping the music carefully, giving each other room, and they produced the hit album *Shaming of the Sun*.

Throughout this time, they both believe the friendship itself was never in question. "Our friendship is unconditional, honestly," says Amy. If they dissolved the Indigo Girls, the friendship would survive. "I do think it exists outside of the Indigo Girls in a way that's unique." Emily nods vigorously. "Yes. Our friendship is sacred."

In fact, it's the one subject they don't write about. They write about love and loneliness, the Southland and "shedding your skin," and they pen political songs, but their relationship remains off-limits. "Everyone thinks we're girlfriends," says Emily. "Our fans would have a feeding frenzy on that, and that makes me uncomfortable."

Friends who collaborate may worry that differences can break up the connection. But Emily sees something else in their own balance. "As we've gotten older, our writing has evolved with more specific images, and we've gone off on our own paths individually in the way we express ourselves." They feel more free now to say different things in their music—and trust that they express those differences in the Indigo Girls.

The vacuum cleaner is gone, someone is lighting the candles on the tables for dinner, and it's time for Amy and Emily to do the last-minute work, deciding which songs they'll sing in which order tonight. We ask them whether there's a "secret" to this eighteen-year run. "A lot of it is deep beyond words, truly," says Emily. "And the best of friendships and relationships are. I mean, you can talk about them, you can talk and talk and talk about them. There's a lot of mystery about what binds two human beings together. And I do think it's remarkable that we've worked together for eighteen years."

We're at the elevator door. Amy punches the down button and gives one of her characteristically crisp observations: "The sum is greater than the parts," she says. "We both know that, and that's what keeps us intact."

An hour later, we are standing on the grass in the Yale quad, surrounded by fans—students, townspeople, all milling around in blue jeans and T-shirts, looking for a vantage point onto the outdoor stage.

Suddenly, music blasts out of the speakers. Amy and Emily burst out from a building, racing onto the stage—no, not Emily and Amy; the Indigo Girls. The crowd roars. Emily begins singing and strumming her twelve-string guitar, then Amy comes in with a tight vocal harmony; they break off into counterpoint and finish with the same strong harmony. The audience is clapping, swaying. There are students up on each other's shoulders, their arms undulating over their heads. The crowd sings along to lyrics—"Standing at opposite poles / equal parts in a mystery." This is where we can see—hear—the sound of collaboration, the rush of being in something larger. The sound spills out over the yard until the crowd is swept into this energy. Much, much, closer to fine.

Because the arts usually attract people dedicated to their own individual vision, the "oneness" that Inga and Gillian talked about is a rare conversation. And the intense togetherness of touring and creating new albums that Emily and Amy experience has pulled apart many similar musical collaborations. If they didn't know and weren't totally up front with each other about the boundaries they need, the partnership wouldn't work. Every relationship deals with the issue of distance and closeness, and these friends are no exception.

We know from the reactions to our own collaboration that working with a friend in a situation where you may rub each other raw on occasion makes women nervous. They worry that if you put too much weight on the voluntary relationship, it could collapse. A friend is supposed to represent the safe place. And that safe place can prove secure for women who are willing to test it.

The friends who transcend a strictly personal relationship don't avoid "bad stuff." Those amazing collaborators, Susan B. Anthony and Elizabeth Cady Stanton, had plenty of arguments, over things as small as their different energy levels, to things as serious as whether they were on the same strategic track in their fight for equal rights for women. After one falling-out, Stanton teasingly lightened the atmosphere by writing to Anthony and asking if she wanted "a divorce." She added immediately, brooking no disagreement, "I shall not allow any such proceedings. I consider our relationship for life, so make the best of it." That's it, you are stuck with me. What confidence it takes to say that, and to know that it is true.

The friends who survive collisions and thrive, like Inga and Gillian, often do so by remembering to take care of the relationship and by continuing to share their "fine feeling news." Amy and Emily did it by giving each other room to breathe. And nothing can survive without allowing the possibility of change.

The two of us genuinely felt exuberant that night at the Democratic Convention in San Francisco when we witnessed one of the footnotes of political history, but that was not the only moment when we felt that easy sense of shared experience. For most of our friendship, the personal and the professional easily dovetailed. We never worked in the same office or on the same paper, but our professional connection was always a comfortable, familiar point of reference. We both knew about editors and deadlines. We read each other's work. ("Does this lead do it?") We traveled on the same turf. ("Are you going to that conference on drug abuse in Detroit?") We argued about the same issues. ("What is journalistic objectivity, anyway?")

But we too had to make room for change.

Ellen

My friend was restless. It was three years after that Ferraro high and she was up on the Hill covering one too many midnight votes on the Congressional budget. She'd learned more about the MX missile than anyone outside of the Pentagon has any right to know. She was getting a case of been-there, done-that. And if there was one thing that Pat isn't, well, it's a stick in the mud.

I could hear the traveling music in her voice and I wasn't surprised when I got the next call. The head of the nascent Dukakis presidential campaign, a guy she knew from the Ferraro days, had asked out of the blue, "Listen, Pat, have you ever considered changing careers?" He wanted to know if she would be interested in working for Governor Michael Dukakis as his campaign press secretary. The job would be based in Boston.

"A press secretary?" Those were the folks we always tortured for information. Those were the folks who were always trying to keep the press in line during some feeding frenzy—"Down, boy, down." They were on the other side of some invisible line that separated us from them, media from candidates. But Pat was intrigued by the idea of learning what life was like on that other side.

To her own surprise, Pat began thinking about it. Anyway, she wanted a stepping-stone out of journalism and into book writing. I got a call from Frank, the man she would—after a few more tumultuous months—finally marry. "She's a hard dog to keep on the porch," he said to me with some alarm. I laughed and sidestepped his nervousness about her move. But when she sounded energized by taking a chance, I thought, "Hey, go for it." And when she took the job, I loved the idea that we'd be in the same town for the first time in years.

I asked around my neighborhood and found a terrific apartment. She grabbed it and we started to talk about what it would be like to run into each other accidentally on the street. Me and my friend the *press secretary?*

Pat

It was an incredibly exhilarating, frenetic time. Setting up a fledgling press office was a daunting task, especially since I was on a plane traveling around the country five or six days a week. And my friend, *the columnist?* Here I was, living in that apartment two blocks from her house, and we saw less of each other than we ever had before. We laughed about the irony of it all. When we managed to talk.

For the first time, we weren't in the same business together. For the first time, we were on different sides. We talked as freely as ever about the kids and Bob and whether or not I was really going to marry Frank. We talked about how I couldn't find time to get a haircut, and we even managed to sneak up to our favorite dress shop, The Studio, to put together a wrinkle-free campaign wardrobe.

But we didn't talk about the campaign. Everyone in the *Globe* city room knew we were friends, as did many people in the campaign, and in a town where that's like being a Serb and a Croat, we developed a self-conscious mutual protection society. All that easy professional sharing we had known for thirteen years was out the window; I didn't want Ellen to be in the awkward position of knowing something she couldn't report. We were playing this one straight, with new rules, mutually accepted.

But working for a campaign is a mercurial thing. I eventually left and moved on to a fellowship at Columbia University. Dukakis won the nomination, but not the election, while I was starting on what I really wanted to do: write fiction. A year later, the news that I had sold my first novel came when I was with a group of friends, including my friend Babs, and her family, in Provence.

"Guess what?" I told Ellen that night when I was finally able to reach her back in Boston. "I've wanted to write stories, and now I'm going to get paid for it!"

Now, after all this time, when we reminisce about the exuberance of the Ferraro moment, here we are, writing about the extra dimension that comes from being involved together once again in something larger than ourselves. Of course: the energy, the challenge of creating something together as partners.

We look at each other in a small writing room perched above Radcliffe Yard where the sun is pouring in, sitting over two desktops laden with coffee cups, pink and yellow Post-Its, file folders, and a half-eaten box of gingersnaps. Of course: that energy and challenge is what brought us to this book.

10

Testing the Limits

Pat

To tell this story, I have to take a big step backward in time—back to the early eighties. Through a series of small catastrophes—high interest rates, an unsold apartment, a bridge loan on my home that I couldn't pay back— I was in financial trouble. I had cashed in all my savings to keep up the two mortgage payments, and the bank was pressing for its money.

All in all, it was not a nice situation, and certainly not one I could hide from Ellen. We already had almost ten years of close friendship behind us, and hiding this particular elephant in the corner wouldn't have worked.

And yet . . . I held back on some of the awful details. When she would ask me how things were going, I would find some way to say, "It'll work out," or "Don't worry, I'll figure something."

She knew better, and I knew better. She offered a couple of times to lend me money for breathing room until a buyer for the apartment finally showed up, and I was deeply grateful that she was willing to reach out and offer to be my safety net. Thanks, my friend, but no thanks.

Borrowing money—serious money, not lunch money—is not on the basic list of what you ask of a friend. I was afraid that doing so might somehow change the terms of our relationship. I worried, would it alter the balance? What does it mean to owe a friend more than affection? My fears were hard to articulate, and I didn't try. Nonetheless, Ellen found a few gentle ways to let me know she didn't think much of that line of reasoning.

As it happened, time did run out. No buyer appeared and the bank was now increasingly persistent. The third time Ellen offered a loan—"Pat, you need the money and I can lend it to you, let's get serious"—I accepted.

This was definitely new territory for us. I kept hearing my father's voice in my head, warning me that lending money often means the end of a friendship, and here I was, on the receiving end. I felt a niggling sense of change—not in her, but in me.

Once the loan was made, it went off Ellen's screen, but not mine. I found myself thinking about it when we were talking about totally unrelated things, feeling in some vague way that I now had to be financially accountable to her. (What business did I have talking about buying new shoes when I owed her money? If I bought new curtains for the kitchen would she wonder why I hadn't paid her back first? Shouldn't I buy the wine, even though she's on an expense account?) Suddenly I was self-conscious about shadings, hidden meanings, examining my behavior, double-thinking—all the stuff that gets in the way of an honest, thriving relationship.

I hated it. It was driving me nuts. Somehow I wasn't operating from strength; I was tiptoeing. I knew the fact of the loan was more important to me than it was to her, and I knew that if anything in our friendship would be altered because of this, it would be because of me. But the old taboos about borrowing money and being "in debt" to a friend were potent and they were seeding troubled feelings.

We came to our friendship as most women do, without a single whiff of responsibility for each other. We had, Lord knows, enough responsibilities to families and bosses. We were each other's spring break, each other's recess, friends with no strings attached. The only thing that brought us together was the pleasure of each other's company, a fine-tuned meeting of the minds. What *kept* us together was comfort, understanding, caring, fun.

This is, of course, part of the delightfully voluntary nature of friendship—we are together because we want to be, not because we have to be. Friends feel lucky, chosen, precisely because there are no constraints, noth-ing between the friend and the door. At the early stages friends are obliged to do almost nothing for each other. Friends play and confide and if things don't work out, they move on.

Sociologist Ann Swidler puts it quite plainly: "Modern friendship works in part because it isn't so demanding. It's turnonable, and turnoffable. Friends are like a line of credit at the bank, but you don't draw on them all the time."

And yet we, like many women friends, moved deeper into our relation-ship rather than moving on. Over time we expanded the borders of our friendship, expanded our sense of responsibility for each other. We gave and got, built up layers of connection and, inevitably, expectation. No, there was no social contract to sign about rights and responsibilities. There were no laws governing this relationship, no agreed-upon hours and wages, no negotiated conditions of continued employment. But gradually, with-out verbalizing it, we made our own rules and guidelines.

Each of us could say it: I'd do anything for her. Yet that assumption is in-evitably tested. The expression friends use so liberally—"She's always there for me"—does get a trial run. The emotional connection, the original ties that are so strictly personal, are tried out in daily life. Is your friend there for you when the mammogram looks dicey? Is she there when you need someone to do you a big favor, beyond a trip to the drugstore, or Fed Ex-ing a package, or jump-starting the car, or watching the kids overnight? You may need someone to care for the kids for a matter of weeks, to help bail out the basement after a flood, to come and stay when chemotherapy has made you sick as a dog, or tide you over a damn bridge loan.

The silent questions mount: How much can I count on you? What will happen if I ask? How would I answer? Am I upping the ante too high? What if she says no? What if I say no? Is it better not to ask?

These questions are posed against a particular cultural backdrop. We do honor the role of friends in our lives and expect them to help us—but only up to a point. There really are a lot of subtle messages in our society about the limitations of friendship.

When Robert Frost wrote that "home is where, when you go there, they have to let you in," he was not talking about a friend's home. There is a threshold that friends aren't expected to cross. "The friendship model is part of the fantastically voluntaristic notion of obligation in the Western and Anglo-American world in particular," as political scientist Jane Mansbridge said. "I voluntarily enter, I voluntarily leave. You enter into friendships so long as they're good for you, and then you leave them. Not like family."

For the most part, middle-class American women are more likely to call upon friends for emotional support than for functional support—or financial support. We call on friends when we can't figure out feelings. But we are more reluctant to call on them when we're in other sorts of trouble. As Mark Twain once said, "The holy passion of friendship is of so sweet and steady and loyal and enduring a nature that it will last for a whole lifetime, if not asked to lend money."

Ann Copeland, who writes a cross-cultural newsletter for foreigners in America, says many newcomers are surprised that American friends are so willing to share feelings—but so reluctant to ask each other for child care help. In the cities, professional couples will hire a baby-sitter before they ask a friend to baby-sit on Saturday night. A mother is more likely to trade such favors with other mothers than to ask a childless friend—often uncomfortable that she might not be able to "pay her back." In fact, the higher people are on the economic scale, it often seems, the more likely they are to pay for help, and the less likely to ask for it from their friends, unless they are pretty sure they can reciprocate. In general, urban Americans are wary of feeling obligated to each other.

This tendency is part of the other cultural message about independence that we have seen in the background of this story of friendship. Friends come to each other as equals, freestanding independent people. Part of the reluctance to push the boundaries of friendship is built on the subtle fear that it will transform a relationship between free agents to one of mutual obligation. It is built on the fear that a relationship between equals will be transformed into a relationship of dependency. And to a great extent in our contemporary society, dependency is still a source of unease, weakness, and even shame.

Dottie and Diane, the two former welfare mothers, had no sense of this unease when they helped each other out with lunch money. They knew they were in the same boat, which mattered a lot more than worrying about who-owed-who-what. Yet when Pat found herself in need of money—the most emotionally loaded of currencies—she brushed up against a potent middle-class cultural message. For if there is a symbol of inequality in our society, it's the dollar sign.

Money is such a loaded topic, people who have known each other for years, who have told each other about affairs or abortions, wouldn't think of revealing their salaries or just exactly how much they've made in the stock market. We felt ourselves far beyond such cautions, which made it even more surprising to find ourselves on such awkward terrain.

We both believed strongly after a decade of knowing each other that friendship was indeed the third leg of the stool that holds up our lives. But would it falter under a different test?

Ellen

The time of the bridge loan, the big, bad bridge loan, looms larger in Pat's memory than in my own. After all, she was the one in trouble. I remember trying to make her laugh—"Bridge loan? Where do they come up with these names?"—but she wasn't amused. The theory is that the bank loans you money to get from one safe shore to another. But the waters were rising over her kneecaps and heading north.

In retrospect I was conscious from the outset of the risks of lending money. She might start editing her conversations about finances. Or shopping. The rough equality of our early friendship when we were both running on empty could become unsettled.

One of the risks of allowing money to enter a relationship between friends is that these friends take on new roles—some with pretty negative titles, like *borrower* and *lender, deadbeat* and *repo officer.* There are lots of ways to introduce an element of awkwardness, self-consciousness, inferiority, or superiority when one person needs the other's help. When all the stuff that surrounds money is brought to the table of friendship, it can make it shaky.

The truth is that Pat always worried more about money than I did. In part it was the difference between supporting four kids and one. In part it was our own family histories. I always had the sense of a safety net. When my dad was in debt after a failed congressional campaign, he handled it, as Anne Lamott would say, bird by bird, or buck by buck. Money had been passed quietly around in my family from haves to have-not-right-nows since I was a kid. I had seen my dad help more than one friend from the old neighborhood.

I knew the rules of the money road. Don't lend the rent money. Don't lend money if you can't forget about it. Don't charge interest—you aren't a bank but a buddy. Fair enough. But after years of barely having enough to pay the bills, I had started syndicating my column and now had some money. Nobody went into the newspaper business then with the idea they would eke out more than a living, but now I had what Pat needed, and while borrowing money is more complicated than borrowing a cup of sugar . . . so what?

I also knew with certainty that if the roles were reversed, she would have been the first in line with that cup of sugar for me.

There's something else. When we started writing about this period in our relationship, I thought, what if I hadn't offered? What if I'd sat there with money in the bank and watched my friend go bankrupt, drown under the damn bridge loan? Nobody would have faulted me. Nobody else would have known. No one would have held me accountable. No one except me.

Had I not come through for Pat, I think it would have been deeply damaging to our relationship. I would have been ashamed that I hadn't done what I could. It wouldn't have fit into my own image of who I am or what I value. I would have been saying to Pat, you aren't worth it.

People don't talk that much about the other side of this story. It's not just one person testing the limits of friendship. We assume that the "good person" is the one who gives. Not so. Not that simple. It's one good feeling to be able to bail out a friend.

Our friendship wasn't weighted nor was the balance tipped by this experience. When Pat paid me back we celebrated the fact that she was out of the woods—or across the bridge—not the fact that she was out of my debt.

The truth is that despite the cautionary signs in this road, friends often really do want to create mutual aid societies. What's a friend for? We ask that not just as a rhetorical question but as a real one. What is a friend for if we can't go beyond having dinner together and sharing the "fine feeling news"?

In any intimate exchange, women share their needs; it's part of building even the smallest society of two or three. But there is a fundamental contradiction between the desire to feel free in relationships and the desire to feel connected. Many want the freedom that comes with distance *and* the closeness that brings responsibility.

Jane Mansbridge, who acknowledges the voluntary nature of friendship, adds another layer, a human contradiction that lies at the heart of the matter: "What people *want* out of friendship is exactly the ties that are beyond volunteering. It's exactly the idea that I can call on you and because you're my friend, you'll do some stuff you don't want to do. We want constancy, depth and, consequently, responsibility. We want to create a dense set of mutual relationships that then oblige us. That make us not free. But we're not willing to realize that that's what we want to do. We want to think of friendship as this free thing: you know, in, out." It is, then, hardly surprising that friends often find themselves stumbling over this contradiction. Do you go to the friendship to relieve burdens, only to burden the friendship? On the other hand, is holding back in order not to put excess pressure on a friendship denying a friend the chance to help?

Paradoxically, part of the particular pleasure of helping a friend is that you don't have to. We were impressed, not long ago, by the story of a woman in Maryland who donated a kidney to her boss and friend. This was an act of great generosity and it was acknowledged that way. But it was also greeted by great doubts. The bioethicists put her through a battery of psychological tests, questioning her motives and how she would feel afterward. This was exactly the opposite experience of family members, who can feel pressured into becoming donors. Indeed, the same ethicists may offer a "cover story" to a reluctant family donor—sorry, not a good match—to keep the family ties intact. The act of friendship is perceived as much more altruistic. No one would dare suggest a friend is obliged to offer a kidney.

We are not suggesting that friendship takes precedence over other relationships. We are, rather, conscious of the boundaries, especially for women who want to help more than they can. We have talked while writing this book: what would happen if one of us were sick at the same time a husband or child were sick? We know the answer. Our families come first.

But in small, less dramatic ways, a lot of friends are stymied from doing what they wish—not only by competing responsibilities, but by the ordinary constraints of that old nemesis of modern life, the time bind.

We have a friend in Philadelphia, a young mother with a full-time job and three young children, who told us that at this moment in her life she can only have friendships that simmer on the back burner. Any friend who wants more than an annual reunion or a birthday lunch is going to be disappointed and drift away. Her idea of a high-maintenance friend is anyone who calls after six. And she admitted as she said this to us, the rules have left her lonely.

Jane Mansbridge remembers her own frantic child-rearing, career-building years. At one point during that time, she had a close friend for whom everything was going wrong at once.

"God, is there anything I can do to help?" she asked.

"If you could take the kids one afternoon this week, it would be fantastic," her friend said immediately.

Mansbridge recalls hesitating for a split second, her datebook flashing before her eyes. "Um . . . is there anything else I could do?" she said.

She still feels terrible. She didn't have an afternoon. She felt she had betrayed her friend or, to use a more gentle phrase, she had let her friend down.

"I had this horrible wrench of, I don't want to live in a world where my friend is up a wall and says can you give me an afternoon and I have to say no. That's not the world I want to live in." It was a memory that would shape her response years later to a friend with cancer.

Most women don't think of helping friends, in Swidler's terms, as a line of credit. It seems somehow too utilitarian, as if you are keeping some internal accounting system that says—let's see, she brought dinner when my back was out, I'll bring breakfast when she has the flu—but in some ways, when the tests come, you are making a choice. You are building a community of friends, that reciprocal mutual aid society, or not. You will be there for them, they will be there for you. Or not.

Protecting yourself from obligation, from responsibility, shielding yourself from other people in trouble, means protecting yourself right out of help. When Patrizia DiLucchio wrote for an on-line news service about friends who step over the limit, she stated flatly, "There are limits beyond which you can't trespass without incurring resentments that can seriously damage the friendship." Fair enough. But she went on to say, "In fact, friendship may operate best as a possibility that is never redeemed, as a psychic coupon without an expiration date entitling the bearer to any number of dramatic interventions, so long as they remain in the realm of the theoretical."

This is, happily, not the experience of women who learn they can cash in those "psychic coupons." When author Anne Lamott was pregnant and single, there was no doubt who would be there for her—Pammy, her best friend of twenty-five years, the "sanest, most grounded and giving person I've ever known." The woman that Lamott describes in *Operating Instructions* as "my guardian" went to Lamaze classes with her, and walked up and down San Francisco's Geary Boulevard while the doctors were waiting for her to dilate, and came with her into the birthing room.

Pammy was literally "there" when Lamott's son Sam was born. She was there for tea and sanity every afternoon and for Sam's first bath and the anxious craziness of first-year motherhood—especially for a mother alone.

Not big stuff. No daring rescue from a rooftop. Just the small daily life-saving and sharing of two women linked since childhood by black humor and cynicism and now connected by a baby named Sam. "It feels good to say 'we' even if that means me and my best friend, instead of me and a man. I could not have gone through with this, could not be doing it now, without Pammy," wrote Lamott.

Yet before Sam could even walk, Pammy found a lump in her breast. The cancer was the rotten, virulent kind that sent her through chemotherapy and a roller coaster of exhaustion and anxiety. When Pammy had to go to the doctor, Anne and Sam took her. "We are always expecting the doctor to say that mistakes were made and that Pammy is actually just fine, but what she said is that they are trying to control the cancer, that she doesn't think it can be cured per se." Now it was Anne who was beside Pammy, taking care of her friend. The terrain had shifted prematurely to illness and death.

It wasn't easy. Even Lamott, in the honest way that she has of never letting herself off the hook, remembers the week when her ailing friend went away with her husband to the ocean. Part of her missed Pammy, but she wrote, "A small, bad part of me is glad to get a week off too."

When a friend is in need, most women try hard to deliver, even when the story sounds like something out of an Agatha Christie mystery—even, as a matter of fact, when it is a *true* Agatha Christie mystery.

Nan Watts went way beyond the limits for her best friend, Agatha Christie, the great English mystery writer. The year was 1926. Christie was having marital troubles and asked Nan to help fake her death so the police would suspect her faithless husband was a murderer. Just for a few weeks. Just long enough to thoroughly scare and embarrass him.

Watts agreed, and what ensued was an eleven-day disappearance that created an international media scandal before Christie was discovered registered under an assumed name in an English country inn.

This quirky and sad caper began the day Agatha drove to London from her home in Berkshire after a fight with her husband, Archie, over his insistence on a divorce so he could marry his mistress. Nan was worried that her friend, an intense, private, and emotionally fragile person, was becoming obsessed with her fiction-writing career. But she also resented Archie's cruelty, and thought he deserved a comeuppance. So she helped spirit Agatha away to a hiding place.

The next morning, Agatha's abandoned car was found. She had driven it to the edge of an embankment and watched it plunge down the hill before taking the train back to Nan's house, where the two friends hatched an amnesia defense, to be used later when she would be "found."

The ensuing uproar shocked them both, and, as the days went by, they didn't know what to do. Finally, two musicians at the country inn where Agatha was staying under an assumed name told the police about a "Mrs. Neele from South Africa" who fit the description of the missing novelist. Agatha and Nan's plot had unraveled.

Archie was furious with them both. Out of his own embarrassment and fear of more publicity, he backed his wife up on the amnesia defense. But the marriage was over.

In the hurtful time that followed, friends took sides. Agatha divided them into categories: those who remained loyal were members of the FOD (Faithful Order of Dogs) and those who deserted her were the FOR (Faithless Order of Rats.) The stalwart Nan never wavered. She even lied to Archie during the time Agatha was missing, professing herself horrified at her friend's disappearance. For this friend, signing on meant following through; even for a scheme as over the top as this.

Did Agatha ask too much? Should Nan have agreed?

There are clear-cut cases when a friend asks or expects too much. It happens with teenagers all the time, when loyalty is demanded above other values. It happens with adults too. When a married friend of freelance writer Sandy Banks of Los Angeles wanted her to pretend they were together as a cover for her extramarital affair, this was, for Sandy, beyond the pale. The friendship foundered.

There are times when friendship isn't deep enough for what is asked. There are times when, with great difficulty, you have to say no. A friend of ours in Washington was touched when a casual friend asked if she would be willing to be named guardian for her children if she died. Some women willingly do this for each other, but it is a responsibility few people take on lightly—and the woman had the delicate problem of saying no.

And there are times when you don't "come through" for a friend because, in fact, you decide not to. You draw the line. As DiLucchio observed, "There is a fine line between friendship and co-dependency." Or, as a friend of hers said, "Everyone is entitled to two calls at four o'clock in the morning. But when that third phone call comes, I turn off the ringer and go back to sleep."

Most of us believe a true friend does not turn off the ringer. Most of us believe we would indeed take that third phone call. But sometimes limits are reached.

Barbara Corday, a striking woman with large dark eyes, began her Hollywood career as a television writer, and achieved her greatest writing success as cocreator of *Cagney and Lacey,* one of the most successful television series of the '70s. Her partner in that endeavor (and many others) was the woman who became one of the closest friends of her life, the late Barbara Avedon. Their collaboration ended in a mix of trauma, confusion, hurt, and loss, just before their show took off and became a hit.

What happened to two women who trusted each other with everything, who took care of each other's children, who forged from their friendship one of television's most storied writing teams? How could there come a point where Corday felt she had to give up and walk away?

It is that story Corday sets out to tell at her spacious home in the Hancock Park neighborhood of Los Angeles. "It still boggles my mind that this happened to us," she says, gesturing with long, graceful, well-polished fingers. She settles back into a plush upholstered sofa in her living room, the lingering glow of a long, warm twilight touching on the richly hued oil paintings that hang on her walls.

"Barbara and I went through the women's movement together, we went through the Vietnam War protests, we were one of the few working writer teams of women in television. Divorce, marriage, kids, everything that you could possibly imagine, we went through together . . . and yet we came to a point where although there was a connection that would always be there, that connection on another level was irreparably broken."

In 1968, Corday was a twenty-three-old publicist staying home with a new baby. She first met Avedon at the jumbled Los Angeles offices of Avedon's anti-Vietnam group, Another Mother for Peace. Corday had come to volunteer and quickly was swept into the excitement, trekking off with the group—her baby strapped on her back—to join an antiwar demonstration in Washington. She was new to political activism and the sight of people writing impassioned press releases and making frenzied phone calls for something they believed in was a powerful draw. Barbara Avedon in particular impressed her—initially with her energy, enthusiasm, and skills as an organizer. "Suddenly I was actually participating in something much larger than I and doing something," she remembers. "For me, the beginning of my politics was Barbara."

Within a short time, the two Barbaras, each with a small baby, became friends. And after Corday's divorce the following year, they were also sharing the problems and travails of single working mothers. At one point, Corday suggested that she and the far more experienced Avedon (who was fifteen years older and already a successful television writer) try writing a television series together. Avedon agreed. "It was really amazing that she took me in as a partner when I was in my twenties and very inexperienced," Corday says. "And she never made me feel like the junior partner."

Each gave the other something she didn't have; Avedon was the one who spilled out the ideas and Corday was the one who shaped them into coherent dialogue. The collaboration clicked. Soon they were getting jobs, working together every day, having the time of their lives. They merged as writers, and even as mothers. After a while, each was comfortable talking with the other's child over the phone, solving problems, arranging for pickups, lessons, whatever needed to be done.

They chose an office by timing the distance from their homes and renting a place exactly halfway between the two of them. "We worked in a room that cost fifty-five dollars a month and was probably about the size of this coffee table," Corday says. "We had half a window, because the room had been divided into two offices, and the people next door got the other half. We had room for two desks, two chairs, one phone, one typewriter, and us, and we would start every single day talking about our lives, our kids, our needs, our this, or that. A piece of us went into everything we wrote, everything we were, because we were so connected to each other."

And here was where these two friends—with the backing of executive producer Barney Rosenzweig—gave birth to a pretty extraordinary pair of fictional friends, two women who were equals, not star and sidekick, whose adventures and tough-minded friendship would eventually capture huge television audiences. Their names were Chris Cagney and Mary Beth Lacey.

Cagney and Lacey were New York City cops. Cagney was hip and single and a recovering alcoholic, and Lacey was a married working-class mother—and nobody had met women like this pair on television before. "There never were shows about two equal women friends," Corday says. "What we wanted to do and did was write a show about two partners, because that's what we were; we were best friends who might not under other circumstances have gotten together—but there we were."

That part of the creation of *Cagney and Lacey* brings back memories of Avedon pacing the floor of that tiny office in her jeans and sweatshirt while Corday banged away on the typewriter, laughing and arguing and putting it all together. "She was so charming and funny and talented, and I felt incredibly lucky," Corday says quietly.

But the luck, if it was luck, turned bad. Avedon and her ex-husband became embroiled in a child custody dispute over their thirteen-year-old son, a dispute so bitter, according to Corday, that Avedon became increasingly anxious and depressed.

Worried, Corday accompanied her friend to the courtroom every day. "To watch someone you really care about go through something so personal and so difficult . . ." Corday pauses, looking for the right words to end her thought. She gives up, shakes her head. "They were both very nice people and they both loved their son very much—it's hard to explain."

Barbara Avedon won the custody fight, but Corday describes the aftermath as a long spiral downward. Indeed, she believes Avedon suffered a major breakdown.

"She had trouble getting dressed in the morning and was in a depression, and would stay home a lot. Our professional relationship was kind of in question because I needed to work, and she didn't want to work. We were really struggling after all those years of being so intensely close."

Avedon took some time off during this shaky period to go to Europe for a couple of months, and Corday in her absence collaborated with someone else on a writing project. "I needed the money," she says, feeling guilty about it even today. "I felt like I was cheating. It was such a big, big decision. It was such a big thing to do."

There's no way of knowing how Avedon, who died in 1994, felt about this, no way of knowing what she thought of what was going on. But the dismantling process of their collaboration was well under way. Corday stopped writing and went to work at ABC as an executive. Without work uniting them, her contacts with Avedon began to dwindle. Stories were circulating about Avedon's behavior, which, Corday says, was becoming increasingly erratic and puzzling. Avedon was taking on writing jobs on her own, but the rumors that came back to Corday were that her old collaborator was developing a reputation for not finishing scripts.

Corday went her own way, from ABC to the presidency of Columbia

Television. And then, ironically, just as their own friendship was in disarray, the brainchild of this friendship, *Cagney and Lacey,* finally took off.

"During the entire span of time that *Cagney and Lacey* was on the air, I was a pretty public person in Hollywood and Barbara was in her worst time," says Corday, who gives credit to her then-husband Rosenzweig for the series' lift-off. "Here we had this hit show on the air, and I was becoming more and more visible, and she was becoming more and more invisible."

There were forced reunions, where the cocreators of one of television's most remarkable teams would be feted on this stage or at that dinner, reunions that felt completely awkward to Corday. On the television screen were the two policewomen they had created—characters who had transformed the ordinary images of women friends in a spectacularly successful way—offering up this icon to millions of viewers. But now, *Cagney and Lacey* only underscored the hollowness of the friendship of Corday and Avedon.

One day, Avedon showed up at Corday's house. But it wasn't to talk about where they were as friends in the aftermath of their severed collaboration. The visit had another purpose.

As Corday replays it, Avedon pulled a manuscript from her bag and handed it to her. "I've been writing a screenplay, and I think it's really good," she said. "You know all these people—will you send it around for me? It is really good."

"Sure, of course I will, I'll do whatever I can to help you," Corday remembers replying.

When Avedon left, Corday opened the script with some apprehension and started to read. The first twelve pages were filled with writing that made little sense—and the rest of the script was literally blank.

A few days later, she began receiving envelopes in the mail with scraps of paper inside scrawled with more illegible gibberish.

"I was frightened and worried," Corday remembers. She called Avedon's ex-husband to alert him (which in itself felt like a betrayal after the custody battle).

As Corday tried to help, she said, the stories about Avedon began to accumulate, stories of a woman seemingly in the middle of a breakdown, a woman who would go on and off medication. There was the time, she heard, that Avedon brought a hitchhiker to a party and ended up taking him to script meetings as her partner, the times she was hired to do *Cagney and Lacey* scripts and never finished them, the time she wrote the president of CBS, demanding the show go on the air Sundays at 7 P.M.

"She just lost her reality," says Corday sadly. "You never knew what she was going to do." She feels what was happening to her old friend was something she could neither control nor cure. But that didn't relieve her own turmoil.

"I felt guilty for being on my own, I felt guilty for being successful, and I felt guilty for not being able to do anything for her. I felt guilty for not being able to give her work," she says softly. "I felt guilty all the time."

Corday remembers only one more significant meeting, which took place about a year before Barbara Avedon died. They met for lunch, and Avedon, all bubbly and looking terrific, told her she was moving out of Los Angeles to Palm Springs. She said she was going to be writing for a magazine there, and she was working on a play, and she was getting her life together. They had a great lunch, Corday said, and she felt enormous relief. They would stay in touch; and she was convinced her friend was in much better shape.

And then one weekend less than a year later, Barbara Avedon's son called. He told Corday his mother had died. She was shocked. "I've known you all your life, how could you not have told me what was going on?" she asked the son. "He said, 'she wouldn't let me. She wouldn't let me tell anybody. She didn't want anybody else except me to be around.'"

After piecing it all together, Corday believes this: Avedon knew at the time of their last lunch that she was suffering from cancer, and she wanted to get out of Los Angeles. And clearly, she neither wanted nor would ask for help from her former friend and partner. "I believe she knew we weren't going to see each other again," Corday says. "I kind of believe that."

Even now, as Corday looks back on the ending of their friendship, she seems to be listening for the "missing words," the language that Avedon could have used to explain what really happened. The relationship between these two women who talked and wrote and collaborated through the best part of a decade, these women who created two friends in their own image, ended in a particularly jolting way: with silence.

Avedon's expectation that Corday could help her may have been as unreasonable as the idea of selling a blank manuscript. We think sometimes of what Letty Pogrebin observed: "Friends are like violin strings: They can make beautiful music, but if drawn too tight, they snap. Unhappy, overly dependant people may need more help than any friendship can provide." Yet Corday still carries a kind of survival guilt, an undertone of regret: Did I let her down? After connections have been shredded, there rarely is a satisfactory answer for this kind of remorse. We have talked to many women about the end of a friendship who wonder, with no clear answer: Did I let her down?

That concern will lead friends to walk the extra mile for each other in exceptional ways. One woman explained to social science researchers why she put aside her opposition to abortion long enough to support a friend who was having one: "I went through the entire procedure with her, from the clinic to the abortion itself . . . I did it because she is my friend and because I just—it was something I felt I had to do and you know, I love her and . . . I knew if I didn't, God knows what would happen to her."

Yet what happens when one friend walks the extra mile for another—right into a confrontation? It's so much easier to carry a pie to a sick friend, to be on her side against the world, to comfort rather than to confront her. Even if she's wrong. But there are times when testing the limits of friendship means telling the tough truth. "Good friends won't let you off the hook when you shouldn't be let off the hook," offers writer John O'Donohue. Is the "hook" the opposite of empathy? Do friends who confront each other no longer "know just what you mean"?

Jane Hickie and Ann Richards.

In our own friendship, we have counted on each other not just for a listening ear and a murmur of assent, but for a reality check. When I'm wrong, tell me. We may not want to hear it, but we listen when the assessment is relayed, we hope, gently but honestly.

Yet we have never had to risk everything to break through a rock-hard shell of denial. We've never had to tell each other something as difficult as—well, listen, you're an alcoholic.

This was the challenge for Jane Hickie, a longtime friend of Ann Richards, the colorful Texas politician with the quick wit and the mother-of-pearl hair who would eventually become governor of Texas. The political powerhouse who could—and does—intimidate with a cool, cadenced stare; the woman who shriveled George Bush from the podium of the 1988 Democratic National Convention with an unforgettable line. "*Poooor* George," she drawled in her Texas twang, "He can't help it." A pause, a slow grin, then her zinger, followed by the delighted roar of the crowd: "He was born with a silver *foot* in his mouth."

But all that came later.

Ann, who is both warm and formidable at the same time, was drinking heavily in the early years of her political career, but nobody—friends or family—felt able to get her to confront the problem. It was Jane who in 1981 finally felt she had to do something. She decided to gather together family members and friends for a carefully planned intervention.

This step was not one for a friend to take lightly. To pull it off, Jane had to lie to her friend, set her up, plot against her, talk about her to other people—all the elements of betrayal. But not to do it? Not to do it was to give up on her. "I thought, well, if she doesn't speak to me anymore after this, at least she won't be dead," Jane concluded.

When we meet with Ann and Jane one hot summer evening in Jane's spacious Washington apartment, they begin by swapping "war" stories of bucking the political system and the political characters that make up the Lone Star state. There was the time Ann got elected county commissioner ("Hell, I had no idea what a county commissioner *did*") and the years they barnstormed the state, stitching together a women's political network. They were making things happen, doing things that mattered, fighting for women's rights, campaigning for liberal causes.

"It was just wild," Ann remembers. "I hope you have the picture here of people who were just burning a candle at both ends—"

"On many ends," interjects Jane. "We were like gasoline and matches."

"We took turns being the gasoline and the match," says Ann.

One story rolls into another, segueing slowly into the heart of the matter. "Ann had an enormous social life, parties you could hardly imagine; Ann, remember the Easter egg hunt for two hundred?" Jane says. "We were always either planning something or doing something—"

"We were drinking," Ann says.

"Yeah, with the same energy and passion we did everything else."

A pause. Jane, who at fifty is fifteen years younger than her friend, peers over rimless glasses, her red hair burnished by the overhead lights.

The mood quiets, the tone changes.

"Things weren't great in Ann's home," Jane begins. "There was a whole lot of suffering. So we were spending a lot of time in a local bar. I worked up the courage to talk to her, and she basically said, 'Butt out, back off.'"

Ann, looking as calm in her classically tidy black suit as she always has, sits at the table, nodding from time to time, crunching pistachio nuts. Almost—but not quite—an outside observer.

"It seemed to me that Ann was getting drunk differently," Jane continues. "She fell, broke her leg—but I was afraid that if I did anything, she wouldn't speak to me anymore. And that would have been terrible." Only when Jane saw Ann driving in her "big gray Olds" at night with the lights off did she decide things had gone too far.

Jane had read about interventions, and she set out to find the people who could make it happen, then kept Ann out of town so her friends and family could have intervention training.

One Sunday morning in September of 1980, Ann walked into the room where thirteen friends and family members waited to confront her. Ann shoves away the dish of pistachio nuts, and drawls: "Sort of like the Last Supper."

"I knew something was terribly wrong when I saw them all sitting there," she goes on. "I immediately assumed something had happened to one of my children."

After being assured her kids were fine, she sat down. After a pause, each person in the room read a prepared statement. One by one they recounted their stories in dreary, hurtful detail, stories of Ann drinking, drinking, drunk. One by one, they asked her to stop.

"It was overwhelming. Unbelievable. A trauma beyond any that you can imagine, and with a dozen people speaking for three or four minutes each, it went on for a while," Ann says. "It was devastating."

Jane lays out her own memories of that day. "I felt horrible. It was my birthday, and Ann had given me a gift—"

"An electric mixer," Ann interrupts wryly. "Probably for daiquiris."

"I was betraying her, lying to her, setting her up," Jane plows on. "Worse, I was talking to her children. When she walked in that door . . ."

Ann looks up at Jane, and adds in measured tones: "It took a lot of guts for Jane to do it."

Richards left that very day to seek treatment at a Minneapolis center for alcoholics. While there, she finally faced up to the fact that her marriage was disintegrating. She knew that Jane had been courageous. But that still left open the question: What would happen to the friendship? Would it be stronger or weaker?

The answer: stronger. Not without tension; not without work. But yes, stronger. "Jane made an almost ultimate sacrifice. She was willing to give up our friendship to rescue me," says Ann. "It was one huge thing to do."

Patching back their relationship when Ann finished rehab was complicated. "I felt very much alone when I came back," Ann says. "I didn't enjoy sitting in bars, telling stories anymore." Her marriage now definitely over, Ann was faced with moving on, figuring out a new life. "I was trying to reinvent myself, to be a person without alcohol, without a husband," she says. And she was determined to do it on her own. "I've never thought it's okay to talk in a way that burdened someone else," she declares.

But Jane remembers this time a little differently. She leans forward, hands folded on the table. "Sometimes you would call and say, come get me," she reminds Ann. To us, she says, "I'd go get her. We'd drive around. Maybe we wouldn't talk."

The two of them sat down with a therapist, and as Jane tells us, they both lighten the story with the shared sense of the absurd. "He wore this elephant tooth on the end of a chain around his neck," says Jane.

"We called him Tooth," Ann says, breaking into a grin. "And he had these big fuzzy cats—"

"And that water garden in back—"

They are off and running again, whooping about Tooth, relieving the pressure of the memories even as they dip back in, spooning more of them out.

There is a postscript to this story. Many years later, the second of these two drinking buddies also crossed that invisible line to problem drinker. Ann's role? One night, after drinking heavily, Jane called to share what she thought was an uproarious joke. "She didn't laugh," Jane says. "She didn't think it was funny. That did it." Ann was her reality check. It was her turn to stop.

An intervention is not what most of us think of as an ordinary act of friendship. Jane risked the possibility that Ann wouldn't listen and would slam the door, a risk that she had overstepped the limits. But sometimes friends can take on a role that even family rejects; it's sometimes harder for families to confront a member about any addiction or trouble—an eating disorder, a drug problem, child neglect. Because a close friend is a chosen relationship, the defenses developed around family may give way and friends may dole out a more powerful dose of reality.

Yes, we have said that family comes first; family is sacred, friendship secular. But in many ways, today friends test and break through the ordinary assumptions and boundaries by functioning as kinfolk. After all, women spend significant chunks of their lives single, divorced, widowed. In middle age, women especially begin to push past the cultural limits. With children grown and often scattered, with time to have experienced the ups and downs of life, this generation of women does not just need but wants to build mutual support systems.

This may be why the baby boom generation, mobile and middle-aged, is beginning to form communities that offer buffers and the help that used to be the business of kinfolk and neighbors. They are crossing the line from the secular to the sacred.

Over the past few years we have heard a growing number of stories— something just short of a movement—about friends who form a caring circle around one person in crisis. It is usually women, often single women, who are creating these deliberately planned support systems. They are offering the support we imagine once grew organically in small towns, doing it as teams in spite of frenetic lives—and the help they give is often provided with as much efficiency as they might use organizing a business.

At one point in her life, Phyllis Katz would have been a prime candidate for organizing that kind of help. Outwardly dynamic and competent, Phyllis was, at that time, the director of employee relations for the state of Virginia. A woman in her fifties with short, gray-streaked hair who favors striking jewelry, she harbored one secret fear. "When I separated from my husband, my greatest fear was a catastrophic illness. If that happened,

I used to wonder—who would be there for me?" she remembers.

That underlying question, that nagging fear of illness, was not one she talked about or thought about too much. But the fear became a reality when she was diagnosed with breast cancer in 1992.

Her best friend promptly came from New Jersey, leaving her family, and moved in

Phyllis Katz and Gail Shea Nardi.

with Phyllis through her surgery, staying for three months, an act of friendship for which Phyllis felt enormous gratitude. She had made it through.

But she wasn't prepared for what came next. The cancer came back and she was told that her best chance of survival was a bone-marrow transplant. This time, her best friend was unable to move back in and her adult daughter was overwhelmed. "She is not a caretaker," Phyllis says with careful delicacy. Her voice is strong, conveying practiced, professional authority. "She is someone I love who loves me, but she is not a caretaker."

Watching on the sidelines was Phyllis's friend Gail Shea Nardi, a woman who had been through similar dark days with another friend. As the two women sat talking together on Phyllis's back porch one afternoon, Gail knew with certainty what had to be done.

"I could see how frightened she was, and how vulnerable she was after her divorce. She was absolutely, matter-of-factly, taking care of her own illness—to a fault. It was pretty scary." Gail told Phyllis she was setting up a care group. "Your friends will be there for you, don't worry."

Gail—the spokesperson for the Democratic Party in Virginia, a person who knows how to get a job done—was not talking apple pies and supportive phone calls. Within short order, she marshaled thirty women for a planning dinner. "My idea was that each of us take a day for which we would be responsible, and that meant calling Phyllis the night before, asking her what she needed."

One of the women piped up: "She told me she needs to laugh three times a day. I'm good for one laugh a day, but I'm counting on the rest of you for the other two."

Knowing her friend's determined self-sufficiency, Gail warned the others: "If you see her refrigerator needs to be cleaned and she tells you to stop, lock her in a closet."

Phyllis, who was not invited to that organizing dinner, laughs at this. "There isn't anything Gail says she'll do that she doesn't get done. I would never take her on."

The group met on a monthly basis to set up the schedule they dubbed Phyllis's Calendar for Getting Well. The practicality of their help, the consistency of their offerings, remind us of nothing more than the old-fashioned bucket brigades.

✦ When Phyllis lay in bed with a high fever, her friend Cindy Aaron and her husband were sitting quietly in the bedroom, committed to staying until the fever broke. She would not be left alone.
✦ When she needed daily injections, a member of Phyllis's group showed up each day to administer them.
✦ When she needed food on the table and her bills paid, it was all done. One bucket of "water" after another, day after day, passed along, until Phyllis was well again.

The women, mostly busy professionals with government and corporate jobs, took time for small gestures of thoughtfulness. "I liked chicken broth and wanted the vegetables strained out. They would do that, and it made me feel as if my mother was caring for me," Phyllis says.

"I was embarrassed by the scale of it at first," she adds. "But they didn't take away my autonomy. The greatest gift these people gave me was the ability to say no when they were ready to help and I felt I didn't need it. I was the most fortunate person in the world. Most people don't get this kind of care until they die."

The core group were friends, but the larger group also included women who came forward unexpectedly. Her ex-husband's secretary, remembering how Phyllis had helped her find a new job, signed on, as did women across political party lines. Even Mary Sue Terry, a political adversary and the lieutenant governor of the state of Virginia, showed up to mow her lawn.

Long after her recovery was complete, long after the cleared calendars of the women had filled up again and they had gone back to their private lives, Phyllis made a significant decision. "I wanted to pay back what was given me," Phyllis says. So she formed an organization to provide legal support for poor women with cancer who need help getting insurance coverage and medical care.

Perhaps the key to a venture such as this one is the fact that no single person was overwhelmed with responsibility; no one friend was weighted down with obligation. Each woman was responsible for one day. And it did something for them, too. According to Gail, they were relieved and happy to see what they could accomplish for a friend. "Think of how many times you've wanted to help someone, but you can't give up your life—you've got your kids, your job, the rest of your life—it gave us an incredible sense of community," she told us.

What is the Woody Allen line? Eighty percent of life is just showing up. People will read into that what they will, but it's amazing and humbling how deeply the simple gestures of life matter. You don't have to be Mother Teresa. After all, Mother Teresa is the one who said that none of us can do great things, but we can do small things with great love.

The two of us are conscious of how geography has kept us from sharing the rhythms of our everyday lives. We haven't been able to be there for each other to pick up the kids or run errands or perform any of the other small "showing up" gestures of friendship. But at times when life hits the hardest and sends you reeling—at times when you need the closest people to be there face-to-face—thank you, we have showed up. Without question.

Ellen

In February of 1991, Bob and I had the early-morning visitor that every family dreads. The police were at our door to tell us that Greg, my stepson, my husband's lovely, funny, troubled son, had committed suicide. I can still describe the policeman on his grim task, my own disbelief, my husband's despair. I can still picture Bob in his navy bathrobe, disintegrating, his head held against the entry wall.

There is no way to describe this pain unless you have felt it. The numbness, the blur, the reporter's knock on the door. We were desolate, in that first moment before desolation becomes an ache, before grief becomes a chronic disease that you learn to live with, a pain that flares up regularly to remind you: Don't forget.

There isn't much friends can do in such a moment. Nothing can make that boy who once ate his way through our refrigerator come back to the kitchen table. Nothing that can make you replay the last months and come up with a different ending. All friends can do is be there.

Our friends were there, though the story of Greg's death is by no means a story of friendship. It's a tragedy that belongs most of all to our family—my husband, my stepdaughter, Jenny, and son-in-law, Bart, my daughter, Katie—and Greg. But if I may put a grid of friendship over death, a grid that says how we find comfort even at the very worst moments, times that seem to defy or even belittle the notion of comfort, I have to remember our friends also.

They gathered in our home to make our own deep sorrow a little more collective, a small bit more bearable. They gathered for ceremony and for mourning and for telling stories. And among them was Pat.

About the time Bob and I were opening the door to that policeman, Pat had just headed to the airport for a plane from D.C. to her daughter Maureen in Seattle. While we were calling and making those horrific arrangements, she was flying west. When I finally called Frank to tell him, she was somewhere over Montana. Pat landed in Seattle and drove to her daughter's small student housing apartment and never unpacked her bag. There was a message on the answering machine from Frank.

When she called me from Maureen's kitchen to my own, we struggled for the words that contain less real comfort than the sound of a voice. And then she simply got back in the car.

That first grim night, Pat drove with the kids back to the Seattle airport and waited for the red-eye that would take her from Seattle at midnight to Chicago at 5 A.M. to my doorstep at eight the next morning. We gathered that night in our living room—Bob, Jenny, Bart, Katie, my husband's family, my own, and all our friends who had known Greg—and we struggled to talk about his life as well as his death. There isn't much I remember from those days, or for that matter those months, but I do remember Pat coming through the door off the red-eye. And in all the horror of the day, it mattered.

W hat you learn as you grow older and life tests you in ways for which you are never prepared, is that showing up matters. The simple, unremarkable, unheroic act of being there, bearing witness, saying in one way or another: I am with you. There is nothing that carries the seal of friendship quite as firmly as being there in crisis.

So many of the women we have talked with stop and remember such moments, sometimes surprising themselves by tearing up at a particularly vivid memory. Maybe it is still a surprise that the person who is not under some prescribed set of "shoulds," the person who doesn't *have* to be there, will be anyway. Maybe it's because the very act of being there is a nonverbal way of saying, "I understand, and I care."

For Nina Totenberg, it is all of the above, and more. From the time one bitter-cold morning in Washington when her husband, Floyd Haskell, slipped on the ice as he walked down the front steps of their home, suffering severe brain damage, to the summer day a few years later when he finally died, her friends—particularly her colleagues Cokie Roberts and Linda Wertheimer—have been there to see her through.

"When Floyd was first hurt, I was just wild, terrified," she said during a conversation in her cluttered office at National Public Radio in Washington. "Through those first six weeks, when Floyd had three brain operations, they would sit with me at the hospital, listen to the doctors' explanations, ask questions, look at the CAT scans—and they made sure I never had to eat dinner alone."

Haskell survived his injury and made a remarkable recovery, but the respite was short. He developed lung cancer. From that point on, life for Nina and her husband lurched from one crisis to another.

Once when Nina was away on assignment in Oklahoma City, an emergency sent Floyd back to the hospital. When she called the intensive care unit she heard news she had both dreaded and anticipated: his blood pressure was plummeting, his heart was in arrhythmia. The nurse told her she didn't think he would make it through. Nina tried desperately to get a seat on a plane, afraid she would not get back in time. She finally flew home on a charter arranged by a producer friend at NBC, crying all the way. "I was terrified Floyd would die alone," she said. When she finally arrived and rushed into her husband's hospital room, Cokie was sitting by his side, holding his hand. "She had been there all morning, because she too had been afraid he would die alone," Nina remembered. Cokie was enough of a friend to know a simple thing: Sit by that hospital bed. Be there. It is things like this that Nina says she will never forget.

Her husband rallied that time, but there were many more points in his last years when she needed the support of her friends. And they came through. "I have never had a friend disappoint me in a pinch," she said quietly. "They proved to be better friends than I deserved." Those who count themselves among that group do not agree.

We talk about going to and through the limits for a friend. But one day we came across a barrier that we had never even thought about. How many people reach out at the very end of their life to create a new relationship?

How many deliberately, delightedly, begin a friendship with someone who will soon leave?

———

We went to talk with Jane Mansbridge as a political scientist. But as often happened in our interviews with "experts," the personal overwhelmed the "political." So we stayed to talk about her friendship with Sharland Trotter. This is a relationship that began and ended in just a year, with Sharland's death.

———

Jane, who is known to her friends as Jenny, settles in with us around the round wooden table in her Cambridge kitchen, mug of coffee in hand. This intense, even romantic, insightful, and sometimes scattered Harvard professor begins to tell us of a connection that began at another kitchen table just a few years earlier.

Jenny first came to visit shortly after she learned Sharland had been diagnosed with liver cancer. The two women knew each other only casually. Sharland's husband, Robert Kuttner, and Jenny's husband, Christopher Jencks, were colleagues, and Jenny was there to pay the classic visit to a sick friend. It was going to be just an hour out of a busy morning, an act of kindness more than an act of friendship.

But from the moment Sharland, a woman just past fifty, opened the door, everything was different from what Jenny expected. Knowing that Sharland had been undergoing a grueling cancer treatment, she was surprised to see her fully dressed. "I had expected to see her looking like a little old lady in a bathrobe, that kind of thing," says Jenny. "Instead here she was, making me coffee."

Jenny smooths back gray hair pulled loosely into an elastic band, then hugs her coffee mug close to her chest. "A cup of coffee, bagels, a table, and two women," she says. "It's the classic scene. If you were to draw a picture of friendship it would be just like that."

She felt immediately that this pale, blond woman had a special aura about her—a kind of quiet, concentrated ability to give attention. She was a wonderful listener, by training and instinct. The two of them drank coffee and munched bagels off colorful Italian painted plates and began sharing the stories of their lives in what Jenny remembers as the most fluid, natural exchange she could imagine. They talked about everything—their young love affairs, their marriages, their children, Jenny's obsession with new curtains for her house (imagine, she says now, telling a woman with cancer about curtains), and of course Sharland's illness. They talked as if it were a beginning. Which it was. But Sharland, a psychologist, was also talking about the difficulty of helping her clients, who had come to depend on her, deal with her illness.

"She was trying to provide for her husband and children and clients. I saw how many people depended on her," Jenny says. By this time, the hour she had allocated for her visit had stretched to the entire morning. When she finally got up to leave, she knew that this energizing, unexpected connection was not going to end with a courtesy call. She had stumbled into a friendship, and she would come again.

At the front door, thinking of how Sharland worried so about being responsible for helping people through her death, she took both of Sharland's hands into her own and said impulsively, "It's okay with me if you die."

She drove home, appalled at her own exit line: "I thought, oh, what a weird thing to say. Ohhh, 'it's *okay with me if you die?*' I don't give a shit? It was ringing in my ears all week, 'It's okay with me if you die, it's okay with me if you die, it's okay with me if you die. . . .'"

When she came over the next week, she didn't know where to begin, what to say, whether or not to apologize. "I have to tell you what I meant," she began.

Sharland's response was immediate. "I knew exactly what you meant. You meant that you could be there for me, but I didn't have to worry about you."

"That is what I was trying to say," Jenny tells us, her eyes filling with tears. "It was such a relief to be completely understood."

The sense of being completely understood seemed to run both ways and became their glue. The "visit to a sick friend" became a weekly or biweekly ritual. They talked about everything, sharing '60s memories, telling about their romances, discovering delicious, even silly, coincidences.

Jenny is the same woman whose datebook was once too full to take care of a friend's children for one afternoon. But this time, it was different. As she says bluntly and yet completely: "Death trumps the datebook." There was, she says, "no time for bullshit."

As Sharland's husband, Bob, remembers it, "They sort of fell in love with each other."

Week after week, says Jenny, "We each got to tell the story of our lives to a very rapt listener. I mean, who wants to hear the story of your life?"

After it became clear that the cancer treatment had failed, Sharland became even more determined to see her family and friends through her death. She was determined to make sure, as Jenny says, that she left everyone "all right."

The remarkable part of this friendship was how little sadness was a part of it, how little it was focused on illness. This was not patient-and-Florence-Nightingale stuff. Jenny insists she got as much as—"more" than—she gave. Together these middle-aged women also seemed to get back some fresh, young idea of themselves, almost as if making a new friend took them back to childhood.

Then came summer, and the final realization that Sharland was not going to make it. The two friends, with their husbands and families, spent time that summer on Cape Cod. Jenny and Sharland would go together to the beach or sit on the dock, Jenny wrapping Sharland in huge, outsized blankets. Together they would smoke the marijuana that Sharland now took for the side effects of her cancer. "It was like being zapped back to the Sixties," Jenny says with a bad-girl delight. "We would sit and feel the breeze and tell each other how it felt. I called it 'time out of time'; it was a wonderful experience of being in a place, together, heightened, beautiful."

One witheringly hot afternoon, they struggled up a sand dune with a wholly inadequate umbrella, and found themselves frying under the unrelenting sun. They had a choice of either going back or running down the other side of the dune, which would be faster, but a bit riskier for Sharland in her weakened state. "Her bones were so frail, and she was so thin," remembers Jenny. "I felt worried; I felt I was in charge, and I asked her, 'How frail are you?' If we go down the dune this way you may trip and fall."

"I'm not *that* frail," retorted Sharland rebelliously. The two of them ran down the dune, laughing all the way back to the car, then sat there drinking water, watching the sun filtered through the trees, feeling totally victorious.

"I thought we'd done an Indiana Jones thing. It had taken on these epic proportions—plowing our way through the Sahara," Jenny says with a laugh. "Sharland felt she had proven she could still have an adventure, and I felt I had helped her have it. We both felt triumphant. These moments when she was so frail were slaps in the face of death." Her voice became intense, as if she were still shaking her fist at the fates. "We felt, we can laugh, we can enjoy the breeze, we can be as open to love and the world and nature and beauty and joy as anyone ever was! Fuck you, Death, we can do it!"

To this day, sitting in the house with "the damn curtains" she finally chose, Jenny says, "I'd have to go back to my teenage years to be that exhilarated."

By the end of the summer, they had compressed a lifetime friendship into an hourglass with time running out. Jenny and her husband were slated for a Stanford sabbatical that fall. She and Sharland talked on the phone several times a week that fall, but it was no substitute for face time. In one last "Fuck you, Death" gesture, Jenny sent Sharland a small wardrobe of elegant clothes—maternity clothes that might fit over her tumor.

Then as Jenny was planning a Thanksgiving trip, she had a call from her friend: "I think it would be a good idea if you came earlier," Sharland said simply.

Jenny flew back immediately and joined the cluster of gathering family and friends at the home where she and her friend had spent so many hours at the kitchen table. She knew she was about to lose Sharland. But she had been also given a great gift. "I gave, but there was no imbalance," she says. "She really was always there for me."

At the end of her last visit, Jenny hesitated as she was about to leave Sharland's room. She did have one last thing to say, and it wasn't good-bye. She leaned over her friend's bed. "You know what, Sharland?" she whispered. "It's not okay for you to die. It's not okay."

They had gone in such a short time from the early bondings of friendship to the deeply connected ties that take women friends to the long run. Jenny thought she could accept ultimate loss as part of the equation. But who can?

"I thought she became one person in not just a million, two million. Instead of falling apart like some people do in an illness, she came together," Jenny says. Sharland Trotter did indeed turn the end of her life into an exploration. "Not a morbid looking under the rocks—she used it to explore the joy and to intensify her relationships and that's what she did with me," says Jenny.

In her eulogy for Sharland, Jenny said she found an odd personal comfort in the honest realization that if Sharland had not been dying they would never have become friends. "Death trumps your appointment book," she says again. "And I would never have had this intense a friendship with her if she hadn't been dying. Because I would have said, let's get together for lunch, maybe in April. But she was dying and she said, 'Can you come over?' And I wasn't obligated but I was loving every second of it.

"It was time. The most precious thing we've got. Prime time. And one message I got out of that very, very unusual relationship is the scarcity of that kind of time in most people's everyday lives, and the extraordinariness of taking it, just saying, "I'm goddamn taking it!'"

We got up from Jenny Mansbridge's kitchen table in a sudden midmorning, midweek rush. We were all late. She was late for an appointment in her office. We were late for work. We'd lingered too long, three women, three cups of coffee, a plate of scones (not bagels), the classic image for the sharing of fine feeling news.

But all that morning, the word *time* still echoed. The two of us started this chapter talking about the expectations of friendship and the anxieties we experienced about changing the terms of our established relationship. We talked about money changing hands, a loan and what it meant in a mutual, voluntary relationship of two independent but connected women. It was not a small moment in our own friendship.

How much larger and harder, though, were the other moments when we put down what we were doing and paid that other coin of the realm: attention. When it was inconvenient. When we were needed. Attention, caring, and time can stretch—not break—the limits of friendship.

It is true that sometimes a friend cannot be helped. And it is true that sometimes there's no choice except letting a friend down.

But the terrain that takes us beyond the limits is there to be explored, even under the constraints of our busy, scrambling society. Friends who give more than sympathy and "I know just what you mean," friends who show up and feed the kids and walk the dog and even risk destroying a friendship with a needed jolt of reality find themselves in a different and deeply satisfactory place. And friends who can let down their defenses, who allow themselves to ask for help, putting aside their fears of being overly indebted, are often surprised at the payoff.

11

The Wider Circle:
Friends and Family

Pat

The first stop on my wedding day was a decidedly unromantic place: the federal courthouse in Washington, where Judge Abner Mikva would take care of the legalities before the "real" ceremony at my sister's farm in Maryland. Frank and I chatted with Ab about the presidential campaign and what Congress was up to and Frank told a couple of jokes in the wonderful, easy style that I love. Then Ab pushed some papers over to us for our signatures. Still laughing and talking, we signed them.

"Okay," he said cheerfully. "You're married."

What? What? No ceremony whatsoever? I felt like someone had diverted my attention while the dentist yanked a tooth. I looked quickly at this man sitting next to me who had suddenly become my husband. Much as I loved him and wanted to marry him, I felt taken by surprise. And obscurely cheated. "What happens if I grab this piece of paper, tear it up, and run for the door?" I asked.

"Pat, you're married," Ab said gently.

Now that's a moment when you need a friend. Fortunately, the one I needed was holding my hand, and he knew what was missing—our community of family and friends.

So, as we drove out to my sister's house, we solemnly agreed we weren't married. The courthouse stuff didn't count. I felt much better.

And then on that snowy day in January of 1988 on my sister's porch, we pledged ourselves to each other in the company of the people we couldn't imagine leaving behind. The ones who were part of what we were creating. The people we loved; the people who loved us.

I was never more aware than on my wedding day of how these relationships overlap and enrich each other. Without family, I would be bereft. Without friends, I would be impoverished.

My memories of the day are like a series of tableaux: my daughter Maureen in her blue dress, playing the flute, as Martin, my brother-in-law, accompanied her on the piano (with the family dog asleep underneath) in that airy, glass-enclosed room with the sun sparkling on the snow-covered landscape outside; my mother, small and sturdy, holding my sister's hand; my other daughters, Marianna, Margaret, and Monica, there to witness this passage in their mother's life. My two sons-in-law, Bob and Steve, my niece, Megan, and my cousins, completed the circle of family I was bringing to this new midlife marriage.

On Frank's side, there was his brother, Don, and my fey, funny new sister-in-law, Carol, and Frank's uncle Joe and his wife, Rosemary.

And then there were the friends without whom I could not imagine making this major life transition. Frank's friend Jim. My sister, Mary. It's a different kind of friendship with a sister. I remember her crawling into bed with me when we were children, howling when I tore up her picture of Montgomery Clift, shocking me by suddenly turning sophisticated and dating older boys. My sister, always funny and wry, the only person in the world I know who has a 97 percent failure rate in getting the right drink when she orders a C. C. dry Manhattan, straight up, with a twist. (They always arrive with cherries.) Who would in too few years be grieving the loss of her husband, Martin. And also the only person in the world who could ever be—as she would be—a full and steady partner during our mother's final illness.

My friend Babs from Chicago was there with her wonderfully irrepressible husband, Burt. My trusted confidante and fashion guru, the woman with more warmth and style than anyone I've ever known. It had been her job several years before to break to me the frightening news that my daughter Marianna had been hit by a car. She had been there to put both hands on my shoulders and say, "First, she's going to be all right. Now sit down and I'll tell you what happened." How could there be a full circle without Babs?

And, of course, Ellen. My friend who could have charted every twist and turn of my relationship with Frank, who had cheered us on, and been there for me when times were rough—could I have "tied the knot" without her and her Bob? No way.

That's the guest list. There were others too far away to come, but these were the people essential to the new community we were creating that would be at the heart of our midlife marriage.

In a very real way, a second marriage is much more complex than an original union: you aren't just committing yourself to a new partner, you are making an act of faith that you can pick up the threads of the rest of your lives and weave them together again. Would I have married Frank if I hadn't trusted instinctively that he would also love my children? I doubt it. Would he have married me without the same trust that I would love his two sons? I don't think so.

A first marriage means creating a whole new world; a second marriage means you come with a whole world—and that means a second marriage can never be exclusive. Part of the joy ahead for me would be Frank sharing a rapid accumulation of grandchildren; part of the joy for him would be me cheering Ben on in the father-son softball games and sharing dinners with the much-traveled Josh. We were both, from the beginning, part of something larger than ourselves.

That "something larger" included not only family but friends. We both valued friendship; after all, we began as friends. That was the glue for our voyage back into marriage (even if the actual transition did catch me by surprise) and is probably why each of us automatically understood the place of friendship in our lives. I married a man who understood he wasn't my only best friend—now there's something that might send some men over the edge. But Frank knew it was all part of the dowry.

For much of this book, we have focused on the intimate, over-the-kitchen-table friendships that we deeply value, talking about what makes these relationships work and stay strong. But here we want to talk about opening up the borders between such friendships and the rest of life, about how much richer it can be if these friendships overlap with family—and enlarge to include other friends. We want to make the simple point that widening the circle in these two directions, as many women know, makes a fuller life.

Sixty years ago, Vera Brittain made this point in homage to her dear friend Winifred Holtby—the creative soul mate who was also "aunt" to her children—in *Testament of Friendship*: "Loyalty and affections between women is a noble relationship, which, far from impoverishing, actually enhances the love of a girl for her lover, of a wife for her husband, of a mother for her children."

Friends can strengthen family just as they can enlarge the meaning of family. But the blending of family and friendship relationships can be uneasy at times. Is the friendship between a husband and a best friend a match or a tense squeeze? Can women remain friends—just friends—with men after marriage or do these friendships trip on the jealousy threshold?

And when it comes to widening the circle of friends, how is that done without friction? How do friends handle feeling "ranked" against each other? How do they contend with strains, sexual jealousy, issues of loyalty, and concerns about exclusion?

Women have many people in their lives—husbands, children, sisters, male friends, work friends, old friends—and they want to maintain a community of caring people. They don't choose between friends and family, friends and husbands, one friend and another; women need them all. How do they keep it all together?

A friend of Pat's told her one evening at a Washington dinner party that, when she was a young wife and mother forty-five years ago, friendship was "the illicit relationship." Friendship had to be sneaked in under the wire, hastily, apologetically. It was necessary to pretend it wasn't important, just something sandwiched into the day among other trivial pursuits. This came from the strong and often unconscious presumption that nothing superseded family. It came from the sense that an intimate relationship outside of the family circle was a kind of betrayal. This presumption still prevails in sometimes subtle ways. One woman we interviewed told us her husband still times her long-distance phone calls to her old college room-mate. Perhaps it is insecurity, perhaps rivalry for his wife's attention, but it leaves her with a chafing sense of having her friendship monitored.

Women friends do talk about husbands. Of course they do. They vent, they tell stories, they share gripes—"Why can't *he* take the dog to the vet sometimes?" "Why do *I* have to buy *his* mother a birthday present?"—and sometimes this makes men wary. They suspect that friends simply support each other's grievances, encouraging each other in some version of self-righteousness. Listen to the words of the sitcom heroine Cybill. When she cannot reach her best friend, Maryann, on the phone to complain about her ex-husband, it doesn't matter—she already knows Maryann's response: "He is wrong, wrong, wrong and you are right, right, right."

Would men be surprised to know what is often *really* going on? Sociologist Stacey J. Oliker reports in *Best Friends and Marriage* that women friends may in fact offer insight into a husband's behavior, as well as the marriage. Instead of trashing a husband with a friend, women are often seeking out their friends for perspective. A friend, as listener or adviser, is often the unheralded support person for a marriage.

We saw that need reinforced by almost every set of friends. There were, to be sure, women who disapproved of their friends' husbands. But for the most part, friends are in the business of understanding, not undermining marriages. And it's a pretty foolish friend who volunteers harsh words about the other's husband. If marriage and friendship is to be a package deal, certain rules of civility apply.

We certainly came to each other's second weddings as part of the package deal. Hannah Arendt once referred to her friend Mary McCarthy's husband as "a friend of the house," an extension of the friendship, someone who comes with the territory. Yet even we still feel great relief that—praise the Lord!—we not only like each other's husbands but are welcomed by them. Not only are we welcomed, we are taken for granted as part of their lives. From time to time, we tease Frank about that retro moment when he said it was great that we liked to have lunch together by ourselves. But dinner? Wasn't that reserved for husbands? He is now the first to laugh.

Yes, there are husbands—and wives—who are not at all comfortable with "others." But we also saw how family and friends can work together. Melba and Linda, the two partners who run a legal recruiting firm in Atlanta, have a friendship that seamlessly connects to both their work and their home life. "She's married to a wonderful guy who I love," says the divorced Linda. "Melba's husband and I are, in a lot of respects, more alike than Mel and I are. If Jim and I hadn't gotten along so well, it would have affected the relationship a lot." To which Melba adds with amusement, "My husband sends her valentine cards."

So women and men can and do fold in the friendships they bring to their union—as long as they are friendships of the same sex. It simply is much harder to weave love and friendship into one seamless web when your friend is a man.

Our culture has come a long way from the days when boys and girls mingled only for the classic mating game. But there are boundaries. The line between friendship and love, or what we used to call platonic friendship and love, has always been sex.

All the advice columns, all the dorm chatter, and many long night discussions are spent trying to decipher affection—when it's friendship, and when it carries a sexual tension, and when that tension becomes the real thing. In one television show after another, it's played out. In *Friends,* a postgraduate collection of coed roommates play relationship roulette; Mulder and Scully of *X-Files* have the classic opposite-sex relationship—with plenty of sexual tension.

The fact that the sexual component is difficult to exorcise raises a larger question. Can men and women really be friends in the first place? We have played this one both ways. In one of those odd symmetries, friendship with our husbands came first for both of us. Pat and Frank would meet for lunch and talk about politics and journalism in the simmering crockpot that is Washington; Bob would come over to make hot-and-sour soup for Ellen's dinner parties, finish with a flourish of sesame oil, and head off before the guests arrived. Just pals.

On the other hand, well . . . we eventually fell in love with our friends. So we are living proof and disproof of the possibility of male-female friendships.

Today, coed dorms are a natural starting place for such friendships. Contrary to what many people believe, there is almost an incest taboo on sex between men and women in close living arrangements. At Harvard, in the current campus jargon, those who break the taboo are guilty of "dormcest." In a tongue-in-cheek article, *The Crimson* warned of the booby traps that await the perpetrators. "There's something weird about being able to walk from your room to the room of your significant other in pajamas," the piece declares. Moreover, everyone knows the intimate details of your relationship. And the breakups can be particularly messy. The *Crimson* says former lovers who live next door to each other often never speak again. This is "like divorcing, but not being able to move out of the same house as the former spouse."

Whether women are in college dorms, working in factories or law firms, if they are in any mixed environment, they almost inevitably forge friendships with their colleagues—which raises the confusing issue of sexual attraction. If you feel attracted, but don't want to be, can you still be friends? Will sex always get in the way?

The movie *When Harry Met Sally* became a classic because it has as good a take as any on this dilemma. The young and callow Harry (played by Billy Crystal) is convinced that no man can be friends with a woman he finds attractive. Then he gets totally mixed up when he asks Sally (Meg Ryan) to dinner just as a friend and, caught in his own ironbound "rule," he struggles to write some amendments:

> Yes, that's right, they can't be friends. Unless both of them are involved with other people, then they can. . . . If the two people are in relationships, the pressure of possible involvement is lifted. . . . That doesn't work either, because what happens then is, the person you're involved with can't understand why you need to be friends with the person you're just friends with. Like it means something is missing from the relationship and why do you have to go outside to get it? And when you say, "No, no, no, it's not true, nothing is missing from the relationship," the person you're involved with then accuses you of being secretly attracted to the person you're just friends with, which you probably are. I mean come on, who the hell are we kidding? Let's face it. Which brings us back to the earlier rule before the amendment, which is men and women can't be friends.

Harry, of course, has in one speech talked himself totally around the circle. Eventually, older and wiser, he does become friends with Sally. And yet, by the end of the movie, they are husband and wife.

If it's awkward to maintain friendship and love in heterosexual lives, it's no easier for lesbian women. Lesbians often put as strong a priority on their female friendships as they do on their love affairs, but the boundaries can blur in equally unsettling ways. The Indigo Girls, Amy Ray and Emily Saliers, know their fans assume they are or have been lovers, but in reality they view romance as a taboo. They both respect their collaboration, want to protect the partnership. Amy describes a state of "constant upheaval" in the lesbian community, with people breaking up and getting together, and the tension of somebody having a crush on somebody else.

"The lesbian community is considered an incestuous community a lot of times," Emily said. "People date the same people over a period of time and end up being friends with their exes and things like that. In fact, my ex-girlfriend is a close friend."

Amy was in a long relationship that was respected by her lesbian friends, but when that relationship ended, she was startled to find that a number of her friends started crossing the boundary, wanting to become intimate. "It was very weird," she confessed. "When some of my friends asked me out, I was like, what I need is friends. I don't need somebody to go out with."

Can we only maintain friends and lovers when sex is off the table? One of the male-female friendships that coexists most easily with lovers and husbands are those between gay men and straight women. More than a few women point out the obvious: they are able to maintain emotionally intimate friendships with gay men—as opposed to heterosexual men—because those relationships are devoid of sexual tension.

We've talked about family and friends and about whether lovers can be friends. But we also want to explore what at first glance might seem to be the easiest way of widening the circle—simply to embrace other women friends.

Friendship is not, after all, monogamous. At its best, as Carolyn Heilbrun said, describing a close relationship between two women in *Writing a Woman's Life*, "They were not enclosed in an isolated relationship, a folie à deux, as some marriages become."

When the two of us signed on to write this book, we had moments of self-consciousness about our other friends. As grown-ups, we don't have to identify "best friends." We don't even especially like the term. If we are best friends, what are the others, second best? But writing a book together was a kind of public announcement.

One day early on, Ellen talked with Otile about this and it was Otile who said with a generous and dismissive laugh, "Don't be silly. I have always thought of us as having an open friendship." As solid as that friendship is, Ellen felt an oversized sense of relief.

Open friendship? "Open marriage," that illusion of the 1970s, turned out to be little more than a prelude to divorce. But open friendship is a necessity.

Pat and Irene walk together every morning in Washington, lacing up their walking shoes for a three-mile route, offering up daily reports on mothers, children, the problems of feeling swallowed up by busy lives and family responsibilities. As we were writing this book Irene became—without missing a step—a thoughtful sounding board for us. She and Pat have been practicing friendship for ten years on those walks, and she knew just what we meant.

Most women have a range of friends, different people with whom they are comfortable in different ways. We all mix and match, depending on our different activities and interests. Pat would not force Ellen—well, she did once—to keep her company while watching the annual Academy Awards show. The truth is, Pat feels Ellen is no fun, because she falls asleep too early. Nor is Ellen about to choose Pat for a round of golf. She can't even calculate her handicap.

The two of us live in different cities, and different social worlds. When Pat comes to Boston, we often eat—roast chicken and potatoes—at Otile's. When Ellen is in Washington, the two peripatetic walkers Pat and Irene make room for a third on the narrow sidewalk. Our lives overlap in many ways, but we do not always walk in sync—and not all our friends even know each other. We also don't know if they would all like each other.

And we, like other women, feel awkward when we seem to be in a position of "choosing" one friend over another. Emotional ranking may be hardwired into our psyches or maybe it comes from that old memory of the clique, of inclusion and exclusion. In one study of grade-school friendships, the investigators found that girls are more likely than boys to narrow their network of friends in the attempt to manage conflicts and rivalries among themselves. It would seem the difficulties of keeping a wide tent are too much for children. The demand for clear and unequivocal "best friends" is too strong.

So when the questions start bubbling onto the screen of adult consciousness—am I the best friend of my best friend? Does she like me as much as I like her?—it feels silly and embarrassing. Women don't like to feel they still have strong childlike insecurities in their adult friendships.

Yet since we began this book, we've noted many tiny but real instances of sensitivity. One fall day, Ellen was driving back from a luncheon with two women who run a Montessori school together. The older of the two was headed west to celebrate her fiftieth birthday with "my best friend." No sooner had that phrase come out of her mouth than she turned to the backseat, saying automatically as if she were ten years old and not fifty, "Of course, you're my best friend in Boston."

Rachel Hamilton, the young actress in Los Angeles, treasures the "balance" in her group of closest friends. "I hate it when women talk about a friend and call her their 'best' friend. All that they're doing is telling their other friends, 'You *aren't* my best friend,'" she says. When one of her group of friends married, the rest of the group were bridesmaids, but no one was officially designated the "maid of honor." "That's the way it should be," said Rachel.

What we know, at least rationally, is that exclusivity denies the real pleasures of a group of friends. It was, after all, a quartet of friends who formed the Ya-Ya Sisterhood. And high school and college reunions are definitely not one-on-one. At birthdays and celebrations, college friends mix—or don't—with childhood friends and work friends. We create communities on this long extension cord of friends.

We have called friends "the chosen family" and yet also acknowledged all the distinctions that society makes between the "real" family and the "chosen" one. But there are times when those distinctions disappear and friends are, after all, family.

We know of no better illustration of this than the story of two Long Island women whose mothers, Lulu and Annie, were best friends. Sally Jackson and Melanie L'Ecuyer have known each other since childhood. What they have together goes beyond simple friendship. They see it as the continuation of their mothers' fierce love and loyalty for each other; it's nothing less than "a cherished inheritance." And it is one they have gone to great lengths to honor, even as far as—well, breaking the law. Or, as they happily prefer to think of it, committing "memorial mischief."

———

Sunlight was just beginning to hit the rolling slopes of the deserted New York cemetery. It was shortly past dawn when Sally and Melanie, dressed in jeans and sweatshirts, pushed open the creaking gates and moved silently inside with a few other family members. They moved carefully, worried about creating too much clatter with the shovels and spades they were carrying. The last thing they wanted to do was attract any attention. After all, if you are about to bury someone illegally, you don't want an audience.

The preliminary work had been done. They carried with them plants and bulbs and annuals and, most important, two tiny ceramic squirrels to be placed discreetly at the grave in honor of its newest occupant, whose ashes they also carried with them in a small box. Annie Jackson, who had wanted no memorial, was about to join Lulu L'Ecuyer.

At Lulu's grave, they dug hurriedly. "Dig until the earth gets warm," whispered Sally's brother. They did, laughing, joking, trying to stay quiet. This was happy work. Finally they placed Annie's ashes in the grave, covered it up, and disguised the site of their digging with new plantings. The squirrels peeked out from behind a tiny jungle of green leaves. Annie had loved squirrels. She used to throw them cashews from the back window of her house, and all she had to do was hit her ring on the window, and the squirrels would come out and wait to be fed.

The sun was getting higher. Finally the job was done and the grimy little crew of gravediggers slipped out of the cemetery, went back to their hotel, showered, changed, and came back for what was ostensibly a rededication ceremony of Lulu's stone.

The priest didn't have a clue.

"I commend the spirit of Lucille L'Ecuyer . . ." he intoned. Under their breaths, Melanie and Sally added, "and Annie Jackson . . ."

It felt wonderful. Afterward they went off together and drank whiskey sours, the favorite drink of their two mothers in their many shared times together. All in all, a perfect day.

"They belonged together," says Melanie, a slight, slender woman with hair cut short and close to her head. "It just seemed like such a right thing to do, that we didn't care about the rules. We couldn't do it properly because Lulu was Catholic, and Annie was not. I mean, this was what had to be. It was meant to be. I never had a question about it."

"Neither one of them had a husband worth being buried next to," adds Sally, a woman with long curly blond hair and a ruddy complexion. "I hate to say that, but . . ."

"And because it was mischief. It was so Lulu and Annie," says Melanie.

"Yeah, it was." Sally grins. "It really was."

We are talking now with these two friends in an oak-paneled, formal restaurant, and it is a long time after their "memorial mischief" caper. Sally is married, the owner of a public relations firm; Melanie is divorced, an officer manager for a law firm, and she has a daughter and grandchild. Their lives are quite different, but they consider themselves almost sisters—the heiresses of their mothers' friendship. And the memories they have of that friendship can still make them laugh—and cry.

The two mothers met just before Christmas, 1951. Sally's mother was in the hospital in critical condition after a problematic hysterectomy, and needed a full-time nurse. The nurse who showed up to help Annie was Lulu, and for reasons that baffled Sally's father, who believed his wife was

Sally Jackson and Melanie L'Ecuyer, 1998.

dying, the two women were soon laughing together, uproariously.

Sally, who was five, first saw Melanie, Lulu's two-year-old daughter, rolling around under her mother's hospital bed, dressed in a camel hair coat and leggings and roaring her head off in a full-blown temper tantrum. "She was flailing around and no one could get her out," remembers Sally. "I was stunned. I was never allowed to behave like that."

It was Lulu who nursed Annie back to health, and their daughters eagerly pull out a picture of the two women taken that Christmas—Annie in her sickbed, Lulu in her uniform, their heads leaning toward each other, clearly enjoying something very funny. Maybe it was Lulu's attempt to wash the ailing Annie's "unbelievably thick" red hair with an awful '50s product, a dry shampoo that she couldn't get out that turned into a gluey mess. Maybe it was just the instant spark between two witty, vivacious women who needed each other more than they knew.

For there was a dark side to this picture. "They both had disappointing marriages, and I think that drew them together," says Sally. "They became confidantes to one another because they didn't have husbands in whom they could confide."

It was worse for Lulu. Her husband drank heavily and was abusive. One of Sally's early memories is of Lulu walking up to their house, seeking Annie, seeking refuge, holding little Melanie and her baby son in her arms.

"Our house was as wild and crazy with alcohol as theirs," Sally says quietly. "But it was a place they could go."

Even so, Melanie remembers feeling very comforted there. "It was a home away from home," she says. "Annie was very loving. You couldn't help but love her. I think she was like another mother to me."

They are both eager to describe their mothers: Lulu's fighting quality, her beauty, her intelligence; Annie's innocent quality, how this could lead people to hurt her. "Nobody ever put my mother first in the family," Sally says. "The only person who did, the only one who really listened to her, was Lulu."

And Lulu opened up Annie's world. She got her friend a job at the hospital where she worked, running the Xerox machine Annie dubbed Harold. Now Lulu and Annie could have lunch together every day—and Annie was able to get out of the house and earn a little money of her own.

When Lulu finally left her dismal marriage, she sold her home and decided to surprise her daughter by renting a house about a mile and a quarter away from Annie and Sally. A glum, fourteen-year-old Melanie thought they were moving to a "horrible, dingy" apartment. Instead Sally, who was in on the surprise, drove Melanie to the new house. Melanie won't ever forget driving in and spying a hand-lettered sign reading: "L'Ecuyer"—then seeing their two mothers waiting on the porch. She was thrilled. Not only did she have a home again, it was close to the people she needed the most.

Sally went away to boarding school, and then to college, while Melanie, after graduating from high school, decided to go to work. But as these two women moved into adulthood, they held on to each other. When Melanie married at twenty, Sally was music director at the wedding. When Melanie divorced twelve years later, Sally was there for her. The glue from the early years, the sense of carrying on the friendship of their two mothers, remained strong through several separations.

Then, out of nowhere, came a terrible loss. Lulu was killed in an automobile accident at the age of fifty-six, when the car being driven by Melanie's stepfather smashed into a telephone pole.

Annie was waiting for Lulu at the beauty parlor that day; she was puzzled when her friend didn't show up, but decided she must have been held up at the hospital. Only when she came home did she and Sally get the news. Devastated, the two of them rushed over to Lulu's house.

Annie Jackson and Lucille (Lulu) L'Ecuyer.
Christmastime 1951.

"On some level, both of our mothers died that night," ventures Sally.

"Absolutely. I know part of me did," replies Melanie.

Annie would live almost another twenty years, but memories of that enduring, lighthearted friendship are what propelled their two daughters to reunite their mothers in the cemetery.

"We don't keep them alive to the point of enshrining them, it's not that," says Melanie. "It's just—it's just they're so much a part of us. I mean, our lives have gone on and—they're so much a part of us."

When Annie died, Melanie went with her friend to help with the sad task of cleaning out her mother's apartment. There was nothing easy about the process of dismantling her mother's life: throwing out clothes and trinkets, sorting papers and letters. But the worst part was finding a worn pair of tap shoes in a box at the back of the closet. The two women sat on the floor and cried, flooded with memories. Annie, who once had dreamed of trying her luck as a dancer in Hollywood, used to put those shoes on and dance for the two little girls, pirouetting around the room, dazzling them with what they thought then was her wonderful skill.

"The killer that day was those shoes," Melanie says softly.

What is it that keeps two very different women with different lifestyles together, now that both mothers are long gone?

They look at each other. They think about the fact that they were, in a sense, raised together by two wonderful women who never quite had the chance for happy lives themselves—except as friends.

"It's like an inheritance, a very cherished inheritance," Sally says simply.

Melanie nods. "That's a good way to put it. It's different. I know that my relationship with Sally is different than with every friend I've ever had. Sally's friendship means more to me than anything. If there was nobody left in the world, and there was just Sally, I'd feel very safe."

Again and again, as we've talked with women, we have seen how family and friendship overlap in more accustomed ways—from friends sharing child-rearing help to supporting each other in the care of an aging parent.

When Mary Gordon had her first child, she knew she wanted her friend, Maureen, a doctor, in the delivery room with her. And when Maureen's daughter was born, she knew there was only one person who could be her godmother: Mary.

When Gillian Brown was faced with the task of finding a home for her mother, who was afflicted with Alzheimer's, it was Inga, her friend and fellow artist, who helped her find the right nursing facility.

And when Dottie Stevens was on welfare and struggling with a difficult teenage son, it was her friend Diane who was there with advice and support. "She always told me, 'If it's the middle of the night, and something happens and you need me, call me,'" Dottie said. Their friendship is so intertwined with family that Diane's mother lovingly refers to Dottie as "my white Diane."

We have had those experiences too. Pat's favorite post-surgical memory is seeing—through the haze of anesthesia—her friend Deborah Howell standing there with Pat's husband and children. Deborah had spent a long day flipping through old magazines in the hospital waiting room. Pat's kids remember the comfort of her presence, and Pat remembers that her ebullient friend was able to make her laugh, even as she was being wheeled out of the operating room.

Throughout life, overlapping friendships become building blocks of larger communities. Sally and Melanie became like "sisters," raised together by mothers who were best friends. There's was an almost organic friendship. But others carefully braid friends and family together into a wider, personal community.

———

When Johnnetta Cole was president of Spelman College in Atlanta, she had a nickname: Sister Prez. A charismatic woman who collects honorary degrees like berries on a country road, Johnnetta takes the word *sister* very seriously. It isn't just a casual greeting between this African-American woman and her friends and colleagues; it encompasses a central fact of her life: family is not a closed corporation separate from friendship. In midlife, Johnnetta and her friend Beverly Guy-Sheftall have created a rich world of friends, families, work, community. Theirs is a friendship about including, not excluding. It's about the creation of a whole life.

Beverly and Johnnetta met—and clicked—in the late 1980s, when Johnnetta was being considered for the presidency of Spelman. "I couldn't figure out why Spelman would even consider hiring this nappy-headed progressive political divorcee," remembers Johnnetta wryly. Meanwhile Beverly, once a Spelman undergraduate and now a history professor, steeped in the college tradition and restless for change, was determined to get this strong and engaging woman onto campus as the first female president.

The surprise was that these two women who traveled in so many of the same circles had never met before. But from the first meeting, they were invested together in a new vision for the college.

We met them a decade later—after Johnnetta's retirement from Spelman—in a house alive with her trademark energy.

———

Johnnetta is standing at the stove, chopping and stirring, throwing together a spaghetti dinner in a kitchen carefully designed to be the heart of a home. Beverly is seated at her place at the table, watching, nodding; her bright polymer earrings catching the light.

These two self-described workaholics, committed—no, wildly overcommitted—academics, describe their childhoods in their African-American communities. There was no rigid line between kinfolk. In the South, especially the segregated South of her childhood, says Johnnetta, an extended family included an unrelated "auntie" up north who would help the kids into a better school. In her own southern family, Beverly's mother's best friend was welcomed in as "Aunt Gert."

This was a model for both of them. Even before they met, Johnnetta believed in creating a life in a personal and political community. Beverly's "fantasy" was of a friendship that was also a meeting of the minds.

So when they met, strategizing for the presidency, "there was this chemistry," remembers Johnnetta. "It was 'I don't have to finish this sentence because you already know the rest of it.'"

But almost immediately after Johnnetta was named president, just as they realized that—at fifty and forty years old—they had set the foundation for a friendship, that circle expanded. This time to include Art.

Imagine the scene. Here is Johnnetta, divorced with three grown sons, newly anointed president of a conservative women's college. At the same time, she has just begun a romance with Arthur Robinson, a man she hadn't seen in thirty-five years. Where could she and Art be together? How could she have a romance in the fishbowl world she had entered?

"I knew," says Beverly, "that she couldn't have him stay at her house overnight. Or be seen going in and out of hotels." And she had a solution. "Yeah, I said, you-all can come to my house."

"That was so Beverly—'you-all just come to my house,'" adds Johnnetta.

Which they did. The courtship of Johnnetta and Art took place on weekends at Beverly's home. A year later, Beverly, who is divorced, "stood up" for Johnnetta at her wedding to Art.

"You know," says Beverly now, "even the most progressive man can sometimes have twinges of jealousy. He has not had any of that and I think it has to do a lot with how we all came together." They were already "family."

By now that chosen family has multiplied. They are kinfolk who feel each other's sisters are their own. Johnnetta's sons expect to see Beverly when they visit—"My sons cannot imagine any holiday or any moment of significance without Beverly"—and Beverly in turn remembers to look for a lamp for the room of one of those sons. Johnnetta has "leapfrogged over Beverly" into a friendship with her cousin, Levi. When someone's niece is in trouble, there is another auntie to lend a watchful eye. The circle grows.

In their overlapping professional lives, late-night faxes go back and forth between insomniac and night owl. Intensely political, they are each other's sounding board. They talk, plot, teach classes together. "There's no question in my mind," says Johnnetta, "that my relationship with Beverly is grounded in intellectual sharing." She stops to list the intellectual connections as if they were genealogical ties: "We're both academics. We're both academics into women's studies. We're both race women. We're both feminists."

And in the overlapping personal world, these "sisters" spend every holiday together at Johnnetta's table. It's just a given. "My first Christmas ever in Atlanta, Beverly was at that table, and has not missed a single one," says Johnnetta firmly.

Like family members too, these women have their different roles. Johnnetta is the one who cooks, whose kitchen is central to her sense of nurturing, whose home is always neat. That's not for Beverly. Her caretaking is of a different sort.

Johnnetta replays the back-and-forth of that first Christmas when she discovered Beverly's secret weapon. "I was desperate," she says. "I have no time. I have all these people I have to shop for. I don't know how to get anywhere and Beverly—if I ever thought this woman was magic, it was that first Christmastime." Now every year, as surely as they will have dinner around Johnnetta's table, they will also get into Beverly's car with Johnnetta's list, set up a combat plan worthy of the Pentagon, and "just blitz it."

As for open friendship?

"One of the things that has struck me over and over again is the absence of a demand on the part of either of us for exclusivity," says Johnnetta. Beverly nods in agreement, deliberately using the language of marriage to describe what they both believe: "If you insist on monogamy, it's just not going to work."

What if one of them moves? After all, these are fast-track career women. That, they tell us, is nonnegotiable. "That is just not going to happen. No, I mean we all move or nobody moves," Johnnetta says firmly.

Beverly says, "We've had that little conversation."

In this overlapping world, made sturdy by its many parts, they find time for innumerable small caretaking gestures as well, from cards to calls. This night, as we leave, Johnnetta extracts her ritual promise from Beverly: "Call when you get home," she says.

Beverly promises.

What strikes us is how directly these two have made a commitment to keeping everything—work, family, friendship—together. And how they have done this reminds us of what we have missed by living in separate cities. We did not, after all, raise our children together. We wonder sometimes now if those turbulent years of child-raising might have been eased if we had been around the corner from each other.

But we were able to offer each other mutual parenting advice and family consolation over the phone and during long visits. And these last years when our attention turned from raising children to supporting elderly mothers, we offered each other insight and advice on the problems of elder care that have driven one or another of us crazy or, sometimes, to despair. Our experiences tell us it is sometimes easier to go outside the family to get perspective on a problem or a relationship, and bring that perspective back in.

We could tick off dozens of examples of the combination of family and friendship, but all we want to do is make the simple point that this combination is one of life's major blessings. Most women live in the circles of relationships that we've described, at home, at work, at play. Not all relationships mix and match, or form a whole. But in the care and maintenance of a whole life, family especially can be strengthened by friendship, and friendship can be strengthened by family. Rather than protecting the boundaries, women benefit by opening them up.

12

The Long Run

Ellen

On a rare spring day, Pat and I are back at the Pewter Pot Muffin House. It's not called that anymore, of course, it's called the Greenhouse Coffee Shop and Restaurant, but never mind. In the evanescent cityscape of Harvard Square, it's miraculous to find that the building is still there, that it's still a restaurant, that there are still oversized muffins in a glass case by the door.

The butcher-block tables are arranged to fit in as many people as possible, and we are seated next to a table of four young women from Malaysia, Japan, and Indonesia. They are eating huge American sandwiches and talking in the only language they share: beginner's English.

It's been a quarter century since Pat and I first spent our long mornings talking—two women, two muffins, endless cups of coffee—over a table in this same space. We are past our silver anniversary. Should we send out announcements?

Toward the back of the restaurant Pat notices two women our age, leaning toward each other, heads nodding, listening, talking. We can almost hear them saying to each other, "I know just what you mean." We order lunch from a young waitress who oozes loneliness—"All of my friends have moved to New York"—and we sip coffee that has, alas, not improved at all over the decades.

I look across the table and imagine a reporter's description of my friend: "Patricia O'Brien, grandmother of six." Dear Lord, who is that? Aren't we the same young mothers and reporters who shared all our ambitions, all our yearnings for love, for work, for a pair of jeans that fit, and for a checkbook that was balanced?

At that moment, I see something I've never seen in Harvard Square. A man comes over to the table of Asian women next to us and offers one a flower. She accepts it. Remember the wine? I ask Pat. She smiles.

By now, we know the cast of characters in each other's lives and keep current the running narrative of children, husbands, friends, bosses— "How's Mary's new apartment?" "How's Helen's hip?" "How's the rewrite going on Irene's play?" We take care of each other—she "saves my life" by grabbing me as we cross the street; I save hers by keeping a sharp eye out for the bones in her fish.

We have become people who knew each other when. We have a mental album of sorts that we can flip through for favorite snapshots. We have layers upon layers of memories.

Two people who rarely have lived in the same town have somehow managed to be there for each other. Not *that* long ago, I drove my daughter to college, delivering her to adulthood and a dorm room. The last thing in the world I wanted was to drive home alone to that nest now emptied of all her energy, so Pat, who had been there and done that, hopped on the train up to Philadelphia.

Together we would drive to Maine, a long ride up the East Coast. We went to bed early that night in a Philadelphia hotel after I, the early bird, extracted a promise from my defensive (and by no means fast) friend that of course she would be up and on the road within fifteen minutes flat after the wake-up call, no doubt about it.

When the hotel phone rang, startling both of us out of a deep sleep, Pat headed for the bathroom. Long after I had hung up on what turned out to be a wrong number, I began to realize dimly that the watery sound I heard was the shower. It was 3 A.M., not 6 A.M., but she had responded to the ringing phone like Paul Revere and was damned if she was going to be late. I managed to roll into the bathroom to deliver my news in great gasping hunks of laughter. And then, after two more giggly and sleepless hours we started a trip back home that I remember, gratefully, more for its high humor than for my emptiness.

How many years does it take for two people to feel known to each other? We have exchanged how many birthday presents? I can go through a store now and just point to an item, with "That looks like Pat." Once on a gray weekend day somewhere between my April birthday and her May birthday, in a shop in Martha's Vineyard, I found a hand-knit sweater reduced to a

Pat and Ellen at Katie's wedding, 1994.

mere 20 percent more than it should have been. In a nearby jewelry shop, Pat found a silver necklace that was over her guilt limit.

We hemmed and hawed. I left the sweater. She left the necklace. We talked sensibly about credit card remorse and consumer guilt. She did not *need* the necklace. I did not *need* the sweater.

Suddenly we came up with the idea of giving them to each other for our birthdays. But this was no Gift of the Magi paean to mutual sacrifice at the end of which one has a fob but no watch, the other a comb but no hair. We gave each other presents and gave ourselves permission. Happy birthday. Happy ending.

And that other memorable celebration? After Pat had written a magazine cover story on Hillary Clinton, she was invited to the White House for dinner on May 25. The White House didn't know the significance of that date, but I did. It was Pat's birthday, and I couldn't resist. I phoned in a hot tip to the West Wing social secretary, and managed to keep my secret for a week—an all-time record. After dinner, Hillary dumbfounded Pat by standing up at the table and announcing it was her birthday; a cake was rolled out, and Pat found herself serenaded by the folks at 1600 Pennsylvania Ave. Happy birthday, toots.

We too have had the kind of coincidences and near collisions that friends remember. Who could have imagined our daughters' weddings would come a mere week apart? There is a picture of the two of us, late on Katie's windy wedding day in Maine, me with my flyaway hair, Pat holding onto her wide-brimmed picture hat, her head filled with the last-minute details of Monica's upcoming wedding, both of us laughing at the serendipity of it all.

A year later, when Katie and Soren decided to move to Montana and the separation hit me with an unexpected and deep sense of loss, Pat was the one who caught me up short. "You just get on the plane and go. This is only a loss if you make it a loss," she said.

Our circle has grown. Frank with his irrepressible humor and passion for politics and parsnips. Pat's grandchildren—not quite my "practice grandchildren," but still . . . there was that night when we became the first babysitters for Monica's baby, little Elizabeth—and never confessed how late we kept her up.

There are some things we will never change about each other. After twenty-five years, she cannot interest me in Oscar Night and I cannot interest her in goldfinches—"What's the little bird at the feeder? Is that a canary?" She will never say *kvetch* right, and I will never get the difference between a high and a low Mass. But she has come to love Maine and I have come to respect nostalgia.

These days we yearn less and value what we have more. It comes with the territory. At the table in the Greenhouse we talk more about aches and less about men than we did at the Pewter Pot. We are no longer getting to know each other. We know each other.

Is there anything good to be said for the passage of time? Here is one thing: it's the only way you get to be old friends. There just isn't any shortcut to the long run.

Pat

Let me put it this way. Ellen and I have reached the point where we know precisely what is on each other's bathroom countertop—Advil, Fosamax, all kinds of vitamins, and plenty of floss. But we've known each other long enough to remember the tampons under the sink, too. We've gone from talking about sex to hormone therapy, from racquetball to knee surgery, from toenail polish to orthotics. We've watched each other's children grow, and had the joy of seeing her Katie and my Monica married just a week apart. We've gone from remembering everything, to having to remind each other what to remember, to forgetting everything at the same time—not a good situation (and rare, we both insist).

I can't think of my life of this past quarter century as separate from this friendship. There would be huge gaps, empty spaces. In truth, if Ellen were suddenly blipped off my screen, anyone curious enough to care would wonder if there had been a computer meltdown. She has been part of every chapter in my life in the last quarter century, every transition, either as a player or a counselor. Who else would I have trusted to shop with me for my first official mother-of-the-bride dress when my daughter Marianna was married? Who else would have understood what a shock it was to see all those silk old-lady dresses being hauled out of dress-shop backrooms for my presumed approval?

It's also been a lot of fun. Especially given the fact that each of us is the sworn repository of a lifetime of secrets and the sworn protector of the other's most obnoxious failings, like our mutual inability to read a map.

A few years ago we set off together for Florida for a work-and-walk week, accepting the hospitality of a friend who offered us his vacation house in Coconut Grove. We headed out of the Miami airport into the nighttime darkness in a rented car with a map, an address, and a set of keys—which would have been enough for most people, except I made a wrong turn onto the highway and headed north instead of south. Ellen was directing me out of this screwup when she realized she was holding the map upside down and heading us straight into the Atlantic Ocean. Admiral Byrd could have found the South Pole in the time it took us to find that house. When we finally got there and stumbled inside, we were hungry, but, of course, there was no food. No way were we going out again in hopes of finding a restaurant. It was too dark. We found an out-of-date yellow pages and called a fast-food restaurant that delivered, hoping as we gave the address that they wouldn't ask for directions. They didn't. When our dinner arrived, we gave each other relieved high fives, two friends who could admit to each other—but only to each other—what bumblers we were. In our own way, we felt successful. After all, we might get lost occasionally, but we were together, and on the same road, and in the long run—where it really mattered—we weren't lost at all.

Ellen and I, though we laugh about our shared quirks, also provide each other balance. I'm the one who goes over the top emotionally; she's the calming, rational voice. I will probably always gasp over the horrible stories of violence in the morning newspaper; she will probably always know when it's best to turn the page. She, like Frank, never tamps me down, she anchors me. If being alike were essential to a long-run friendship, we would have run out of gas long ago.

We've never had to reshape the foundation of this friendship. There's been no point where we've had to renegotiate the basic shared principles. When I began writing novels, Ellen, Frank, and Irene were the three people I trusted to keep me on course. Instead of reading her friend's newspaper stories, Ellen was reading my plot summaries—and never missed a beat.

The most important change in my life, the one that has separated me most from the rhythms Ellen and I have shared, has been the rapid-fire accumulation of grandchildren. I used to head through airports rushing to connect with a campaign; now I'm cashing in my frequent flyer coupons to visit all those little kids growing up in the four corners of the United States. I am an expert on *Star Wars* trivia, courtesy of my two grandsons, Sean and Brendan. I've pitched balls to Sophie, climbed jungle gyms to retrieve Anna, watched Charlotte at ballet, read stories to Elizabeth, and sung songs to all of them. When Ellen and I go shopping, my eye is likely to be turned by Pokémon displays and size 6x dresses in a store window, and I can't seem to browse in a bookstore without gravitating toward the children's section.

My dear friend will coo over the dresses and glance at the books, but she does so in much the same way I exclaim over the sighting of an upside-down woodpecker—or whatever it is—at the bird feeder outside her kitchen window. It isn't that we're feigning interest, it is that we can delight in each other's pleasures without having to share each and every one.

For all of our two-city existence, through all of our years as friends, talk—either through visits or telephone or e-mail—remains at the core of this long-running friendship.

And as we have grown older, the truth about the importance of "showing up" has taken on greater weight.

It was Ellen who accompanied me on that long-ago tough trip back to South Bend, a trip I needed to make to come to terms with that period of my life. Ellen puts up with my nostalgia, and never dismisses its importance to me.

And when my mother died, I felt as I had felt when my father died—a hole had opened in the sky, and in my heart. I remember my sister reaching for me and saying, "We're orphans now." It was a profound moment of loss, the loss of mother as a person and as a parent, and my family gathered quickly.

When I called Ellen, she and Bob were vacationing on their island in Maine. Dropping everything and getting to Los Angeles wasn't easy; there was no quick nonstop flight to the West Coast. They took a car, a boat, a bus, and two planes to make it to my mother's funeral. (I'm not even counting the taxi.) It is a very long way to come, "just for a friend," on a few hours' notice. But we have shared too many milestones at this point to miss any of the ones that matter, and I will not forget the comfort of her hug as she came in the door of the funeral home in time for my mother's wake. As Ellen said, there is no shortcut to the long run. You get there by taking a car, a boat, a bus, and two planes.

We know in a thoroughly satisfying way that an enduring friendship is one of life's best payoffs. It takes time and focus, and it is frequently a juggling act, but in a world of so many tumultuous transitions, it can be a sustaining pleasure of surprising force. We think of that often as we walk along the sparkling Charles River to the office where we are writing this book, watching a new generation of college athletes rowing through the waters. It's startling to realize we have been friends longer than the people in those boats have been *alive.* That realization is both weird and funny, but mostly it gives us a deep respect for the process that got us here. We have been with each other, talking, laughing, helping, and supporting, covering together many miles of shared history. In a way, our relationship is like a long-distance marathon.

We use marathon as a metaphor because it seems apt for long-run friendships. First there is the energizing start, the terrain that sometimes seems daunting, the steady pace—all the phrases that runners use apply, including "hitting the wall." But one day, we met two women for whom marathon is more than just a metaphor.

These are two real-life marathoners, two pals who are more than running friends. They are life friends who grew up together, live in the same neighborhood, and have seven children between them. They've shared family vacations at Disney World and plenty of beers together at Joe's Bar and Grill. But most of all, since childhood, they've seen each other through bad times and good times, and their shared joy of running has become a metaphor for the central themes of their lives: survival and celebration.

We first meet Pauline Clancy and Nancy Bulger on a Sunday afternoon, the day before the 103rd Boston Marathon. We know that the next morning, these women from Milton, Massachusetts, will be just two of the thousands of people running the classic twenty-six-mile race. They'll be starting way back in the pack, wearing black shorts and white tops and the flapping cardboard signs that identify them as numbers 10,944 and 10,884. They will have a long way to go, but then, they've come a long way already.

Pauline and Nancy grew up in Field's Corner in Dorchester and attended St. Peter's grammar school. They come from large, connected Irish families—especially Pauline, who is the fifth of thirteen children—in an era of disconnection, when frequently friends are substitutes for kin.

"When we were kids, I would go over and say, 'Pauline, can you come out and play?' And she would say, 'I can't, my mother had another baby,'" says Nancy, a lithe, trim woman with short hair capping her small face. The fourth of five kids, Nancy describes herself in a broad Boston accent as feeling a bit left out of the fun in those days, so much so that she remembers trying to convince her own mother to have another baby, too.

In part because of their large families, each woman wanted a friend who viewed her as an individual, who would know her in a way different from relatives. "It's different with Nancy; I feel I have more leeway than I do inside my family," says Pauline, a small-framed redhead with the bouncy look of a woman too naturally exuberant to sit still. "She's more forgiving. In friendship, you tend to work a little harder."

Early on, they discovered the comfort of being understood. One Christmas, after opening her own abundant pile of gifts, Nancy ran over to Pauline's only to learn that her friend had found virtually nothing for herself under the family tree. "She was so sad," Nancy remembers. "She'd kind of been lost in the shuffle, you know? Her mother, God, a heart of gold, but . . ." The two friends look at each other, shrug, and smile. There were so many children, so little organization. In the scheme of things, it was no big deal, just one of those oversights that can't be uncommon when you are one of many. "I'll never forget leaving there that day, feeling so bad," Nancy says.

The next year, Nancy took her own steps to make sure Christmas was different for her pal. She presented an impressed Pauline with her first tube of lipstick ("Oh, it was wicked orange") and her first pair of pierced earrings ("They were awesome").

After Nancy's brother died in Vietnam, her parents chose to leave Dorchester for Milton. "Too many memories," Nancy says simply. So the girls were separated during high school, but Pauline would get on the bus and go see Nancy almost every weekend. They smoked their first cigarettes together, and went with each other to Beach Boys concerts, a bottle of Southern Comfort hidden under their belts. And, they tell us laughingly, they still don't want their parents to know.

Nancy graduated in 1974 and was married by age nineteen, four years before Pauline. When Nancy produced two babies in quick succession, Pauline was no tuned-out single friend without a clue. "I'd walk in and pick up the kids, and I'd put one on my hip and say, 'This one needs a diaper change,'" she says, and she would take on the job.

Pauline Clancy and Nancy Bulger.

After Pauline married and had a baby herself, the two friends were caught in the time crunch: too busy for friendship; too busy, in fact, for anything except family and work. "We wouldn't hear from each other, and then that phone call would come at just the right time," Pauline says.

Then Pauline got hooked on running, and began begging Nancy to join her. Nancy didn't relish getting up three or four times a week at 4:30 in the morning and heading out into the dark streets to *run,* for God's sake, even with her best friend. Who had time for that?

But when Pauline and her family went off on a two-week vacation, Nancy hatched a plan. "I had it in my mind, I'll get so I can go two miles around the post office and back. I wanted to be able to do that," she said. "I wanted it to be a surprise gift, to be able to say, 'I can run with you.'" So she took to the streets and within those two weeks, without even investing in those "funny sneakers," she was up to three miles. She was quite literally going "the extra mile" for a friend.

Pauline came home and found to her delight that she had the running mate she wanted. The two of them started a daunting early-morning routine: up before Pauline's 7 A.M. shift at the hospital and Nancy's job at the town hall, before feeding the kids and husbands, before getting them off to school and work.

On running mornings, exactly at 4:15, Nancy would call Pauline's house and let the phone ring once, the signal for Pauline to slip out the door and meet her friend at East Milton Square, where they set out on their run, talking all the way, about kids, about husbands, about everything.

"The husbands sometimes say we're crazy," Nancy admits.

"But I don't think we're selfish," Pauline interjects. "Nobody else is up at 4:30. We do everything else for everybody; this is for ourselves."

About a year after Nancy first joined her for those morning runs, Pauline suggested doing something *really* adventurous—trying for the Boston Marathon. When Nancy balked, Pauline persisted: "I told her the worst thing that would happen would be she'd get an expensive T-shirt."

"I had no intention of ever running a marathon," Nancy emphasizes. But with Pauline's urging, she got out there and kicked up from fifteen to twenty-two miles, and decided this was looking possible. Before she knew it, they were registered for the race; then she was in the runners' bus with Pauline on her way to the Hopkinton starting line, watching with muted apprehension as the miles zipped by on the Massachusetts Turnpike.

"I'm looking, how am I going to get home?" she says, waving her arms in a mock gesture of hopelessness. "For me to go home and have a cup of tea, I had to run all the way! God, the pictures we got? I look like a scared little kid." She shakes her head. "God, out there watching men do funky things with Band-Aids, everybody covering their nipples—"

"You have no idea the uses for Vaseline!" Pauline chimes in.

They laugh. They love the fact that they ran together, and that they crossed the finish line twenty-six miles later—together. "By the time we got to the finish line, the winners had already gone home and showered," Nancy says drily. And when the high fives and the shouting were over, they were off again for their morning runs, determined to really burn up the miles in the next marathon.

But life has a way of intervening. After a routine Pap smear, Pauline discovered she had cervical cancer. The diagnosis was, unbelievably, given to her over the phone at the hospital where she works as a radiation therapist, and the shock was profound. She reached for the phone and called Nancy right away. "I had to tell somebody, I was losing it," she says quietly. "She was like, it'll be all right." Except maybe it wouldn't be, and they both knew it.

When Nancy hung up, she turned to her husband and said with finality: "I'm not running in the marathon."

"I begged her to run," says Pauline.

Nancy was adamant; she would not run without Pauline.

Pauline's surgery was scheduled for a Friday in February of 1997, and that evening Nancy was in a quandary. Should she go see her friend, or was this a time just for family?

"I didn't want to feel that I shouldn't be there. Then I just said, I'm going to go," Nancy tells us. So she stopped at Brigham's ice cream store and bought a quart of maple walnut ice cream and headed for the hospital, cursing the traffic, knowing Pauline would have known all the shortcuts, afraid she'd get there too late, that visiting hours would be over. She got to the hospital and ran for Pauline's room.

"She was all by herself. She looked at me, and she looked like she was twelve years old again. And I cried, and she cried."

Pauline's eyes tear up. "When she walked in, it was wonderful," she says.

"I'm so glad I went," Nancy says quietly.

Recuperation was slow, but Nancy stayed the course. It took eight weeks before the two of them were able to run together again, and Pauline had a hard time getting back up to speed. Nancy urged her on, feeling that running was the route to health, the way her friend could put the cancer behind her.

"Put it in gear!" she'd shout to her lagging friend, as she altered their course to stop at a Dunkin' Donuts so Pauline could get a coffee break.

"I'm warming up, it's only four-thirty in the morning!" Pauline would shout back.

Slowly, steadily, the two of them were back in training. Slowly, steadily, they moved back into racing—with one change. Always before, they had run side by side. Now they were running with Pauline two paces behind Nancy's right shoulder. But Nancy knew how to keep her friend energized: "See that fat ass up there?" she would whisper, "Let's go get her!" Off they would go, picking up a few seconds, feeling great.

"We're a team. People don't get it. Our friends don't get it. Maybe they're not lucky enough to have this," declares Nancy.

"She takes care of me," says Pauline with a grin. And they talk. "We'd probably win something, if we'd shut up and run."

And now, here it is, the day before the 103rd Boston Marathon, and Pauline and Nancy are ready to go again. Revved up, excited, happy. "They're saying tomorrow will be sixty degrees, that's hot. I can't decide whether to wear a T-shirt or a tank top," says Nancy.

"Nancy always gets too hot, and starts peeling clothes," Pauline says, laughing. "We go on long runs and have to go back and pick up her stuff."

Their goal this year is to run the marathon in three hours and fifty minutes. If they can, that will qualify them for better placement next year. The problem is those assigned numbers: 10,884 and 10,944 are going to be running shoulder to shoulder with a huge number of people during the early part of the race.

"That puts us far back in the pack. If we can hit the halfway mark by 2:05 and we're feeling good, then we're doing good," says Pauline. Her voice is now very animated. "Once we come over the hills, that's when we hope to have some energy. If we make the twenty-one-mile mark at three o'clock, we have a good shot."

"We'll give it our best," says Nancy.

Pauline nods firmly at her friend. "She can do it."

"We both can do it."

"Just be at the finish line when I get there, I'll be right behind you," says Pauline quickly.

The two of them jump up from the table and say good-bye. We tell them we will be on Beacon Street tomorrow morning to cheer them on.

There is one more important stop on their schedule in preparation for the big run tomorrow. Simultaneously they hold up their hands. "We've gotta get our nails done!" Nancy says. "We always run with red fingernails. When we saw Uta Pippig cross the finish last year with those bright red nails, it was awesome," chimes in Pauline.

"We'll both stand out, too," Nancy says.

"You know something?" says Pauline, turning back as the two of them are about to leave. "Less than one percent of the entire world has ever run a marathon. We're the elite!"

Laughing with each other, talking, planning, still strategizing, they disappear from view. Tomorrow will be a very big day. . . .

Sometimes we fantasize about gathering together in one room many of the women friends with whom we have talked for this book—childhood friends Mary and Maureen, artists Inga and Gillian, business partners

Linda and Melba, welfare mothers Diane and Dottie, and many others—
to hear them share with each other the collective warmth, wisdom, and experience that has brought them this far, and that will sustain them for the
long run. In the absence of that kind of all-inclusive round-table discussion, we'll take another look at what we think are the ways women friends
manage to expand "I know just what you mean" into lifetime friendships.

One thing we know: friends don't just show up at the station, get their
tickets punched, and settle in for the ride. Attention must be paid. A long-
run friendship needs the honesty that builds trust, and the flexibility that
allows friends to change. They have to manage both distance and closeness.
Women often falter when they can no longer say, "We are so much alike."
Friends who are in it for the long haul, however, expect things to change
along the way, and to adjust and adapt.

We have no illusions about the constancy of friendship. It's no easier to
maintain this relationship than any other. Just as marriages can dissolve
after years of commitment and comfort, so can friendships. Many women
talk wistfully or angrily about friends they have left by the side of the road.
Maybe the barriers of distance and lifestyle become too formidable, or
maybe there isn't enough glue to keep them going.

Nearly all the long-run friends we have met have a solid base, a strong,
even intense beginning of time and attention. That is certainly true for us.
We could not have sustained a "commuting friendship" without that first
year in Cambridge.

But we are conscious of what we do not share: childhood. If one of the
joys and jobs of women friends is to grow in connection with each other,
how lucky those women are who have known each other for decades. The
friends who grew up together have a grab bag of memories always at hand,
a way of talking, a shorthand patter and mental list of names and places
that strike chords as familiar to each of them as the old camp songs nobody
ever forgets.

While writing this book, Ellen's cousin and oldest friend, Judy, came to
dinner one night with a packet of childhood photos wrapped in a small
pink towel. The two of them smiled—no one had to remind them of what
that piece of pink terry cloth represented. Back when they were sixteen-
year-olds and spending the summer together on the Cape, Ellen was always
wrapped in a big, bright pink towel—to the point where Judy's mother
once complained she was spending her entire *summer* in that towel. Who
else would know why they smiled? They knew each other when.

As we talked with Maureen Strafford and Mary Gordon, the doctor and writer who have known each other since they were adolescents, we could see them simultaneously both as teenagers breaking out of the narrow confines of their childhood, and as grown-up mothers with children the same age they were when they met. In their fifties, having lived in different cities for most of their adult lives, they carry on a morning ritual whenever they still have "sleepovers." As only childhood friends could, they bring their coffee mugs into the bedroom and hop under the covers for coffee and talk.

By now, they have the "goods" on each other. Maureen can remember vividly the "autostrada" period in Mary's life, a time when she watched her friend putting on European airs. Mary can relay with horror the time she found Martha Stewart's book on napkin folding on Maureen's shelf. And they love telling the story of the time as teenagers when they hitchhiked to Cape Cod—"my God, we were crazy"—with two Irish Western Union workers who took an unwelcome interest in them.

But the pleasure of "knowing each other when" isn't just nostalgia. "We knew each other, and we knew each other's parents," says Mary. "We can interpret the present in a very rich context because of that. I think about how a lot of people have stories in their childhood they go back to, but that's all they can do. They get together and they can tell stories. But that's it." The friendships that last must allow for change, for the childhood friend who keeps you locked in an image as outgrown as your old school uniform is not the friend of adulthood.

These two friends understand that distinction very well, and have always pushed each other. Without Maureen, Mary says she could have become self-isolating. Without Mary, Maureen agrees, she might have settled for being "a crowd pleaser." As it is? "I have become more mellow and Maureen has gotten more definitive. One of the things about staying in relationships is that even if you start out in boxes, you have to have the capacity to go back and forth and not get stuck in roles. But we are actually aware of those boxes, and it's very liberating to break out of them," Mary said.

When we first talked with them, Mary had written a romp, a sexual adventure story called "Spending." She was breaking out of the serious writing expected of her, treading on the turf of male writers, and she felt vulnerable to critics. But as she said to us, smiling widely, "Who needs John Updike if you have Maureen?"

It's like that with friends who are the repository of each other's past. If they've got each other, they're okay.

In Cathleen Schine's novel *The Evolution of Jane,* the main character is suddenly flooded with memories of an old friend: "Friendship is context, at least ours was. It was what ordered the world. And even though I was an adult myself, even though it had been so many years, even though I had made many friends in the interim, I could somehow not let go of that first real friendship."

How many can? Many old, dear, best, first friends get left by the side of the road, but in mid or later life, the impulse to regain that past can become a strong desire to reconnect. When the Canadian magazine *Chatelaine* offered readers a way to relocate long-lost pals, they were flooded with letters from women looking for childhood friends. One woman wanted to thank an old friend for setting her up with the blind date thirty years ago who became her husband; another wanted a friend to know she felt anguished because she had let her down rather than admit "my choices and my life were not perfect."

A desire somewhere between curiosity and loss can prompt anyone to reach back and mend a broken connection—or want to fill in the blank pages of personal histories. And sometimes memories of a friend echo through one's life in a way that cries for resolution.

Pat

This story needs a split screen. First, my version.

Her name is Margaret, and she was my roommate, a small-town girl from eastern Washington with long, blond hair and an infectious laugh I never forgot. We met in 1954 when I was a freshman and she was a sophomore, and we marveled at the fact that our "great" age difference of one year didn't matter. Margaret was smart, wonderfully smart, and she was also funny, which I was not, but she didn't care. Sitting in our pajamas in Seattle University's Marycrest Hall, our hair in tight, wet pincurls, we talked about the world and who we were and what we wanted to become. I would put Mario Lanza's *Student Prince* album on the turntable in my room and we would roar happily with the chorus, forgetting both homework and the fact that we didn't have any dates that night. When we were morose about our love lives, we would sit cross-legged on twin dark green bedspreads, cigarettes tucked between our fingers, listening to something appropriately sad, like "Unchained Melody." Margaret would chew on a strand of her hair; I preferred Hershey bars.

I thought then that those memories would become the basic grist of friendship for a lifetime. And I spent years wondering why they hadn't.

I dropped out of school, married, and moved to Eugene, Oregon, seeing Margaret only once more after my own wedding—at hers, a few years later. She seemed quite still, and somehow remote. I felt closed out.

But when my second child was born, I named her after that vibrant friend with the wonderful laugh. I called Margaret in Seattle, asking if she would be my baby's godmother, hoping that would be the bridge to reconnection.

She said she was flattered, and how nice it was to have a baby, and she was sorry, but she wouldn't be able to come for the christening. It still didn't make sense to me. But it was clear finally that this relationship had gone off into the realm of memory and anecdote.

Fast-forward twenty-five years. By now I was divorced and living in Washington, and the house had become very quiet after my youngest daughter had left for college. It left just me and Ginger (the cat Ellen remembers so fondly).

Why do we do things on impulse? One night I picked up the phone and, with the help of Margaret's parents, who still lived in the tiny town whose name I managed to remember, placed a call. I reached her on my first try. I knew her voice the second I heard it. "It's Pat, do you remember me?" I asked. And then I heard that wonderful laugh. "Do I *remember?* Oh,

Pat O'Brien and Margaret Hall Cohoe, 1955.

my God, this is WONDERFUL," she said. We talked on that first reconnection for three and a half hours.

Now we go to the other side of the screen. The version of our friendship
that I never knew.

Margaret told me on the phone that night that she has had multiple
sclerosis for many years. Her seizures began while we were roommates. She
couldn't tell anyone, not even me. It sounds unbelievable now to us both,
but she thought God was punishing her for "going too far" with a
boyfriend. After she married and began having children, the seizures grew
worse. Her mind would blank out, and afterward she couldn't remember
things. She would then avoid the people who had been with her when it
happened. She hadn't dared risk a trip to come see me when my Margaret
was born, she confessed. At that time, she was still trying to keep secret her
increasing seizures.

She said she was now bedridden, and I tried to visualize the ebullient
Margaret confined to bed. Down came the barrier of twenty-five years for
both of us; and we could hardly stop talking. We started by coasting on old
times, but the threads of connection were stronger than that. We could
pick them up and go on, walking through the rooms of our lives, sharing
what we each had come to be. And not doing too bad a job of it.

I visit her in the Northwest whenever I can, and when I can't, we talk
via e-mail. And we talk about everything, with one rule she laid down immediately: "Don't hold back on the details of the interesting things you
do," she told me. "If you do, you'll be editing yourself because I can't do
the same things—and then we'll be reduced to just swapping old memories."

I have heeded her advice. And yet in a very real sense, reconnecting with
Margaret has meant getting back a substantial part of my history. She is a
friend who remembers my mother and father as they were when they were
young, someone who knows what it was like to walk a tightrope through
the rigid conservatism of the '50s. Who failed, as did I—though as earnest
Catholics we tried together—to complete successfully the Nine First Fri-
days. Who remembers ironing five-yard "circle" skirts and the medicinal
smell of Noxzema on our pillows. Who knows how I cried when the man I
was crazy about didn't ask me out. Who knows I wanted to be a writer—as
did she.

At times over the years, as someone who has lived in many zip codes, I
have felt like a permanent nomad, repeatedly packing up my tent and mov-

ing on. Reconnecting with Margaret was like throwing an anchor back into the past and finding my ship once again secured.

W e have finally reached that point in the life cycle when we are comfortable reconnecting with our younger selves. We are long past the embarrassment of the zits that always appeared the night of a date. Maybe that's a demarcation line in itself.

Our children have almost all reached—or passed—the ages we were when we first met. Those two thirtysomething single women with men on their minds—something our children can't and probably don't want to recall—we remember through a shared rearview mirror.

Children often see their mothers as real, separate people ("Mom, you did *that?*") only when they hear them sharing stories with their friends, only when they see them in the context of their own chosen relationships. And sometimes the younger generation only gets a peek through that rearview mirror. Pat and her sister laugh now at the old photos of their mother, Anna, and her lighthearted gathering of friends—they called themselves "The Girls"—on their annual trek to Palm Springs. They wish they could go back and eavesdrop on the fun. What were they like, this small band of housewives, off on their own, temporarily freed of child care and housework? What did they talk about?

"*The Girls*": *Pat's mother, Anna O'Brien (right front), with friends.*

And how must it feel when there's no one around anymore to listen? How unceremoniously many elderly women are put in their place: old, "out of touch," dismissable. There comes a time when the world and even their families don't see them as they remember themselves. At that moment, older women lose a large chunk of who they are. "The old live in a different country from the rest of us," writes Mary Pipher. One of the things that segregates them is history. When our generation says "depression," we are thinking of Prozac; when their generation says "depression," they are thinking of bread lines. Only with friends can they reexperience that history and get back to that sense of self.

Ann Crossman and Edith Holtz, 1952.

Ellen

One morning I take my mother to visit her friend Ann. What did a classmate call them in high school? Mike and Ike / They Look Alike—referring to comic strip characters popular in the '20s. Of course they didn't really look alike. Ann was tall and forthright, while my mother, Edith, was short and shy. These two old friends who had met in seventh grade were friends as girls and friends as wives, and now they were friends as widows.

In retrospect, I realize how important their friendship was, even to my own life. My mother, after all, modeled herself as a mother after Ann's mother, a patient, lively woman who had sandwiches on a plate for both girls when they walked home from grammar school together. It was Ann's mother who created the kind of home my mother would imitate.

But in 1998, both women had reached the age of eighty-four. Ann had cancer and my mother was in a wheelchair, and it was clear there wouldn't be many more visits. So Mother and I set off to Ann's apartment for "tea." I helped her carefully into the car, hauling her wheelchair into the trunk. Ann's apartment was less than a mile from Mother's and a half mile from the grammar school where they met.

How can I describe the scene? I pushed my mother in the wheelchair up the ramp and into the elevator and down the corridor. When a clearly fading Ann opened the door, I saw how startled my mother was. They hadn't seen each other in months. Illness did what life hadn't done—it had separated them.

I made tea and spread out the lemon and chocolate desserts they both loved, but Ann could only pick at them now. This lovely woman who had held on to her natural brown hair until chemo—yes, there are eighty-year-olds without a stitch of gray hair, I have known one—now had her head covered with a turban.

But however frail these women, their liveliness revived as they talked—giggling, I swear—reminiscing in front of a new audience. "Remember the boy who had a car and followed you home from high school, Edith? You couldn't get into the car because your grandmother might have seen you, so he drove slowly beside you all the way home." "Oh my Lord." "Remember the times I used to go on dates with you and all three of us would have bacon, lettuce, and tomato sandwiches, Ann? What on earth did they ever think of me, tagging along?"

Willa Cather once described old age as being like "going to a play after most of the characters had died." Mother and Ann were remembering their parents, their husbands, their old beaus—telling stories out of school. And there were stories *of* school, too. How Ann was rushed for a high school sorority before Edith. Why they chose the same college—and why they dropped out. They told stories of the coats Ann's father made for them and how they were, frankly, the prettiest girls in their class.

I could see them as they were then. More to the point, *they* saw each other as they were then. The turban and the wheelchair dropped away for an hour, and laughter and good old days entered the room.

Not long after Ellen took part in that afternoon tea with Edith and Ann, her mother lost that best friend. Gone were the daily phone calls and seventy years of history. One morning Ellen sat with Edith, ruminating about that friendship. She asked her a question: How did Ann ever get you in that sorority anyway?

"I don't remember," Edith said, and then added wistfully, "I can't ask Ann."

Again there is that old song about friends, a simple round: Make new friends, but keep the old; one is silver, and the other is gold. Old friends carry that wash of sun color, the gilt edge of childhood. When women have them, they work hard to keep them. They provide themselves with all sorts of "reasons" for getting together: they meet to eat lunch, to play bridge, to talk about books. When Pat's friends in Washington created a book club, it was Irene's idea—why don't we get a group of women, all writers, to read Shakespeare together? Well, Shakespeare was the text, but friendship was the content. The group has long since become a treasured place to explore fine feeling news as much as *Hamlet*.

The "Stitch and Bitch Club," a group of women in the Harrisburg, Pennsylvania, area, began getting together to play cards once a month twenty years ago. By the 1980s, they had switched to needlework, getting together over cross-stitch canvas and knitting needles. But even this subterfuge didn't work: in the span of a year, they produced only one sleeve of a man's ski sweater. They had been knitting something else.

Women will go to great lengths to put friends first in the datebook. They will do it with long-range hopes, but not necessarily long-range expectations. Sometimes, though, they can surprise themselves.

Pat once met with a group of four women in Maryland who have managed to maintain friendship for almost three decades, simply by following the simple ritual of meeting every Monday night. They never tried to give these meetings a "purpose." They don't sew, read books, play cards, or eat lunch. They meet only to talk. How do they manage to clear their calendars for each other so frequently and so consistently? What does it mean to have been together through the birth of children, the end of marriages, career changes, menopause, the death of parents?

"Look at the pictures I found!" says Sarna Marcus one Monday night. The tall, dramatic graphic artist with white hair and wide expressive eyes tosses a pile of old photographs on the table in front her friends, exclaiming, "Oh, God, we were so young!" Yes, they were young. Very '70s. One photo shows the group of four gathered around a baby tucked inside a brightly colored quilt. "That's my first child," says Susan Drobis, the curly-haired social worker with the high polished forehead of an Egyptian queen. "She's in college now."

Claudia Lipschultz, a biologist, pulls out another photo, turning it around in her fingers like some archival treasure. In the snapshot this reserved woman has on a crown with stars and glittery ribbons; it's from her fiftieth birthday celebration. "I look a little bit silly," she murmurs, a smile belying the words.

Juanita Weaver pours the ritual tea while they describe how the group came together, in a larger gathering then, their espoused goal consciousness-raising. It was a heady time in the women's movement; after a while, though, the meetings lost fire. "We had exhausted all the topics," Sarna remembers, going down the prescribed list of '70s feminist issues. When the group was winnowed down to the four of them, Sarna recalls, "We decided first to share our sexual histories. It was the most intimate thing we could do to push ourselves to another level." She looks at the others. "Remember how hard that was?"

Suddenly all four are talking, interrupting, layering in memories. It was at that time they first made a commitment to meeting Monday nights. Over the weeks and years, each woman faced some unresolved issue in her life. For Sarna it was panic attacks, a regular occurrence, until one Monday night meeting she finally understood their cause: "Anger that I couldn't express. And they pointed out the connection."

"I remember," murmurs Claudia.

Another night, Juanita brought her mother. This was a woman she saw as long-suffering, weak, and insecure, but the image that bounced back out of her friends' eyes surprised her. They saw her mother in an entirely different light, agreeing that she was neither a martyr nor an introvert. In one funny/painful moment, Juanita felt released from an enormous fiction. "I didn't understand that my world was so much bigger than hers," she says. "They helped me see her as a real force in my life, and it was a big moment."

Sharing their histories, giving each other feedback, wasn't always easy.

Left to right: Juanita Weaver, Susan Drobis and Claudia Lipshultz, posing for Sarna Marcus.

"It took us a long time to trust feedback from one another because it wasn't always what we wanted to hear," Susan volunteers. Claudia seconds that. They began to function as a trusted memory bank for each other, a repository of what each needed to understand or explain, a private inviolate place.

Monday after Monday, they built on their commitment and shared history. It was something else, however, that transformed this group into friendship. "I think what happened," begins Susan, "is we realized we were in there for each other."

A few years ago, when Claudia's long marriage came to an end with painful abruptness, "They all decided not to let me be alone. They made out a schedule where one person would stay with me each night of the first week. Sometimes it was just to sit in a room and read, or maybe to go to a movie. It was marvelous. It was a gift."

There were crises of the everyday sort. Susan, the only mother in the group, needed help deciding such issues as whether she should allow her teenage daughter to go to a rock concert in a friend's car. The group gave her a place to get unstuck, to reexamine her instincts and responses. They gave Juanita the courage to leave her government job and go into private consulting. And when Sarna's father was dying, they gave her the strength to talk with him.

"When we work hard together to help one of us figure something out, there's a great sense of satisfaction," says Susan. Juanita runs a hand through her gray-flecked hair. "I've said everything in this group. I haven't protected myself, not when I'm ashamed, lost, or scared. If I were dying they would be here with me."

Four friends. Every week. Twenty-seven years. Sharing rituals complete with birthday crowns and poems and evenings out. "People don't get it," Sarna says with a laugh. "They see it as a secret cabal or something." Susan nods and adds, "They say, '*every* Monday night'?"

The women turn their attention back to the old photographs that Sarna has piled on the middle of the table. Sue holds one up: her daughter, Becca, is the baby tucked in that quilt; her birth was their first shared celebration. Susan, who has brought the wand that she kept all these years, picks it up from the table and gives it a practiced twirl. "Everybody passed the wand around, making wishes for my baby's future. It was a lovely beginning."

What were the wishes? "Strength. Courage," Sarna remembers. "Self-awareness," chimes in Juanita, "a long and interesting life. That she know and like herself." Claudia adds, "That she be joyous and able to overcome adversity."

They sit silently. "Didn't we wish for good health?" Susan asks. They puzzle over that. "We never would have thought of it," says Sarna, "We were too young to worry about THAT."

Susan, Sarna, Claudia, Juanita—partners in this practice of friendship—created their group very carefully. Every Monday night? For twenty-seven years? But their last words this night are, "This is possible for other women too, we are sure of it."

———

These women, baby boomers all, have systematically created a community based on a particular mix of politics and therapy that grew out of the women's movement, but over time they have taken on all the coloration of friends who connect more organically, whether from childhood, college dorms, or neighborhoods of mothers.

Building "kinship" with friends is a slow process at any age. But once in place, these relationships can be vital support systems as women grow older. If demographics tell us anything, it is that aging women will need each other. They will be what each other has.

In all the movies, in the lyrics of all the songs that play the familiar refrain of romance, there is little room for the reality that the average woman in America will spend many years on her own, without a lover or a spouse or a dependent child. Women are single longer, single more often, more likely to be divorced than ever before, and—finally—more likely to be widowed. Old age, Pipher's "another country," is overwhelmingly a female terrain. There are five times as many widows as widowers. By the age of 69, there are 120 women for every 100 men and by 85, there are 257 women for every 100 men. To put it even more starkly, almost 50 percent of women over 65 are widows. These demographics translate into whole colonies of condominiums in such sunny places as Florida, inhabited largely by women whose husbands have died.

We see how the current generation of elderly women support each other. Though many came of age in a generation that put family first, this often changes as children grow busy and move away. We know from one study that when elderly people are depressed, friends are second only to spouses in making the biggest difference. Research tells us too that elderly people value what they give *to* a friendship even more than what they get *out* of it. They become each other's support system. They are there to fill social time, and very often, to help take care of functional needs. They run errands, pick up the medicine, go to the dry cleaner, water the flowers. Indeed, friendships that begin late in life sometimes have certain advantages.

Friendships among older women are less likely to trip up over the bad stuff of envy or competition. One study suggests that women over sixty show more tolerance and have fewer confrontations with their friends. Both the prom queen of a half century ago and the "four-eyed" honor student are now getting senior discounts at the movies. The youthful ambitions and romances and differences of clothing and class recede into memory. Elderly women who are alone are no longer subject to the anxieties and guilts of being too busy to respond to a friend. They are less likely to wonder, Will this friend ask too much, does this relationship come with strings attached? As one old woman in Mary Pipher's book said, "Honey, life ain't nothing but strings."

Old age can be the time when women most fully reap the benefits of their skills at forming and maintaining relationships. Yet at the same time, old age is also when friends can become frail or sick. They may not be able to get on a plane and go visit each other. They can't always head for the beach, the book club, the mall. We wonder ourselves what will happen if someday we are both alone, living in separate cities and unable to travel. The phone? E-mail? Smoke signals?

Old age can separate old friends. They may find themselves in separate retirement homes, nursing homes, surrounded by strangers. How many older women have the resilience—and the need, despite losses—to reach out again, to make a connection, to seek out friends who will understand them and whom they can trust?

———

Gretchen Swidler, a slender, classically beautiful woman in her mid-eighties who wears her gray hair pulled straight back into a severe bun, lives at a retirement home in Washington that is part of a chain called Classic Residences. Gretchen, who is from Knoxville, Tennessee, and was a realtor in the Washington area until her retirement, hates the home's fancy name. "I can't stand telling people what they call this place, I simply give them the address," she says, smiling her greeting in the lobby.

It is an elegant address, in a tranquil setting, with trees and a lovely pond surrounding the high-rise building. There are game rooms, a comfortable library, tapestry-covered chairs in the dining room, an art room, a hair salon. It is a place that could pass as a resort hotel, but for the fact that the people moving through the rooms and corridors are often bent and gray, and many maneuver with walkers.

Gretchen is not bent. She walks with erect carriage, and is dressed in a neat mauve suit with purple blouse, jade necklace, and highly polished shoes. As we walk to the dining room, she confesses she isn't feeling too well; she had a stroke a few years ago and is now awaiting the results of a recent MRI. "I seem to function, but my head feels full of fluff," she says. She doesn't like talking about her physical problems, though, and quickly switches the topic to her real concern: her close friend Nell fell yesterday. She's nervous about what this accident might mean. "At least she didn't break her hip," she says.

A woman with red hair and chunky gold earrings waves and comes over to Gretchen. "Got the results of the MRI yet?" she says. They commiserate about what it is like to have the test, of how claustrophobic it feels to be inside the machine. "The first time I had one, it was like being in a sewer pipe," Gretchen jokes. The woman laughs, looking down at her own slender frame and then at Gretchen's. "We could both fit in together," she says.

Gretchen smiles politely and threads her way through the tables filled with people, settling at an empty one. She doesn't consider herself particularly gregarious, and is acutely missing Nell today. "We've been the basic two, if we want someone else to join us for dinner, we call them first," she says. Last night, when Nell fell, Gretchen decided not to come down for dinner—she might have had to eat alone. The elegance of the dining room belies its politics, which are remarkably cliquish, not all that different from the pairings-off of childhood friends in the school lunchroom. People form groups that only grudgingly accept a stray without a companion. The women who are most ostracized—the ones today who are eating alone— are the ones who are deaf.

Gretchen looks around, picking at the food a brusque waiter has plunked in front of her. She is feeling fragile today in the wake of Nell's fall, and she talks about how quickly things can change at this age and in this place. There was one friend, a psychiatrist who took up sculpting, and now she can't get her out of her mind. "We were going up to her apartment to see her sculpture when she died. You could see her in those last weeks getting smaller. If you flicked her with your finger, she would shatter." Gretchen pauses. "That's the worst thing about friendship at this age. You build one up, and then they're gone."

She brightens. She wants to talk about how her friendship with Nell has thrived in an environment that must make room for illness, change, and death. She talks about their getting out of the home as much as they can, going to movies, out to dinner in real restaurants, shopping, having fun. They refuse to be overwhelmed by the institutional setting within which they live, escaping it in much the same way as women who forge friend-ships in boring jobs. They have found room for play—their equivalent of the escapades of younger women, the two-of-us-against-the-world theme of youth. "We talk about everything," she says. Not just gossip, and not just how Gretchen's arthritis is today or what's happening in Nell's china-painting class. They talk about money matters. They talk about men—both have confessed to each other they miss being desired. They trust each other with their secrets, big and small. And in that talk is the echo of younger voices, the voices of their children and grandchildren, who might not quite believe that "Grandma" still talks this way.

Just the other day, Nell said something Gretchen described as a "little off-color," and immediately leaned forward to whisper, "Don't tell anybody I said that. You know, when I'm alone in my apartment, I cuss."

"I do too, but I don't use the 'F' word," Gretchen whispered back.

"Well, I use all of them!" Nell laughed.

Gretchen leans back in her chair, delighted with the memory, the rub-bery omelette in front of her forgotten. "It was so funny, because she's so feminine, more feminine than I am."

Gretchen first met Nell in the corridors of the retirement complex sev-eral years ago when both their husbands were alive and were living there as well. They liked each other immediately and soon became "couple" friends, meeting in each other's apartments for drinks before going down to the dining room as a foursome. Nell was widowed first. Gretchen and her hus-band reached out to Nell, making sure they kept her as part of their dinner group in the rigidly choreographed culture of the dining room.

Then Gretchen's husband died. "That's when we became close friends," she says. "We were in the same boat, and each of us felt the other would un-derstand." Gretchen grieved for her husband, but found herself unable to cry. "Every time I felt like it, my throat hurt too badly," she remembers. She ran across a poem in *The New Yorker* that finally released her tears, a poem about loss she immediately shared with her friend. And Nell, who had been unable to grieve openly, was finally able to cry, too.

It is the bond of shared grieving that Gretchen believes gave them a sense of taking care of each other, which they do, in basic ways. When Nell was suffering from a bladder infection, Gretchen took her to the doctor, knowing her friend was in too much discomfort to wait for one of her children to take her. These two women, both feeling shaky, took a cab together, a trip neither of them would risk independently. Together, they thought they could do it, and they did.

Lunch is over, and Gretchen is hoping to find out some more news about Nell. She's relieved that Nell didn't break her hip, but she is trying to brace herself for another transition. Maybe Nell will have to leave Classic Residences. "I never used to think about this impermanence of life before," she says. "It makes people reluctant to establish a friendship." She starts wending her graceful way past the other diners, then stops to say over her shoulder with some firmness, "But not me."

Gretchen and Nell created an intimate personal space in the midst of what is—even at its best—an institution. The deepest human need, Margaret Mead once observed, is to have someone who cares if we come home at night. And "home" can be the room at the other end of the hall. Cornel West once called America a "hotel society," a transient place where people don't knock on the next door—they just check in and out without a greeting or a wave.

But there still are places where elderly women work to maintain their communities. They show up again and again, often filling a functional need as their testament to caring. They may not talk about their feelings, but they pick up the prescription, take the gang out for lunch, bring over dinner. In the last years of Pat's mother's life, she was known in her apartment building at Park LaBrea in Los Angeles for her homemade apple pies. If a great-grandchild was visiting or a neighbor was sick, she was, at the age of ninety-two, still determined to roll out her pie dough. "You don't understand, this is what I *do*," she said to Pat, when she once tried to talk her mother into settling for a store-bought pie.

In old age, losses accumulate relentlessly, especially the loss of peers. One of the rewards of living a life connected to friends is that it provides a buffer against loneliness, and the satisfaction of helping others as well as being helped. And these friends remind us how important it is to the human soul to be on the giving end of support as well as the receiving end. In old age we still have the need to be needed. It is our peers sometimes who best see us whole, who really understand the choices we've made and the lives we've led, because they have been fellow travelers. As Anne Lamott writes, "We're not here to see through one another, but to see one another through."

It is Monday, the day of the 103rd Boston Marathon. The sky is a clear, sparkling blue, with only a few tiny puffs of clouds; it promises to be a beautiful day. We hurry through lunch, an eye on the television set, so we can know when the race begins. At noon, the sharp report of the opening gun echos through Hopkinton and thousands of television sets. And there they go! On the screen, we see crowds of people swarming down the street, many of them laughing, waving at the television cameras, at the onlookers. Only twenty-six miles to go.

The temperature is climbing into the 60s—a little warm for the runners, but perfect for all the people thronging to the streets to watch. We stroll down to Beacon Street, finding a place to watch the runners go by. Water stations, complete with stacks of paper cups, are being set up. The streetcars have throttled down, crawling slowly along Beacon Street, the drivers keeping a close eye out for excited kids spilling onto the tracks as they look for a spot along the already crowded route.

All through Boston, designated streets have been closed to traffic. The route for the runners will take them from Hopkinton through Wellesley to Newton up over Heartbreak Hill (the killer stretch that weeds out the faint-hearted), down Beacon Street through Brookline to Kenmore Square to Commonwealth Avenue. Then a right on Hereford Street and left onto Boylston, finishing at Boston's historic Copley Square.

Back at the starting line, our pals from Milton are on their way. "I can't believe we're here again," Nancy shouts to Pauline as they start to run, the two of them slathered in sunscreen. Pauline leans forward, and gives Nancy a big hasty kiss. "Hey, you got me here," she shouts back.

They run the first three miles slowly, almost running in place, waiting for the crowd of runners to stretch out. They talk, they run, they talk some more.

"Ah, Nancy, my quads are really screaming here," Pauline says several miles later.

"Come on, come on," Nancy urges.

"You go ahead!"

"I want to get you to the hills."

Thirteen miles . . . Pauline is loving the run, enjoying the crowds; hugging friends and waving as she passes them by. She doesn't want to push, she wants Nancy to push.

"Nancy, go!"

"No." Nancy squints at the sun. "Where's that cloud cover they promised us?"

Seventeen miles . . . Patty, another friend running with them, is ready to make the push. She turns to Nancy. "You wanna come?" she asks.

"Naw, not before the hills," Nancy says.

"If you think you can do it, *go,*" says Pauline.

"Pauline, trust me."

They grab a high-sugar boost drink, what they call goo-stuff; they drink water. They hit the hills, still together. Going up the third hill, a friend standing in the crowd hands each of them a banana.

"I can't eat," says Pauline.

Nancy takes a bite of her banana. "Here, take it," she says.

"This is tough," murmured Pauline. The heat is catching up with a lot of runners. A woman ahead of them throws up. Some people are crying.

Twenty-two miles . . . Heartbreak Hill. Pauline and Nancy exchange glances.

"Come on, you gotta kick in *right now,*" yells Pauline.

Nancy takes off. She runs the next four miles like eight-minute miles, pushing, pushing.

We are waiting on Beacon Street, watching for them both. We see Nancy running toward us, head up, still energized. "Hey!" she yells, waving when she sees us. "Pauline's just a few minutes behind me!"

And indeed she is. We yell and catch Pauline's eye. "Oh, my God!" she yells, laughing, running over to grab us. "This is terrific that you came!"

"Go!" we find ourselves yelling and laughing. "Don't slow down for us!"

Nancy hits the finish line, running just slightly over a four-hour race. Not what she wanted, not quite, but a good race. Officially, she is the 7,956th runner to complete the marathon. There are still several thousand people behind her.

She turns to face the course, exhausted but unbudging, watching for Pauline. Her time wasn't all that she wanted, but what the hell—there's always next year. Marathon officials tell her she has to move away. They are insistent.

"Look, you don't understand, I'm waiting for my girlfriend!" she yells. Nobody is going to move Nancy.

And here comes Pauline, to the finish line. This is no cancer "victim," this is officially the 8,239th runner to finish. The two friends embrace, laughing, the strain and the worry of the last year gone; the challenge met; the celebration just beginning. They made it.

Maybe they'll run faster next year; maybe not. But it never was about winning, it was about friendship. Women and friendship . . . it's about being stronger together than alone. It's about shared history, laughter, courage, and consolation. It's about being together for the long run.

Pat and Ellen, off to work.

Epilogue

We can't close this book without answering the questions that followed us all along this journey. When we set out to write together, people offered up more warnings than the Weather Channel. We heard the same wondering tone, the same queries repeated again and again:

Are you still friends?
How are you doing? No, I mean *really* . . .
Are you still friends?
This is a test of friendship!
You guys still talking?
Are you still friends?

It was like being faced with cynical guests at a wedding who keep reminding the happy couple, "Do you know that the divorce rate is one in two?" There was, to put it mildly, a running anxiety in the jokes and questions; an underlying worry about what can happen when one ups the ante on friendship.

As the jokes rolled along, and they did, we began to imagine the item in Liz Smith's column or *Publisher's Weekly:* "Well, guess which two galpals went splitsville while, *ahem,* writing about women and friendship. Columnist Ellen Goodman and novelist Patricia O'Brien were seen throwing hissy fits and computer disks at each other over a table at the Harvest in Harvard Square. Sayonara, Simon & Schuster!"

By undertaking this project, we were, it's true, putting our friendship on the line. But along with the running gags from others, we saw genuine curiosity. The same people who gave us those cynical looks also wanted to know the secret: how on earth, quite frankly, can you do this?

It was a question that pointed to the very heart of friendship. Women want to secure relationships and to trust the staying power of their friendships. What is a friend for? What can you count on? How much weight can a friendship hold? We lived this book, and the process of writing it mimicked the themes of our chapters. What we learned from the women we talked with, thank you all very much, helped us to keep track of our own relationship as we dove into deep waters.

How did we do it?

Seamlessly.

No, no, let's try that again.

After a year of conducting interviews, after months of taking turns collaborating at our homes in different cities, we took a leap. We couldn't write this book through shared e-mail, shipping chapters back and forth across the Internet. These friends writing about friendship needed to be in the same space. We needed a room of our own.

Radcliffe College generously offered us that room, a perfect fourth-floor garret in Agassiz House. That meant Pat was heading back to Cambridge for several months, and the two of us were heading back to college, full circle, to the place where we'd met twenty-six years earlier.

More to the point, we would be working in one office, living in one house, integrated into each other's lives and marriages in an entirely new way. It would be a twenty-four-hour relationship with time off for sleeping.

On a January day, Ellen flew down to Washington to drive up to Boston with Pat, to share the adventure from the beginning. For years, Pat's husband had referred to Ellen with straight-faced good humor as "the Boarder." Now Pat, with some trepidation, was putting her own life on hold and moving to Boston. Or as Frank said all too quickly, "You're not *moving* to Boston, you're going up there to write a book."

People looked askance at Frank when they heard Pat was headed north, as if he were being deserted. Frank took to telling them that he was sending Pat to Boston with orders that she couldn't come home until the book was done. Shades of Colette in our garret office.

As for Bob, not deserted but invaded? Playing squash two nights before the move, his friend John looked at him in amazement when Bob said that Pat was moving in until June. "Well, if anyone can handle it, you can," John said. Bob had signed on for this boarder without reservation. And also booked two trips out of town.

The drive that we had planned as a lengthy talk-filled experience turned into the trip from hell—a white-knuckled trip through a snowstorm that turned the New Jersey Turnpike into a stall-and-crawl disaster; a one-day trip that turned into two days, with the blessing of a motel in Connecticut. We did find ourselves wondering, what kind of an omen is a snowstorm, anyway? But it turned out to be a great migratory trip for two partners in an ad-lib collaboration. It was an entry into our great adventure series, the sort that require no Everests, no oxygen, just the ability to make life, and tough patches, more fun.

So we moved in together. Pat pulled out the photographs of her husband, children, and grandchildren and lined them on the mantel in her room, and began to fit in. When's the best time to use the washing machine? Where do you keep the toilet paper?

Bob kept the refrigerator filled with orange juice, enough for a family of five or a family of Pat. But did she actually want instant coffee? Ellen is deeply committed to her espresso machine and shade-grown, bird-friendly organic coffee. Would Pat rather have good coffee than that instant stuff? No? Oh. Okay.

One day Bob, a man who takes food as seriously as Ellen takes coffee, found something in the freezer that had never been there before: EEEK! A Stouffer's frozen dinner.

There were times Pat felt a little like a kid at camp with two nice counselors trying to keep her from getting too homesick—but then Frank began sending weekly care packages of *The Washington Post*'s Sunday comic pages. He knew what his camper needed.

The saving grace of this adventure was that we already knew each other down to the bones, though not down to all the daily quirks. In some ways, moving in together shook some of the old assumptions and cobwebs out of our relationship and kicked it up a notch. Actually, several notches.

We've talked about the importance of empathy, the ability to see, really see, what someone else is going through. Ellen knew how Pat felt when she had to cancel plans to visit granddaughters Sophie and Anna in Seattle because of that first snowy trip to Boston—a not-insignificant side effect of this two-author stress test. And Pat knew what Ellen was juggling when in the midst of two day jobs—book and column—her mother also ended up in the hospital. There were many times when we were each distanced from our own anxieties by the simple act of helping the other.

We were also faced with the need to stay, quite literally, on the same page. Both us were used to being responsible for 100 percent of our work. It took more than a little while to realize that 50 percent was enough. Fifty percent? We'd always thought that was a failing grade. Now we learned that 50 percent was equal sharing. It was both hard to let go, and a real relief. We went from being very careful of each other's prose—"Mind if I make some changes?"—to being absolutely direct—"Hey, this doesn't work; fix it please." Ellen, who works on columns in her head, learned to talk out ideas. Pat, who needs to talk them through, learned when not to break in with, "Ellen, I think the interesting thing about what that psychologist said is . . ."

We would sit in our loft above the Agassiz Theatre, listening to the student singers down the hall, hearing the crash of the thespians thumping their way through something billed as "combat choreography," while we passed chapters back and forth from the laptop to the desktop.

It's not an accident that we used three voices in this book: Pat and Ellen and Ours. It reflects that truth about friendship itself: there are always two I's and a We.

The search for the "we" was not always as easy as it looks. "We" think? We had to wrestle that down. Getting to a joint voice meant working our way toward a level of honesty—keep it real, not nice—that people who care about each other's feelings don't usually have to plumb. We learned how much energy is generated in this friendship because of our different points of view.

There was the morning when we were loudly thrashing out a difference and only later realized that someone was working in the unoccupied office next door. There goes that Liz Smith item.

All those people who asked archly, "Will you still be friends?" were thinking about the inevitable friction of sharing both living and working space. They were thinking of little daily tensions that accumulate and are heightened under the tension of deadline. They worried about twenty fingers on one keyboard, and about staying on the same page. But there was also an undertone of concern that somehow or other one of us would fail the other. There was mistrust in trust itself.

The truth is that we learned to trust each other in new ways. The take charge mentality we each admit to—more so after writing this book together—had its ticklish underside. We sometimes barreled ahead because we were also afraid of letting each other down. We are two women who are overly responsible and disgustingly reliable, and we know how to "do it all" ourselves. But at the heart of so many failed collaborations and failed relationships is the complaint of one person that the other wasn't carrying her own weight.

We had, in the end, quite the opposite experience. If one of us ran out of energy, the other one would take over. On one given day, Pat was the engine. On another, Ellen. One of us would run out of steam or get sick or have to leave town. The running joke became, "The best part of having a partner is that while I was gone the book was being written." We didn't keep score. In one way or another, we knew that over the long haul it would even out. Besides, keeping score is for umpires, not friends.

Ellen's uncle Mike has a wonderful expression about how he and her aunt Charlotte have sustained their fifty-nine-year marriage. "I get up in the morning, look in the mirror, and say: 'You're no bargain either.' " When one of us screwed up on the computer, taped over an interview, dangled a participle, forgot to pass on a message from a husband, got testy, got tired, forgetful—well, the other wasn't any bargain either. It could have been me. Next time it may be.

Did we have our bad days? Yup. There were times when we got sharp with each other, sharper than we'd ever been before. There were times when we were running on empty, devoid of all that nice liquid that oils relationships.

We had never before been part of the problem. But more than once Pat felt the odd loneliness of not being able to talk out something with her best friend—because it was *about* her best friend. More than once, Ellen stopped herself from burdening Pat with her feelings of being overburdened—because their work was part of the burden.

But we refused to be aggrieved. And we learned that, most of the time, it really did get better in the morning.

One of the most important things that sustained us was that old standby, empathy. For Ellen, the toughest part was two full-time jobs. For Pat the toughest part was a commuting life in two cities. But we didn't blame each other. By grace of a long history, we didn't get so deep into our own private woes that we couldn't appreciate what the other was going through.

We were determined, consciously, to retain the good stuff of an everyday friendship while expanding onto this new terrain. Remember Inga and Gillian, the two artists? They had to take time out for the fine feeling news and so did we. The sustaining rhythms included the walk back and forth to Cambridge, the dinners when we put the book aside, had one dessert with two spoons, and got back to talking about children, friends, husbands, Al Gore, George W. Bush, the Supreme Court, and the movies.

One of the hallmarks of women's friendships is the way they take care of each other. Pat "saved Ellen's life" from a marauding bicyclist on Memorial Drive, and Ellen forced Pat to go to the dentist for the jaw problem. And, oh yeah, we reminded each other about the roots. As in hair, not genealogy.

What did we learn? Several things. We learned that friends can be and have to be flexible—that they can freeze each other in place, hang on to rigid ideas about the other, or they can trust and accept their ability to change. We learned to do something that sounds a bit like patting your head and rubbing your belly at the same time: we learned to provide each other with a comfort zone while pushing each other out of those comfort zones.

We learned also—two women who have built their friendship around talking—that not everything has to be talked out. This gave us some insight into the classic silence that often baffles women about male friendships, where we wonder how they can be friends and not express their feelings. We have learned that sometimes you respect the friendship by not talking, and this is not always a barrier to intimacy. Sometimes things that are hard to talk about don't fester, they just go away.

We learned anew that the solid thing friends get out of a long-term friendship is truly knowing someone and being known. There are few enough people in life who can freely reveal themselves to each other, who keep each other's interests at heart. When you find it, well, cherish it. Friendship is worth it.

What did we miss? Play. During the serious writing phase, the only time we went shopping together was through the catalogs on the kitchen table. We felt we couldn't break for play or take time off with each other. We were too busy working on friendship *for* friendship.

One day toward the end of our stay at Radcliffe, when we were backing up disks and printing out pages and downloading e-mails and checking voice-mails, Ellen turned to Pat and said, "Hey, when can my friend come out and play?"

We can't wait to go out and play again.

Pat: So what do you want to do when we finish the book?

Ellen: I don't know, how about taking a vacation?

Pat: Great. A balloon ride over the Serengeti Plain?

Ellen: Are you kidding? How about my front porch in Maine?

Oh, well. We'll work it out.

Acknowledgments

This is our chance to thank all the people in our lives who kept us afloat, nurtured our project, encouraged us, and put up with us when we were cranky or stressed. They saw us through.

First, our families. Especially the guys we are married to: Bob Levey and Frank Mankiewicz. They did more than just tip their hats to the importance of their wives' friendship. They lived it. This wasn't just a dinner-out with a girlfriend, it was years-out. How do you measure the importance of such a cheering section? To them we say, "Thanks, love," and "Honey, I'm home."

We thank our sisters as well, Pat's sister, Mary Thaler, and Ellen's sister, Jane Holtz Kay. Hey, guys, you've been just like sisters to us. Thanks for the encouragement and the fine editing.

Much love to our daughters, who shared their experiences with us and learned more about their mothers in return. Pat's daughters, Marianna, Margaret, Maureen, and Monica, fired off their thoughts all along the way. Ellen's daughter, Katie, tore through the first draft with exuberance, doling out both praise and tough critiques.

Pat wants especially to thank six little people who waited more or less patiently for their grandmother to finish writing and get back to the important stuff—like reading Harry Potter, trick-or-treating, and going to soccer games.

One of the ironies of our book on friendship is that we managed to neglect virtually all our other friends while we were writing it. To them we say, thanks for the encouragement and patience. You know who you are; we love you. Special thanks to Otile McManus and Irene Wurtzel who combed this manuscript, offering support and the insights we count on from them.

We also must thank all the women we interviewed. It's a gift to be allowed into other lives, and we hope we have treated that gift with respect. A word here about our technique. Almost all of these interviews were conducted by the two of us together. We talked with some of the women once, some twice, both in person and on the phone. At times, life intervened, and some of the interviews were conducted by only one of us. For the sake of simplicity, however, we used the editorial "we" throughout the book.

In this project we were helped enormously by two researchers. Laura Doyle worked with us, doing research and transcribing interviews, while building her own family—as we gave birth to one book, she gave birth to two sons. Jamie Jones was the cheerful and agile Harvard College researcher who came back, fast and furiously, always with more information than we asked for. We hope we didn't do too much damage to her grade point average. And thanks to Flora Brown, our guide to the Indigo Girls.

That leads us to those people who gave us not only "a room of our own," but the space, the time, the gift of being let alone to write. In 1999, Radcliffe College—now the Radcliffe Institute for Advanced Studies—appointed us Writers in Residence. We can't thank Tamar March, Dean of Radcliffe Educational Programs, enough for her friendship and confidence.

For keeping the rest of our lives running, we thank Celia Lees-Low, Ellen's assistant. When Ellen was working two day jobs, Celia was the linchpin back at *The Boston Globe* office. In Washington, Laurel Laidlaw, who has been there for Pat through several book launchings, gave us invaluable support copying and sending the manuscript.

Our thanks go to two men who especially applauded this friendship. Chuck Adams and Michael Korda, our editors at Simon & Schuster, have our deep appreciation.

Okay, Esther, your turn. We shared one agent, Esther Newberg, long before we shared this book contract. She's our friend first. When you have Esther on your side, you have an absolutely honest fan, who wishes you well and tells it to you straight. Go, Sox.

Bibliography

BOOKS

Alpert, Barbara. *The Love of Friends: A Celebration of Women's Friendship*. New York: Berkley Publishing Group, 1997.

Ambrose, Stephen E. *Comrades: Brothers, Fathers, Heroes, Sons, Pals*. New York: Simon & Schuster, 1999.

Apter, T.E. *Best Friends: The Pleasures and Perils of Girls' and Women's Friendships*. New York: Crown Publishers, 1998.

Atwood, Margaret Eleanor. *Cat's Eye*. Toronto: McClelland and Stewart, 1988.

Badhwar, Neera Kapur, ed. *Friendship: A Philosophical Reader*. Ithaca and London: Cornell University Press, 1993.

Banner, Lois W. *Elizabeth Cady Stanton: A Radical for Woman's Rights*. Glenview, Ill.: Scott Foresman, 1980.

Bateson, Mary Catherine. *Composing a Life*. New York: Atlantic Monthly Press, 1989.

Beauchamp, Cari. *Without Lying Down: Frances Marion and the Powerful Women of Early Hollywood*. New York: Simon & Schuster, 1997.

Bellah, Robert N., Richard Madsen, William M. Sullivan, Ann Swidler, Steven M. Tipton. *The Good Society*. New York: Alfred A. Knopf, 1991.

Bellah, Robert N., William M. Sullivan, Ann Swidler, and Steven M. Tipton. *Habits of the Heart: Individualism and Commitment in American Life*. New York: Perennial Library, 1985.

Bernikow, Louise. *Among Women*. New York: Perennial Library, Harper & Row Publishers, 1980.

Blackman, Ann. *Seasons of Her Life: A Biography of Madeleine Korbel Albright*. New York: Scribner, 1998.

Bok, Sissela. *Secrets: On the Ethics of Concealment and Revelation*. New York: Pantheon Books, 1982.

Brightman, Carol, ed. *Between Friends: The Correspondence of Hannah Arendt and Mary McCarthy, 1949–1975*. New York: Harcourt Brace, 1995.

Brittain, Vera. *Testament of Friendship: The Story of Winifred Holtby*. New York: Macmillan, 1940.

Cott, Nancy F. *The Bonds of Womanhood: "Woman's Sphere" in New England, 1780–1835*. New Haven: Yale University Press, 1977.

Diliberto, Gioia. *A Useful Woman: The Early Life of Jane Addams*. New York: Scribner, 1999.

DuBois, Ellen Carol. *Elizabeth Cady Stanton and Susan B. Anthony: Correspondence, Writings, Speeches*. New York: Schocken Books, 1981.

Eichenbaum, Luise. *Between Women: Love, Envy, and Competition in Women's Friendships*. New York: Viking, 1987.

Gilligan, Carol. *In a Different Voice: Psychological Theory and Women's Development.* Cambridge, Mass.: Harvard University Press, 1982.

Gilligan, Carol, Nona P. Lyons, Trudy J. Hanmer. *Making Connections: The Relational Worlds of Adolescent Girls at Emma Willard School.* Cambridge, Mass.: Harvard University Press, 1990.

Gilman, Charlotte Perkins. *Herland.* New York: Pantheon Books, 1979.

Gordon, Mary. *Final Payments.* New York: Random House, 1978.

Heilbrun, Carolyn G. *The Last Gift of Time: Life Beyond Sixty.* New York: Dial Press, 1997.

———. *Writing a Woman's Life.* New York: Norton, 1988.

Hochschild, Arlie Russell. *The Time Bind: When Work Becomes Home and Home Becomes Work.* New York: Metropolitan Books, 1997.

Huizinga, Johan. *Homo ludens: A Study of the Play-Element in Culture.* London; Boston: Routledge & Keegan Paul, 1949.

Jordan, Judith V., ed. *Women's Growth in Diversity: More Writings from the Stone Center.* New York: The Guilford Press, 1997.

Jordan, Judith V., Alexandra G. Kaplan, Jean Baker Miller, Irene P. Stiver, Janet L. Surrey. *Women's Growth in Connection: Writings from the Stone Center.* New York: The Guilford Press, 1991.

Kenyon, Olga. *800 Years of Women's Letters.* London: Alan Sutton, 1992.

Lamott, Anne. *Operating Instructions: A Journal of My Son's First Year.* New York: Pantheon Books, 1993.

Luce, Clare Boothe. *The Women.* Newly revised edition. New York: Dramatists Play Service, 1966.

McClatchy, J. D., ed. *Anne Sexton: The Artist and Her Critics.* Bloomington, Ill.: Indiana University Press, 1978.

McCreadie, Marsha. *The Women Who Write the Movies: From Frances Marion to Nora Ephron.* Secaucus, N.J.: Carol Publishing Group, 1994.

Miller, Jean Baker. *Toward a New Psychology of Women.* Boston: Beacon Press, 1976.

Miller, Jean Baker, and Irene Pierce. *The Healing Connection: How Women Form Relationships in Therapy and Life.* Boston: Beacon Press, 1997.

Montgomery, L. M. *Anne of Green Gables.* Toronto: McClelland and Stewart, 1989.

Morrison, Toni. *Beloved.* New York: Alfred A. Knopf, 1987.

Muller, Melissa. *Anne Frank: The Biography.* New York: Metropolitan Books, 1998.

Nardi, Peter M. *Gay Men's Friendships: Invincible Communities.* Chicago, Ill.: University of Chicago Press, 1999.

Nelson, Mariah Burton. *Embracing Victory.* New York: William Morrow, 1998.

Oliker, Stacey J. *Best Friends and Marriage: Exchange Among Women.* Berkeley: University of California Press, 1989.

Pearlman, Mickey, ed. *Between Friends.* Boston: Houghton Mifflin, 1994.

Pipher, Mary Bray. *Another Country: Navigating the Emotional Terrain of Our Elders.* New York: Riverhead Books, 1999.

———. *Reviving Ophelia: Saving the Selves of Adolescent Girls.* New York: G. P. Putnam's Sons, 1994.

Pogrebin, Letty Cottin. *Among Friends: Who We Like, Why We Like Them, and What We Do About It.* New York: McGraw-Hill, 1987.

Rawlins, William K. *Friendship Matters: Communication, Dialectics, and the Life Course.* New York: Aldine de Gruyter, 1992.

Rubin, Lillian B. *Just Friends: The Role of Friendship in Our Lives.* New York: Harper & Row, 1985.

Schine, Cathleen. *The Evolution of Jane.* Boston: Houghton Mifflin, 1998.

Shem, Samuel, and Janet Surrey. *We Have to Talk: Healing Dialogues Between Women and Men.* New York: Basic Books, 1998.

Sherr, Lynn. *Failure Is Impossible.* New York: Times Books, 1995.

Shields, Carol. *Happenstance.* New York: McGraw-Hill Ryerson, 1980.

Souers, Philip Webster. *The Matchless Orinda.* Cambridge, Mass.: Harvard University Press, 1931.

Streitmatter, Rodger, ed. *Empty Without You: The Intimate Letters of Eleanor Roosevelt and Lorena Hickok.* New York: The Free Press, 1998.

Tannen, Deborah. *You Just Don't Understand: Women and Men in Conversation.* New York: William Morrow, 1998.

Tickner, J. Ann. *You Just Don't Understand: Troubled Engagements Between Feminists and IR Theorists.* Canberra, Australia: Research School of Pacific Studies, Australian National University, 1996.

Welty, Eudora, and Ronald A. Sharp, eds. *The Norton Book of Friendship.* New York: W. W. Norton, 1991.

Woolf, Virginia. *A Moment's Liberty: The Shorter Diary of Virginia Woolf.* Anne Olivier Bell, ed. London: The Hogarth Press, 1990.

Wyse, Lois. *Women Make the Best Friends: A Celebration.* New York: Simon & Schuster, 1995.

MOVIES

All About Eve. Dir. Joseph L. Mankiewicz. Perf. Bette Davis, Anne Baxter, George Sanders. 20th Century–Fox, 1950.

The First Wives Club. Dir. Hugh Wilson. Perf. Bette Midler, Diane Keaton, Goldie Hawn. Paramount Pictures, 1996.

The Full Monty. Dir. Peter Cattaneo. Perf. Robert Carlyle, Mark Addy, William Snape, Steve Huison. Channel 4 Films, 1997.

Harriet the Spy. Dir. Bronwen Hughes. Perf. Michelle Trachtenberg, Vanessa Lee Chester, Gregory Smith, Rosie O'Donnell. 1996. Based on the book of the same name by Louise Fitzhugh.

Hope Floats. Dir. Forest Whitaker. Perf. Sandra Bullock, Harry Connick, Jr., Gena Rowlands. 20th Century Fox, 1998.

Julia. Dir. Fred Zinneman. Perf. Jane Fonda, Vanessa Redgrave, Jason Robards. 20th Century–Fox, 1977.

Living Out Loud. Dir. Richard LaGravenese. Perf. Holly Hunter, Danny DeVito, Susan Reno, Queen Latifah. New Line Cinema, 1998.

My Best Friend's Wedding. Dir. P. J. Hogan. Perf. Julia Roberts, Dermot Mulroney, Cameron Diaz, Rupert Everett. TriStar Pictures, 1997.

9 to 5. Dir. Colin Higgins. Perf. Jane Fonda, Lily Tomlin, Dolly Parton. 20th Century Fox, 1980.

One Fine Day. Dir. Michael Hoffman. Perf. Michelle Pfeiffer, George Clooney. 20th Century Fox Productions, 1996.

Walking and Talking. Dir. Nicole Holofcener. Perf. Anne Heche, Catherine Keener. Good Machine, 1996.

When Harry Met Sally. Dir. Rob Reiner. Perf. Billy Crystal, Meg Ryan, Carrie Fisher. Castle Rock Entertainment, 1989.

ARTICLES

Cade, Jared. "Solved: The Mystery of Agatha Christie's Disappearance." *The Daily Telegraph* (London), 24 October 1998: 1.

Cohen, Patricia. "A Woman's Worth: 1857 Letter Echoes Still; Some Basic Disputes Over Feminism Persist." *The New York Times,* 18 July 1998.

Fox, Margery, Margaret Gibbs, and Doris Auerbach. "Age and Gender Dimensions of Friendship." *Psychology of Women Quarterly* (1985).

Lehmann-Haupt, Rachel. "In Women's Groups, Back to 'Girl Talk.'" *The New York Times,* 11 April 1999, section 9: 1.

Roberto, Karen A. "Qualities of Older Women's Friendships: Stable or Volatile." *International Journal of Aging and Development,* vol. 44 (1) (1997): 1–14.

Roberts, Paul. "Goofing off; playful behavior," *Psychology Today,* vol. 28 (4) (July 1995): 34.